LIPSTICK ON YOUR COLLAR

Dennis Potter's numerous television plays include *Blue Remembered Hills* (1979), *Brimstone and Treacle* (commissioned in 1975 but banned until 1987) and the series *Pennies from Heaven* (1978), *The Singing Detective* (1986) and *Blackeyes* (1989). He has also written novels, stage plays and screenplays. His film *Secret Friends*, which he both wrote and directed, opened in 1992, and he is currently working on other projects for screen and television.

Lipstick On Your Collar

DENNIS POTTER

faber and faber
LONDON · BOSTON

First published in 1993 by
Faber and Faber Limited
3 Queen Square London WC1N 3AU

Photoset by Parker Typesetting Service, Leicester
Printed in England by Clays Ltd, St Ives plc

© Dennis Potter, 1993

Dennis Potter is hereby identified as author of this work in
accordance with Section 77 of the Copyright, Designs and Patents
Act 1988

A CIP record for this book is available from the British Library

ISBN 0-571-16874-4

4 6 8 10 9 7 5 3

To Renny Rye
who made the difference . . .

Lipstick On Your Collar was first broadcast on Channel Four television in February 1993. The cast was as follows:

FRANCIS FRANCIS	Giles Thomas
MICK HOPPER	Ewan McGregor
SYLVIA BERRY	Louise Germaine
LISA	Kymberley Huffman
LT. COL. HARRY BERNWOOD	Peter Jeffrey
MAJOR WALLACE HEDGES	Clive Francis
COLONEL 'TRUCK' TREKKER	Shane Rimmer
MAJOR ARCHIE CARTER	Nicholas Jones
MAJOR JOHNNY CHURCH	Nicholas Farrell
CORPORAL PETER BERRY	Douglas Henshall
HAROLD ATTERBOW	Roy Hudd
AUNT VICKIE	Maggie Steed
UNCLE FRED	Bernard Hill
BRIGADIER SANDERS	Frederick Treves
YOUNG MAN IN CINEMA	Damian Dibben
MRS ATTERBOW	Ysanne Churchman
MR FLETCHER	John Cater
MANAGER OF PALAIS	Sean Baker
DANCE INSTRUCTOR	Jean Fergusson
MAN AT PALAIS	Michael Nielsen
CAPTAIN	Jay Villiers
POLICEMAN 1	Benedict Martin
POLICEMAN 2	Che Walker
GENERAL	Terence Bayler
FIRST SOLDIER	Andy Laycock
SECOND SOLDIER	Daniel Ryan
BRIGADIER	Tim Seely
PARACHUTE OFFICER	Rupert Baker
PRIVATE MASON	Darren Lawrence
INSPECTOR	Jim Carter
LT. COLONEL	Roger Hume
VICAR	Geoffrey Drew
NINA	Debra Beaumont
TRIGORIN	James Snell
MASHA	Carol Starks

ARKADINA	Allison Hancock
MEDVEDENKO	Geoffrey Larder
SANDFORD CLARK	Steven Tremblay
OLD GENT IN CLUB	Wensley Pithey
Producer	Dennis Potter
Co-Producers	Rosemarie Whitman
	Alison Barnett
Associate Producer/Accountant	Michael Brent
Director	Renny Rye
Editor	Clare Douglas
Production Designer	Gary Williamson
Costume Designer	Sharon Lewis
Make-up Artist	Sallie Jaye
Choreography	Quinny Sacks
Music Supervisor	Bob Last
Music Arranger	Dave Cooke

Author's Note

Some of the nicks and tucks of the cutting room have been
ignored in this text, as well as a few other slices. The editing stage
is the last rewrite, but this was a happy production and there are
few changes.

Dennis Potter

One

Opening titles, in colour, as for a big fifties musical –

LIPSTICK ON YOUR COLLAR

The music wa-wa-waas out, fifties-style, in a movie-title sequence
that ends on a big, glitzy juke box, drawing all eyes into its shining
depths, where three girls dance and a private soldier in uniform
endures stiff embarrassment.

The cinematic titles take us into a real cinema, in 1956, where
there is a newsreel showing a revolving globe, black and white,
with banal, predictable newsreel 'dramatic' music, and the
caption –

'New York's realistic air-raid drill'

Busy streets, New York. The gabble-gobble newsreel voice begins.
NEWSREEL VOICE: New York in the rush hour. Eight million
people in a hurry. But the very first civil defence exercise pulls
them up with a jerk. And the streets very soon become deserted.
Sirens sound. People run.

Pulling back from the newsreel to its audience, in a typical, big,
slightly rococo 1956 cinema.

Blue cigarette smoke curls and twists in the dancing, flickering
projection beam. The newsreel voice continuing:
Buying and selling on the Stock Exchange reaches zero. And
with a scare like this on, no wonder.
On the screen, dealers scramble for every exit, leaving an
abandoned litter.

Leaning against the wall of the auditorium, at the edge of the
glistening flickers, an attractive young woman, Sylvia, has her
arms folded: torch held languidly in hand, jaws desultorily
chewing gum. She gives no attention to the screen, as the voice
gabbles on –
Schoolchildren get a welcome break from the classroom to get
a much more vital lesson about self-preservation during
atomic warfare.
On the screen the newsreel shows children sitting, covering their
heads and cowering.

And then a White House spokesman appears in what was meant to be a solemn juxtaposition.

POLITICIAN: I am very unhappy to conclude that the hydrogen bomb should be developed and built. I do not think we should intentionally lose the armaments race –

Sylvia could not care less, as she continues to chew her gum.

To do this would be to lose our liberties. And with Patrick Henry, I value my liberties more than my life!

The newsreel comes to an end.

The cinema auditorium resonances yield to the war office in Whitehall.

Inside one of its large rooms, windows looking across Whitehall, Colonel Harry Bernwood (OC), Major Wallace Hedges, Major Johnny Church, Major Archie Carter and US Lt Colonel 'Truck' Trekker are stooped in apparent diligence over their big desks.

At lesser and lower desks bend Corporal Berry, general clerk (and regular soldier) and Private Hopper, National Serviceman, the Russian Language clerk.

The officers and men are in civvies – yet they are unmistakably military, blade-creased and shoe-shiningly stiff. Major Hedges is the only one with his jacket off, revealing red braces which give him an amiably rakish air.

Scratch-scratch-scratch of fountain pens on paper. Then Hedges lets out a mannered sigh, pointedly throws down his pen, looks steadily and comically all around the big room.

HEDGES: Bum holes.

Nobody takes any notice: this must be an old routine. Hedges, miffed, looks around again with evident disdain.

Scratch-scratch-scratch.

Bum holes, say I. In the plural. I conjure up for your delectation the image of row upon row of bare arses. A whole choir-stall of them. Eh? Eh?

Colonel Bernwood rustles paper in slight irritation, but the others bend still closer to their work.

Ah. I see. I see. No one interested in my state of mind this bright morn.

No response. Peeved, he picks up his pen again, with a sigh of comic anguish.

Now why is that, do you think? Mnn? Do you consider,

2

perhaps, that I am being provocative? Is that it? Eh? Eh? (*No response: so, utterly relentless*) Or *boring*, even?

Have I become a bore without even knowing –

Bernwood lifts his head and stares hard. Hedges, in mid-flow, makes a little gesture of partly satiric deference, sighs, and resumes writing.

Scratch-scratch tedium.

Private Hopper is translating from the Soviet Army newspaper *Krasnaya Zvezda* ('*Red Star*') with dictionary and boredom, sighing bitterly to himself.

HOPPER: (*Thinks*) Boring? Boring? Nah – nah – nah – of course
not! – It's thrilling in here. Bloody heart-tingling. Shaggin'
wonder-ful –

But then he becomes aware of the sardonic stare of his Language Officer, Major Church, and tries to adjust his expression.

CHURCH: Keen, are we, Hopper?

HOPPER: Yessah!

CHURCH: Keen and eager?

HOPPER: Yes, sir.

Hopper searches for a word in his dictionary with comic diligence. He waits for Church to stop examining him. Then – he lifts his head and almost with a snarl of disaffection, enters his own fantasies, where he can conjure up music at will, seeming to 'sing' to the original recording – and makes those around him do so too. He releases the opening lyrics of the 1956 hit by the Platters, 'The Great Pretender'.

Soon, though, the music leaves his head. There is no space for anything but his boredom. He is making an illicit line of strange little symbols on his foolscap paper:

UU uu UU uu UU uu

He gets up rather cautiously and shows the line of symbols to Corporal Berry, at the next desk.

(*Whispers*) Look, Corporal. Drum music.

Berry, laboriously collating foolscap sheets, is reluctantly interested.

BERRY: (*Whispers*) Yeah?

HOPPER: (*Whispers*) Yeah. See. Can't you read it?

BERRY: (*Whispers*) You know bloody well I can't.

HOPPER: (*Whispers*) Nothing to it. Look – (*Runs his finger along the line*.) Bum. Tit. Tit. Bum-tit-tit – !

Berry swallows a snigger, then glares.

BERRY: (*Whispers*) Very shaggin' funny.

HOPPER: (*Smirks*) Good. Ennit?

But across the vast room, under a portrait of the young Queen Elizabeth II, Colonel Bernwood has become irritated.

BERNWOOD: Less noise there!

BERRY/HOPPER: Sir!

Berry glares again at Hopper, then crisply rises and begins to distribute the sheets he has been collating into each officer's in-tray.

Major Hedges watches the Corporal's brisk progress with a baleful attention – until a single sheet drops into his own overloaded tray.

HEDGES: Bum holes!

BERRY: Sorry, sir.

But no sooner than Berry resumes his seat, Private Hopper rises to distribute *his* sheets into each in-tray.

Hard-eyed, raw faced Major Carter glints up as his sheet arrives.

CARTER: And what is it, Hopper?

HOPPER: (*Nervously*) '*Krasnaya Zvezda*' – I mean, '*Red Star*', sir.
Article in '*Red Star*', sir.

CARTER: What's it say?

HOPPER: Um. 'Army footballers must play better', sir.

CARTER: Hopper!

HOPPER: Sir!

CARTER: What have you got between your ears? Use your bonce,
will you! Once in a while! I've got more than enough bumph.

He tears the new sheet into pieces and drops them straight into his waste-basket.

HOPPER: Sir. I was told to translate every – (*Wilts under cold stare*)
Yessir. Sorry, sir!

He moves on quickly, on his way to Major Hedges, but Hedges fixes him with a steady, almost sardonic stare.

Sir? You . . . ?

He hesitantly proffers the paper.

HEDGES: Bum holes.

HOPPER: Yessir.

Hopper returns to his desk, and looks covertly sidelong at Berry. Scratch-scratch-scratch.

4

Hopper sighs, seriously bored, looks around with enormous discontent, and then, side-of-mouth to Berry –

HOPPER: (*Whispers*) Bum tit tit bum tit-tit.

Berry returns a *sotto voce* snarl, anxious about Bernwood.

BERRY: Shaddup.

Hopper sighs, heavily, looking as though he'd rather be anywhere else in the world but here.

HOPPER: (*Thinks*) Am I asleep? Or what? How do you tell for sure? Christ. What a dump. Roll on. Roll on.

Almost without realising, he is drawing a music stave, and starting to put in the notes.

Faintly at first, or even mockingly, a familiar boo-wah-ba fifties pop-chorus begins, then Hopper opens his mouth and uninhibitedly releases himself into 'Earth Angel' as the solo singer in the Crewcuts' original recording from 1954/5.

During the song, his sexual yearnings are made flesh, so to speak, as a nubile, virtually naked, yet sometimes winged young woman appears, disappears, appears on various of the desks in a provocative, sinuous progression towards Hopper himself. The rest of the office, of course, continues to work as normal, unaware of the sexual angel.

Eventually, though, the half-erotic fantasy is punctured, for Colonel Bernwood is staring across at Hopper, affronted.

BERNWOOD: Hopper. What are you doing?

HOPPER: Sir. I – (*Gulp*) Sir?

BERNWOOD: Get on with your work!

HOPPER: (*Relieved*) Yes, sir. Sorry, sir.

Across the road, the clock on Horse Guards Parade begins to strike a thin but rapid eleven in the morning –

As the notes continue and conclude, Major Hedges nods his head in time to the last few in wearily satiric exaggeration. And then –

HEDGES: Bum holes!

Bernwood puts down the chart he is annotating, and glares.

BERNWOOD: What?

Hedges pretends surprise.

HEDGES: What – ?

BERNWOOD: (*Sighs*) Wallace –

HEDGES: Sorry. It was just the sound of a human voice. Startled me, y'know. I think I said bum holes. Yes. That was almost certainly it. Bee-you-em. Bum holes.

Corporal Berry and Private Hopper try to avoid looking at each other, and bend their heads lower.

BERNWOOD: Wallace. Please. I wish very much that you wouldn't *do* this. Not every five – (*Suddenly*) Corporal!

This because Berry, despite himself, has started to snigger.

BERRY: Beg pardon, sir!

HEDGES: It's that clock. That deuced clock. Striking eleven like that.

Cold-eyed Major Carter responds, irritably.

CARTER: What about it?

HEDGES: Oh, chatty are we?

CARTER: Actually, no.

HEDGES: Well – I wish it were striking twelve, that's all. One more hour on. Christ in shitty napkins, what a life. Nine to five, eh? Stooped over a bloody desk like a bloody box-wallah – eh? That's what I joined the army for, eh? (*As they half-laugh*) Corporal!

BERRY: Sah!

HEDGES: What about the barely bloody drinkable?

BERRY: Sah! (*To* HOPPER) Hopper. Coffee.

HOPPER: Corporal!

Hopper puts down his Russian dictionary and, with regulation briskness, goes to a side-table where the fifties tin of Nescafé, squat bottle of milk etc. repose.

HEDGES: I mean if we've got to put in office hours, we slaves, then we ought not to deviate one bloody jot or one bloody tittle from office bloody routine. Eh? Coffee at eleven. Tea and bicky-wickies at four. And three two-minute wee-wees in between.

Some amusement, but Bernwood is increasingly annoyed.

BERNWOOD: Wallace.

HEDGES: I know. I know. But –

BERNWOOD: They're champing at the bit upstairs. They need that new Battle Order. You know that, and yet –

HEDGES: Oh, look here, old thing.

BERNWOOD: How in heaven's name are we going to get it out on time if you keep up this non-stop barrage? It's worse than dysentery. Time and place! Please!

HEDGES: All right, Harry, all right. Let's keep some sense of – ah –

6

of – ah – ah – God Almighty! This place is beginning to upset the balance of my mind. I can't drag up the right word when I want it.

CARTER: (*Almost hostile*) Prop-or-tion.

HEDGES: (*Comically*) What?

CARTER: The word you want.

HEDGES: (*Stares at* CARTER, *with no love lost.*) Absolutely not.

CARTER: What?

HEDGES: No, no. That's not a word I care for, old fruit. I was digging down into the bog for a much more – 'Prop-or-tion'? No, no.

BERNWOOD: (*In despair*) Please!

HEDGES: Perspective! That's the word. Yes, Harry. I'm sorry.

BERNWOOD: (*Angrily*) Sorry. Sorry!

HEDGES: All I was saying was –

BERNWOOD: No!

HEDGES: – was – to keep a – a sense of – of –

CHURCH: (*Mischievously*) Perspective?

HEDGES: (*Smirking*) Pro-por-tion.

Hopper, meanwhile, has laid out the cups and put the kettle on.

At Hedges' last line, Hopper ill-advisedly lets out a small bark of a laugh, which he suppresses – but not quickly enough.

The officers turn, almost as one, to stare at such impertinence. Hopper gulps.

The sudden drum and heavy clap of the introduction to 'Little Bitty Pretty One' by Thurston Harris begins, oddly menacing and heavily rhythmic.

Almost immediately (at, say, the second clap) the officers, staring hard at Hopper, join in and the beleaguered Private winces as the music crashes on in heavily rhythmic menace.

Each Officer, except Bernwood, rises at his desk and begins the slow, threatening, 'singing', clapping advance upon Hopper at the coffee table. Hopper goes rigidly to attention, but his eyes swivel in alarm as they come nearer, nearer – touching him, threatening him, even manhandling him in a dancing whirl.

The pitch and tempo change again, as they tighten into a circle around paralysed Hopper. Then, with a menacing leer of camp sexuality, Hedges reaches out and plucks Hopper's cheek, briefly, between his thumb and forefinger, as he apparently 'sings' the blatantly sexist lyric. The others keep up the heavily insistent clapping, throughout.

Colonel Bernwood is still sitting at his big desk, anxiously turning over pages, clenched-up inside with some unnamed foreboding or slowly growing distress. Yet even he is made to take part in the ludicrous but heavily rhythmic and sexually aggressive chorus as it further tightens around the young man.

Suddenly, and comically, Hopper himself bursts into 'song': but his face is a picture of anxiety, and his eyes roll in panic.

At the escalation of the chorus, the officers, facing Hopper, retreat back towards their desks, still clapping. And then, abruptly, the music stops.

Colonel Bernwood lifts his burdened head from his papers at the exact moment, before the song, that Hopper let out his quickly suppressed laugh.

BERNWOOD: (*Frowns*) Hopper. Where the hell do you think you are?

HOPPER: I–I'm sorry, sir. I swallowed the wrong way, sir. Sorry, sir.

BERNWOOD: (*Snaps*) Get on with your work, man! Get back to your desk!

HOPPER: *Sah*! (*But he moves away from the coffee table –*)

HEDGES: Hopper!

HOPPER: Sah!

HEDGES: What about the barely bloody drinkie-winkie?

HOPPER: *Sah*!

With an uncertain swift glance at Bernwood, Hopper returns to the coffee table, his back to the others, spooning coffee powder. Hopper seethes inside.

(*Thinks*) Roll on. Roll on. Roll bloody on.

The kettle, whistle-spouted, begins its boiling shriek.

He begins to slop the boiling water on to the powdered coffee in each of the cups. *Sotto voce*, and transatlantic side-of-the-mouth style, he adds –

Shoot me a slug from the wonderful jug.

At the cinema, the newsreel has come round again in the continuous performance programme.

NEWSREEL VOICE: – million people in a hurry. But the very first civil defence exercise pulls them up with a jerk. And the streets very soon become deserted . . .

Moving from bored usherette Sylvia to a young man at the end of

8

the row nearest or very near to her. He, too, is not remotely interested in the newsreel but is eyeing her with appreciative speculation.

Sylvia becomes aware. They look at each other.

YOUNG MAN: (*Stage whisper*) When do you finish?

SYLVIA: Why?

YOUNG MAN: Come on. What's your name?

SYLVIA: Why?

But she seems interested, in a cautious way.

YOUNG MAN: 'Cos everybody's got to have a name, 'ent they?

MAN IN ROW BEHIND: Sssh!

The young man winks at her. She smiles. He raises his eyebrows, and signals.

YOUNG MAN: I'll be waiting for you, sweetie-pie.

Back at the war office, it is afternoon now, on another boring day in the big room.

Scratch-scratch-scratch of fountain pens biting into paper.

Hopper distributing tea, now, with one digestive biscuit in each saucer.

Scratch-scratch-scratch. A congealing sense of tedium.

HEDGES: (*Suddenly*) Do you know what they call those little black things between an elephant's toes?

CARTER: (*Sigh*) Go on. If we must.

HEDGES: Slow niggers.

There is some laughter, but, throwing down his pen –

BERNWOOD: Major Hedges!

Such an angry shout that everyone is astonished.

HEDGES: Now, now, Harry.

BERNWOOD: Look here, Wallace. I've just about had enough of –

HEDGES: (*Overriding*) We're all working too damned hard. I mean – oh, come on! – it's all bullshit, this new battle order bumph –

BERNWOOD: Wallace –

HEDGES: We might just as well give them the old one. They fuss far too much upstairs. Christ, the Battle Order doesn't change, not in three months it doesn't. The Russians never do anything different. In fact, if you –

BERNWOOD: Bunkum!

HEDGES: What?

CARTER: You're talking through your hat again.

HEDGES: I'm what?

9

TREKKER: They're moving the infantry, fella. And they're moving the tanks.

His American accent comes as a surprise.

HEDGES: What? No, no. Not west they aren't. Not through *my* section they aren't.

TREKKER: South.

HEDGES: (*Suddenly alert*) What?

Bernwood, too, shows a sharper interest.

BERNWOOD: I've lost near enough a whole tank regiment from those new barracks outside Magnitogorsk. The Eighth.

TREKKER: Gone south.

BERNWOOD: That's my impression too, Colonel –

CARTER: And some of the infantry have gone. Decamped!

TREKKER: Going south.

CARTER: (*Dubiously*) Maybe. Maybe.

Bernwood shows a slightly British paranoia.

BERNWOOD: Have your people got more on this, Truck, than we're –

TREKKER: You people have just about everything my people have, Harry. (*Looks at him: measured tones.*) But – well – it's how you read it, I guess. My opinion – no our opinion – is that the status of all this is hardening. You can elevate it from surmise.

HEDGES: You can what?

Trekker looks at him, correctly picking up the tinge of still imperial British condescension.

TREKKER: They're moving men and material south, *old bean*. And you'd better believe it.

HEDGES: All right, all right, old fruit. No offence. But I think –

BERNWOOD: (*Interrupts, testily*) And until we can collate all these new papers, we won't really know what the h. is going on, will we? This could be the – I mean the – Good Lord, Wallace, the next b. war! So let's have an end to these disturbances. If you don't mind!

They bend to their charts and papers again, much more solemnly, as a faint whiff of hell momentarily passes over them.

Scratch-scratch-scratch.

The distant clock chimes the brief, thin quarter.

Suffocated by boredom, Hedges lifts his head, comically, like a hound scenting prey.

HEDGES: Mmm. Quarter past. (*Then, when nobody looks up.*) Time Marches On.

His little device does not work. Morose, he bends his head again.
Scratch-scratch-scratch.

Private Hopper all but clenches his teeth.

HOPPER: (*Thinks*) War? *War*? Shagging *war*? I've only got six
weeks – Hey. Leave me out. Let me go. *I'm* not joining in – no
more shagging war. No!

Way across London, rather too intently studying the stills in their
frames (fifties style) outside the cinema's pillared entrance is the
young man who had whispered and winked at the usherette Sylvia.

The stills are perhaps showing scenes from the Wedding of the
Year: Prince Rainier of Monaco and film star Grace Kelly.

Sylvia, changed out of her uniform, comes out of the cinema.
The young man, who has obviously been waiting, quickly leaves
the framed stills to catch her on the cinema steps.

YOUNG MAN: So here you are then.

SYLVIA: (*Startled*) What you mean?

YOUNG MAN: Bloke at the front told me you only work afternoons
on a Monday and Wednesday.

SYLVIA: That's my business.

But she has stood still. They look at each other.

YOUNG MAN: So – what do you do evenings?

She looks at him, half-speculatively.

SYLVIA: Depends.

YOUNG MAN: Ever go to the Palais, then?

SYLVIA: (*Shrugs*) Not much.

YOUNG MAN: I could take you.

SYLVIA: Nah.

YOUNG MAN: Wouldn't hurt you, would it?

SYLVIA: My old man wouldn't like it, would he?

YOUNG MAN: Yer dad?

SYLVIA: Me *husband*.

A would-be humorist, he takes a swift step back, in exaggerated
shock and horror.

YOUNG MAN: Cor – Christ!

SYLVIA: Wha – ?

YOUNG MAN: Thrown yourself away, entcha! And all this time
there was *me*. Waiting!

He laughs, not sure of the possible response. But then she laughs.

SYLVIA: I didn't know, did I?

YOUNG MAN: Well, you do now. Dontcha?
She just looks at him. He shuffles a bit.
　　　You – but you got a minute?
SYLVIA: What for?
YOUNG MAN: Well. You can do a lot in a minute.
SYLVIA: Yeh. Lotta damage.

Back at the War Office, and Crash! The big door from the corridor outside bangs open.
　　In thump-clumps Private Francis (Frank) Francis, heavily burdened in Full Service Marching Order (FSMO): boots, gaiters, ammunition pouches, bayonet, large back-pack, small back-pack, webbed steel helmet on top of back-packs, kit-bag.
　　Francis, awkward by nature, looks around, momentarily terrorised into mindlessness by the stares, and utterly confused by the absence of uniforms.
　　He looks at Hopper, the nearest. Then – in an ankle-jarring British Army bang – thump of studded boots – *hup-two-three*! – a rigid armed salute, complete with automaton gabble.
FRANCIS: Two – two – nine – two – zero – zero – seven – one –
　　　Private – Francis – F – reporting – for – duty – *Sah*!
And it is Private Hopper he has saluted.
　　Hopper twitchily jerks his head, embarrassed, in an attempt to indicate that Francis should be doing all this to Colonel Bernwood.
BERRY: (*Hisses, to Francis*) You bleed'n git.
FRANCIS: (*Helplessly*) S. sir –
BERNWOOD: Does Private Hopper really look like your new
　　　Commanding Officer, soldier?
Francis quivers.
FRANCIS: Oh . . . I . . . –
Pulling himself together, Francis marches to the front of Bernwood's desk, clump-thump smashes his boot down, and spring-action salutes.
(*Again*) Two – two – nine – two – zero –
BERNWOOD: Yes. Yes. We've had all that. And one of your
　　　shoulders is higher than the other!
FRANCIS: S. sir . . . ?
BERNWOOD: Give me your movement order, man!
FRANCIS: (*Still confused*) Sir – ?
BERNWOOD: Are you a cretin?

Hedges has been hugely enjoying the diversion.

HEDGES: Well, of course he is, Harry. It must be the new
    Language clerk. Not likely to be able to read nor write, now is
    he?

Bernwood is not quite amused.

BERNWOOD: Well, I hope he understands Russian a little better
    than he seems to understand English. (*To* FRANCIS) Come on.
    Movement order. Sharp about it!

All fingers and thumbs, Francis has found, and now timorously
hands over, the correct scrap of paper.

FRANCIS: S.sorry s.sir –

BERNWOOD: Do you stutter?

FRANCIS: N-nun – no, sir – (*Makes effort*) I mean, no sir!

But Bernwood is glaring at the movement order.

BERNWOOD: But look here – your movement order says you are to
    leave the Intelligence Corps depot at Maresfield at 0800 hours
    and report to this room at the war office at 1500 hours.

FRANCIS: Sir. I –

BERNWOOD: (*Utterly astounded*) It's way past 1600 hours.

FRANCIS: Sir. I –

TREKKER: Sixteen hundred twenty one.

BERNWOOD: (*To* FRANCIS) *Well?*

FRANCIS: I – sir. I'm sorry, sir –

BERNWOOD: What do you mean, sorry?

He is genuinely appalled. Orders are orders are sacred. Francis
fidgets, scared.

FRANCIS: I – I – was d.dud. Delayed, sir . . .

BERNWOOD: Delayed? What do you mean, delayed? Late on
    parade is what you mean, soldier!

FRANCIS: (*Twitching*) I – sir – I – *sah!* – Permission to speak, *sah!*

He salutes again. Bernwood looks at him.

BERNWOOD: Speak.

FRANCIS: Sir – I – I've never been to London before sir, except to
    pass through, sir, and I – (*Stiffly trying to straighten even more*)
    got lost, sir.

BERNWOOD: Lost?

Gleeful, Hedges cannot restrain himself.

HEDGES: He's in the Intelligence Corps, isn't he? Of course he
    bloody well got lost.

The others laugh: this happens to be to Francis' benefit, even though it increases his discomfort.

BERNWOOD: In London. You got lost in London.

FRANCIS: Sir.

BERNWOOD: Good God above. (*Studies him.*) Look here. You don't
have to wet your thumb and hold it in the air, soldier. But
you've got a tongue in your head, haven't you? Here we are,
slap in the middle of Whitehall!

FRANCIS: Sir. I asked a policeman, and he –

BERNWOOD: (*Incredulous*) You what?

FRANCIS: I asked him where Whitehall was, sir – where the war
office was, sir – and and – um –

BERNWOOD: And where was this? Where did this encounter take
place?

FRANCIS: Trafalgar Square, sir. (*Stupidly*) With the big stone lions.

HEDGES: And the sticks with horse-head handles!

All laugh, except Bernwood.

BERNWOOD: Half a mo', Wallace. (*To* FRANCIS) Well? And then?

Francis shifts from one boot to the other, heavily burdened in all
senses.

FRANCIS: He pointed to this big building, sir, and it seemed, well –

BERNWOOD: Keep still, man!

FRANCIS: *Sah*!

BERNWOOD: Yes! Go on!

FRANCIS: It had pillars and steps and – and I – but . . . (*Wretched*) It
was full of pictures, sir.

BERNWOOD: Pictures?

FRANCIS: Yessir. And – (*Gulps*) – by the time I realised it wasn't
what the policeman had said it was, sir, I –

He stops, dreadfully unhappy.

   Major Church, the Language Officer, younger than the other
officers, is the first to get it. He points across at Francis.

CHURCH: National Gallery.

A startled pause. Then everyone roars.

HEDGES: National Gallery – ! Hoo! Hoo! National bloody Gall-er-
ee-eee – hee!

His braces-snapping excess of delight increases the laughter.

FRANCIS: (*Above laughter*) Permission – to – speak – *sah*!

BERNWOOD: (*Gasping*) Yes – go on –

He flaps his hand at Francis, temporarily unable to speak for
amusement.

14

FRANCIS: Sir. I would like you to accept the proposal, sir, that I am
    not as big a fool as I must seem, sir.
Which sets off further paroxysms. On the ebb of the laughter, and
not wholly unkindly –
BERNWOOD: I suppose I must take note of that on this one
    occasion. But I hope you will quickly learn, soldier, that in
    this office your opinions are of little or no relevance, and in any
    case should be kept to yourself.
FRANCIS: Sir.
BERNWOOD: None of us here is in uniform, but that does not in any
    shape or form imply the slightest derogation of normal army
    disciplines and procedure. Exactly the opposite! Do you
    understand?
FRANCIS: Yessir.
BERNWOOD: Then get your shoulders into alignment.
FRANCIS: *Sah*!
He stiffens into yet more awkward attention.
    Bernwood studies him, severely.
BERNWOOD: If you arrive late again – and if you continue to make
    such an ass of yourself, you'll – Corporal! Make it clear!
Corporal Berry stands like a ramrod.
BERRY: Sah! (*To* FRANCIS, *in NCO scream*) Ha – bout *turn*!
Francis executes a regulation about-turn – clump, thump – but
with the inexpertness of an awkward young man, bringing himself
to face the screaming Corporal.
BERRY: (*Again*) Sol-dyah!
FRANCIS: Corporal!
BERRY: Yeww – are – a – *twit*. What – are – you?
FRANCIS: A twit, Corporal.
Berry is on NCO-autopilot.
BERRY: I'll – put my – dingaling – in – your – *ear*-a-a! – And – shag
    – some *sense*-a-a – into – you! Understand-d-d-a?
FRANCIS: Corporal!
BERNWOOD: (*Mildly*) Right you are, Corporal Berry. Return him
    to me.
BERRY: Sah! (*Screams*) Ha – bout-t – *turn*!
Francis thumps around, to face Bernwood again.
BERNWOOD: Let us hope things will improve a bit from now on.
    Right. Now, then – (*Seems to consider, for too long.*) As I said –
    aah – none of us in this office is in uniform, for reasons that

may become apparent to you. I'm – ah – I'm afraid the same will have to apply to yourself. No uniform.

Francis cannot quite control a little jerk of utter delight – which Bernwood, fortunately, misunderstands.

FRANCIS: No, sir . . . !

BERNWOOD: Yes, I know, I know. But there it is – you will have to wear your civilian clothes to work.

FRANCIS: (*Controlling delight*) Yes, sir.

Bernwood becomes remotely aware of some (to him) puzzling, held-in enthusiasm.

BERNWOOD: Neat and tidy! Collar and ties. No coloured shirts, or – (*Barks*) plain socks!

FRANCIS: Yessir!

BERNWOOD: Good. Now – neat and tidy, neat and tidy – well. We are extremely busy this afternoon – very busy – The world doesn't stand still, um, Francis – understand?

FRANCIS: Sir.

BERNWOOD: Perhaps you wanted adventure. Malaya, eh? Or Cyprus. Or, in the – ah – forests, eh? Teaching the Mau Mau how to behave themselves. But this little place here – it's even more – (*Ominously*) The Soviet Union, Francis.

FRANCIS: (*At a loss*) Sir.

BERNWOOD: Exactly! Got to be ready for when the bally thing goes up, mm? The balloon.

FRANCIS: Yessir.

Bernwood looks around the office, seemingly distracted and not quite sure what to say.

His gaze falls on Private Hopper, who quickly lowers his head.

BERNWOOD: Briefly, then – this section of Military Intelligence – MI (*Coughs*) bracket BO bracket is – Do you know what BO means?

They all lift their heads in expectant amusement.

FRANCIS: Um – it's when you don't – (*Some alertness saves him.*) No, sir.

BERNWOOD: Battle Order.

Comic half-beat.

FRANCIS: Yessir.

BERNWOOD: In this case, the Battle Order of the Red Army, Francis. Where they are. Where they've been. Where they're going. Got the point?

16

FRANCIS: Yessir.

BERNWOOD: Now, then. This info comes to us at these desks by a variety of overt and covert – pretty damned hush-hush, and – but I won't go into – Yes. Pretty clear? Mm?

FRANCIS: (*Comically*) Sir.

BERNWOOD: Right you are. You are to be the new Russian Language Clerk to Major Church, there. The Language Officer. He will explain.

CHURCH: Explicate the inexplicable.

Bernwood frowns a little, disliking frivolity, but continues to addess Francis.

BERNWOOD: Now. I am Colonel Bernwood – over there, Major Carter. That is Major Hedges in the – ah – the – (*Wants to say red braces.*) And – now listen to me very carefully. You see the gentleman sitting there?

He indicates the American Lt Colonel, who nods back.

FRANCIS: Yes, sir.

BERNWOOD: Well. He's not there.

A beat.

FRANCIS: No, sir.

BERNWOOD: (*Glinting*) Where is he?

Francis looks at Trekker and then at Bernwood, in dismay.

FRANCIS: Sir – ?

BERNWOOD: He's – not – here!

FRANCIS: Sah!

BERNWOOD: His name – ah – which of course you will need to know even though he's not – ah – (*Looks at* FRANCIS, *vaguely puzzled*) Lieutenant Colonel Trekker. From G-2, United States Army. (*Stares hard.*) You have signed the Official Secrets Act.

FRANCIS: Yes, sir.

BERNWOOD: And you are aware of the consequences of breaking it.

FRANCIS: Sir.

BERNWOOD: Hanging.

FRANCIS: Sir?

BERNWOOD: You don't want to be hanged, do you?

FRANCIS: No, sir.

BERNWOOD: One stray word. One wink across the top of your glass of sherry – understand? A nudge is as good as a – Anywhere outside this room, soldier. Anywhere at all is the wrong place.

17

Is that perfectly clear?

FRANCIS: Yessir!

BERNWOOD: Good. Then you won't have to be buried in
quicklime. Now – who is that sitting over there?

He indicates Trekker again.

FRANCIS: (*Uncertainly*) Nobody, sir.

Bernwood nods, satisfied.

BERNWOOD: And *that* is the first thing to tuck away and keep dark.
The military intelligence services of the United Kingdom and
the United States are to all intents and purposes – (*Severely*)
You understand?

FRANCIS: Sir!

A beat.

BERNWOOD: Well. I think that covers things pretty well.

He bends abruptly to his work.

Francis is left at attention in cumbersome FSMO and with no
idea of what to do.

Scratch-scratch-scratch go all the fountain pens at all the desks.

FRANCIS: (*Croaks*) Sir? I – Excuse me, sir . . . ?

Bernwood looks up, testily.

BERNWOOD: Don't stand around, soldier! Get those packs off.
Present your idle self to Major Church.

FRANCIS: *Sah*!

Church, who has been watching with sardonic amusement, affects
a weary reluctance.

CHURCH: Over here. Sharp about it. Sit down.

Francis divests himself of his packs, very awkwardly, getting
strap-tangled and flustered.

Aware of Church's gaze, he looks for a chair, all but knocks it
over with ever-increasing clumsiness and awkwardness, and sits.

Church waits, making Francis twitch, then lobs a word.

CHURCH: A gazelle.

FRANCIS: Sir – ?

CHURCH: Like a gazelle.

FRANCIS: (*Mumbles*) Sir.

CHURCH: Name. Say again.

FRANCIS: Francis, sir. Francis F.

CHURCH: What's the F?

FRANCIS: Francis, sir.

CHURCH: Yes, yes. What's the F!

FRANCIS: (*Twitches*) Francis, sir. Francis Francis.

CHURCH: How very economical. Well, Francis. Get this clear. When we call you Francis we mean Francis, not Francis. No familiarity.

FRANCIS: No, sir.

He is not yet equipped to pick up Church's style, which is usually sardonic.

CHURCH: Ability. That's always at issue. What was your final mark on the Joint Services Russian course?

FRANCIS: 92 per cent, sir.

CHURCH: Is that a smirk I detect?

FRANCIS: No, sir.

CHURCH: Clever Dick are we?

FRANCIS: No, sir.

CHURCH: Mm. I wonder. Graceful movements. Superb brain. An economical name. Well, let's hear it.

FRANCIS: Sir?

CHURCH: Your brilliant Russian.

FRANCIS: Um –

CHURCH: My God. Whiplash Willie.

FRANCIS: (*Stung*)

   Ya pomnyu chudnoye mgnovyenye –

CHURCH: What?

FRANCIS: 'I remember a wonderful moment – '

CHURCH: Yes. Somewhere in the valleys. I'll bet you do. Some Megan or Blodwen, I'll be bound.

FRANCIS: Pushkin, sir.

Church knows quite well what he means, but –

CHURCH: What do you mean, Pushkin? What do you think you are talking about, Francis?

FRANCIS: Well, sir –

CHURCH: Go on, then!

Francis is not quite sure he understands and cautiously continues.

FRANCIS:

   Pyeryedo mnoy yavilas ty
   Kak mimolyotnoye vidyenye . . .

CHURCH: What?

FRANCIS: (*Uneasily*)

   'You stood before me
   Like a momentary vision – '

19

CHURCH: Did I?

But Francis has an awkward young man's suddenly flushed imagination.

FRANCIS: Sir. He is remembering the very first time he –

CHURCH: Had a bunk-up.

FRANCIS: No, sir!

CHURCH: No?

FRANCIS: (*Twitches*) No, sir. The first time he met this – this enchantingly lovely young lady Anna, sir. And how now that he has seen her again, his heart is – is – (*Falters under the stare*) Sorry, sir.

CHURCH: (*With precision*) Tosh.

FRANCIS: Sir.

CHURCH: Caterpillar tracks, Francis. Artillery ranges. Calibrations. Each sort of shooter. Tanks. Those are the words you need in this office. Military words. Not mush.

FRANCIS: Yes sir.

Church contemplates him, secretly amused.

CHURCH: Enchantingly lovely young lady. Is that what you said?

Hedges, way across the vast room, lifts his head to a promising new scent as Francis near-adolescently squirms.

HEDGES: What's that, Johnny?

CHURCH: Private Francis here. Obsessed with pretty young ladies.

FRANCIS: (*Twitches*) Sir. I –

HEDGES: Jolly good! Nice fluffy things, eh?

CHURCH: (*Mock severely to* FRANCIS) If you feel an overwhelming need to masturbate, young man, I suggest you do it in your lunch hour.

Francis is appalled, and half-rises.

FRANCIS: Sir – !

CHURCH: Yes?

FRANCIS: Permission to speak, sir.

CHURCH: No.

FRANCIS: (*Deeply upset*) Sir. I must – sir, this is . . .

CHURCH: (*Mildly*) Be quiet.

FRANCIS: Sir.

And he drops his head.

Church looks at him, with a glint of amusement tempered by sympathy.

Meanwhile, Private Hopper, watching, listening, conjures up

20

some more music. And the enormous room instantly becomes a set for a musical number, with everyone, even the humiliated Francis, taking part: 'The Garden of Eden', as sung by Frankie Vaughan with Wally Stott, his orchestra and chorus, but 'sung' here – lips moving in synchronisation with the original – by everyone in the office.

Hedges is out of his seat, making mock lewd gestures, wiggling pretend breasts and lascivious hips at hapless Francis.

The apparently ever-available, fantasy young woman who had been the distinctly carnal angel in 'Earth Angel' glows again as a blasphemous Eve, complete with every physical provocation as well as the additional armoury of a phallic snake and an apple that goldenly glows, in surrounding greenery and exotica.

The green and steamy sequence ends with Major Church 'singing' – but then, as the music disappears, he carries on talking as though nothing unusual had happened.

CHURCH: Have you located a lodging? A place to dream.

FRANCIS: Yes, sir.

CHURCH: Suitable?

FRANCIS: (*Fidgets*) With my mother's relatives, sir. In Walham Green.

CHURCH: Walham what?

FRANCIS: Fulham, sir.

CHURCH: Relatives, you say?

FRANCIS: My mother's sister, sir. She –

CHURCH: (*Briskly*) Good. Good.

FRANCIS: Sir.

Church looks at his watch.

CHURCH: What you do the rest of the afternoon, Francis, is to take yourself off there – if you can find it!

FRANCIS: Yessir.

CHURCH: Get settled in. Stow your kit. Wash behind your ears. Stand close to the razor. Forget your Pushkin. And present yourself here in sober clothes – sober – at 0850 in the morning. On the bloody dot.

FRANCIS: Yes, sir.

CHURCH: And then Private Hopper there – who has the misfortune of being soon to be demobilized – Don't smirk, Hopper!

HOPPER: (*Grins*) No, sir.

CHURCH: (*To* FRANCIS) Where that smirking oaf will begin in his

21

own dozy way to hand over his duties to you. And then, who knows, you may get some faint glimmer of what it is we are up to in this little room.

FRANCIS: Yes, sir. Thank you, sir.

CHURCH: Toddle off, then.

FRANCIS: Yes, sir. Thank you, sir.

Church studies him as the young man awkwardly rises.

CHURCH: You can go and look for it, can't you?

FRANCIS: Sir . . . ?

CHURCH: That wonderful moment.

Francis has arrived at his new home in Fulham. In the front room, middle-aged aunt Vickie pulls down the sofa bed.

AUNT VICKIE: You see, that's all you do. Good, ennit? 'Course I haven't made it up yet. But it's a nice piece of furniture. Had it a good long time.

FRANCIS: It's – splendid, Aunt Vickie.

She looks at him. Splendid is an alien term of praise. She thinks he might be putting it on.

AUNT VICKIE: That's where your Mum and Dad spent the first night of their honeymoon – if that's what you could call it.

FRANCIS: Really?

AUNT VICKIE: It's sagged a bit in the middle ever since. (*Observes, and is amused by his shy twitch.*) Should be all right, shouldn't it?

FRANCIS: (*Rather stiffly*) Yes, thank you.

AUNT VICKIE: There's nothing wrong with the springs. A very nice Put-U-Up.

FRANCIS: It's splendid, Aunt Vickie.

She looks at him again.

AUNT VICKIE: If it comes to that, *you* might have been first thought of on that Put-U-Up –

FRANCIS: (*Quickly*) If you'll show me where the sheets and that –

AUNT VICKIE: Yes. I wouldn't be surprised if – let's see – (*Calculates on her fingers.*) No. Bit later. But not much. (*Moving to door.*) Still – that's where they had their first go, ennit? *As far as we know.* How is your mum, anyway? Buried down there in the back of beyond.

FRANCIS: (*Not at ease*) Oh, she's – Yes. She's splendid.

AUNT VICKIE: 'Splendid'.

22

FRANCIS: I mean –

AUNT VICKIE: My God, she's changed then – must have.

FRANCIS: (*Quickly*) She's very well.

AUNT VICKIE: 'Splendid' is what you call a hotel, ennit? At the seaside.

Francis, a bit sheepish, follows his bustling Aunt out into the narrow hall, from which stairs steeply rise, facing the front door.

FRANCIS: I mean – yeh – she's all right, Aunt Vickie. Well, except for her feet, she says.

AUNT VICKIE: Her feet?

The front door is opening.

FRANCIS: When she cut herself on that milk bottle, it –

He stops dead. Sylvia is coming in. She shuts the door, loudly.

But Aunt Vickie seems to take no notice whatsoever of the lovely young woman.

AUNT VICKIE: What do you mean, milk bottle? I haven't heard of this.

Francis is not listening. He gapes, swallows –

FRANCIS: (*To* SYLVIA) Um. Good even –

AUNT VICKIE: (*Sharply*) Frank! No.

So unexpectedly, that Francis is astounded. Sylvia takes no notice at all. It seems very odd.

FRANCIS: W.what ?

AUNT VICKIE: Oh, I remember now. That broken bottle. But that was months and months ago. She wrote and said. (*Without looking at* SYLVIA) Don't slam the door, young woman.

SYLVIA: (*Flatly*) And up yours too.

AUNT VICKIE: Noise, noise. You must love it.

SYLVIA: (*Flatly*) Kiss mine.

Confused, embarrassed, Francis all but presses himself against the wall to let Sylvia pass.

She gives him one small flicker of attention as she passes him and goes on up the stairs. But it registers – for her, too.

Aunt Vickie resumes talking to Francis as though nothing has happened.

AUNT VICKIE: She shouldn't have gone out on to the step in bare feet, but that was a long –

FRANCIS: Aunt Vickie.

AUNT VICKIE: – time ago, wasn't it? I mean –

FRANCIS: Aunt Vickie – who was that?

23

AUNT VICKIE: Who was what?

FRANCIS: That – that girl –

Aunt Vickie looks at him as though he has sworn, and goes on through into the tiny living-room and kitchen.

    Francis follows her in, astonished. He looks at her.

    (*Puzzled*) Aunt Vickie – ?

AUNT VICKIE: She used to be a very good dancer, your mum. Very, very good. All the blokes standing up against the wall – you know, looking and looking and sniffing –

FRANCIS: Who was – ?

AUNT VICKIE: (*Sweeping on*) All eyes. You know what they're like. *Young men.* When she was dancing, your mum – God, talk about your Grace Kelly and who'sit – Prince um –

FRANCIS: (*Doggedly*) Aunt Vickie. Who was that?

AUNT VICKIE: What?

FRANCIS: That girl.

AUNT VICKIE: What girl?

FRANCIS: Going up the stairs. Just now. The one who – *that girl*.

She looks at him, lips pursing in disapproval.

AUNT VICKIE: I didn't see nobody.

FRANCIS: (*Blinks*) What – ?

AUNT VICKIE: And even if I did, I don't talk to her. Waste of bloody breath.

FRANCIS: But –

AUNT VICKIE: (*Sweeping on*) Might just as well talk to a bitch on heat. The cow. No, Frank, we don't have nothing to do with her. Not no more.

FRANCIS: But – why? I mean – why?

AUNT VICKIE: (*Indignantly*) Whatchewmean, why?

FRANCIS: Well – I – well – she lives upstairs. Doesn't she?

AUNT VICKIE: Why do you want to know?

FRANCIS: Doesn't she?

AUNT VICKIE: Your Uncle Fred won't want you asking about Sylvia. He'll be very –

FRANCIS: (*Too lyrical*) Sylvia.

AUNT VICKIE: (*Stares*) What?

FRANCIS: Is that her name, then? Sylvia.

AUNT VICKIE: Common as muck.

FRANCIS: Sylvia.

AUNT VICKIE: What you looking like that for?

FRANCIS: (*Dreamily*)
    'Who is Sylvia?
    What is she?'
AUNT VICKIE: Your Mum used to look like that sometimes.
FRANCIS: Sorry?
AUNT VICKIE: Soppy.
FRANCIS: (*Offended*) What do you mean – ?
AUNT VICKIE: And look what happened to her!
FRANCIS: (*Swallows*) Aunt Vickie?
AUNT VICKIE: See somebody who takes your fancy and end up
    hundreds of miles from home with a – (*Pulls back*) Anyway.
    We don't talk to her upstairs. Not no more.
FRANCIS: But why?
AUNT VICKIE: (*Indignantly*) Why!
FRANCIS: Yes. Why?
She purses her lips again, and studies him.
AUNT VICKIE: Your Uncle Fred won't want you asking about her –
FRANCIS: But –
AUNT VICKIE: He says she's a – Well, never mind, there's some
    words you don't – And your Uncle Fred is a very upright man.
    Being neighbours is one thing – We had *words*, her and me,
    about the noise upstairs. Talk about a herd of elephants! We
    had words, and then she was bloody cheeky to your uncle.
    The sauce! We don't talk now.
FRANCIS: But what was it all about?
Aunt Vickie is filling the kettle in the tiny kitchenette off, which
has a pullable curtain instead of a door.
AUNT VICKIE: Anyway. What's all this about our Betty's foot.
    Didn't it heal up proper, or what? (*At his non-answer*) I
    wouldn't pass the time of day with her. And there's not many I
    don't get on with.
FRANCIS: *Why* don't you talk? I mean – what was it all about?
AUNT VICKIE: Expect you're ready for a nice cup of tea, aren't you?
FRANCIS: (*Near whisper*) I'd talk to her.
But Aunt Vickie is unexpectedly looking at him from the
kitchenette entrance. He twitches.
AUNT VICKIE: What's that, Frank?
FRANCIS: I – yes. Cup of tea.
AUNT VICKIE: Interested in her? Are you?
FRANCIS: I – no, I was just –

AUNT VICKIE: It's not a good idea.

FRANCIS: No, no, I just – Well. If she lives upstairs and uses the same front door and –

AUNT VICKIE: Hard as nails, her bloke. Nasty little bugger. And a bit of a mystery.

FRANCIS: In what way?

AUNT VICKIE: He's a spy.

FRANCIS: A what?

AUNT VICKIE: Leastways, that's *one* of his tales. (*Looks hard at him.*) I wouldn't tangle with *him*. Not if I was you.

FRANCIS: I wasn't proposing to.

And he looks miffed.

There is a budgerigar in a cage on the table, which is up against the half net curtained window. The window looks out on to the tiny backyard.

Francis looks at the bird, with an obscure sense of fellow feeling.

Then, from upstairs, a fairly loud blast of music, from a just switched-on radio – midway or so into 'Lipstick on Your Collar', as sung by Connie Francis.

Aunt Vickie puts her head around the curtain, affronted by the noise.

AUNT VICKIE: There! You see!

FRANCIS: (*Reluctantly*) Yes – but it's a nice song, though. (*At her expression*) Sort of.

Upstairs, Sylvia dumps some potatoes into the ancient sink in a similarly curtained-off subsection of what is already a small room.

She half-sings to the continuing music from the radio on the other side of the curtain in the living-room, as she peels the potatoes.

Almost immediately below, Aunt Vickie has hold of a broom. She starts to bang on the ceiling, as 'Lipstick On Your Collar' continues to spill out from the radio above.

SYLVIA: Oh, shut up.

She begins to chip the potatoes, and the thumping stops.

A little later, in the street outside, a bespectacled middle-aged man – Harold Atterbow, cinema organist – parks his car and looks up yearningly at Sylvia's window.

An hour or so later, in the cramped spaces downstairs, Uncle Fred, a morose Londoner whose lugubrious melancholy hides a deeper eccentricity, is eating egg and chips, as are Aunt Vickie and

Francis. The budgerigar twitters in its cage on the table.

UNCLE FRED: (*Eventually*) We shall be glad to have you here, Frank.

FRANCIS: Thank you, Uncle Fred.

UNCLE FRED: Bit of educated conversation.

Francis does not know whether sarcasm lurks.

FRANCIS: Well, I don't know about that.

UNCLE FRED: It's what I don't get. It's what I miss.

AUNT VICKIE: Thanks very much.

UNCLE FRED: See what I mean, Frank?

FRANCIS: (*Embarrassed*) Um.

UNCLE FRED: I talk to that bird sometimes. Do you know that, Frank? I talk to –

He breaks off at the heavy bang of the street door, off, which is immediately followed by –

MAN'S VOICE: (*Off*) Here I am sweetheart! Norwich!

Uncle Fred puts his fork down with a clatter on the plate of egg and chips.

UNCLE FRED: Why does he do that? Every bloody time he comes home! It's enough to put you off your tea.

Feet on stairs, off.

AUNT VICKIE: Noisy sods.

UNCLE FRED: Language!

AUNT VICKIE: Yes, well – (*Sniffs*) They should go back there, shouldn't they?

UNCLE FRED: What?

AUNT VICKIE: Norwich.

Francis makes a noise.

Uncle Fred looks sidelong at Francis, comically furtive, as though he already knows why he has choked back a guffaw.

Frank? What's the –

UNCLE FRED: It's you. It's what you say. You daft pudding.

AUNT VICKIE: What?

UNCLE FRED: It's dirty. Ennit?

There is a strange anger and aggression about him now.

AUNT VICKIE: Dirty? What you mean?

FRANCIS: (*Half-smirking*) 'Knickers off ready when I come home'.

Silence. Uncle Fred puts down his knife and fork. Aunt Vickie makes an urgent signalling expression with her eyes and face at bewildered Francis.

27

It's – well, it's childish, ennit? You hear it in the army. See it, I mean. N.O.R.W.I.C.H. – some of the blokes put it on the flap of the envelope when they write to their – (*Slight falter*) girlfriends or – And S.W.A.L.K. Sealed With A Loving Kiss. Or –

UNCLE FRED: (*Suddenly, sharp*) That's enough!

FRANCIS: Pardon?

UNCLE FRED: I don't want filth with my food, thank you very much.

Francis looks at him, utterly astonished.

Upstairs, in the tiny kitchen, Corporal Berry, standing close behind Sylvia, pressing into her, cups his hands over her breasts.

BERRY: You're the best, Sylv. Best looking bint I seen all day, Sylvia.

SYLVIA: Don't say that.

BERRY: Well, it's true.

SYLVIA: Bint. Don't say that.

BERRY: Oops. Sor-ry.

He turns her, and kisses her eyelids. But she is clearly not very responsive.

What's the matter?

SYLVIA: I'm not a bint.

BERRY: No – but what's the matter?

He goes to kiss her lips.

SYLVIA: Not now, Peter. And you smell of beer.

BERRY: Hey. One pint. *One.*

SYLVIA: I'm – tired. That's all.

BERRY: (*Indignantly*) Tired!

She looks at him evenly.

SYLVIA: Fed up.

BERRY: What with?

SYLVIA: This place for a start.

BERRY: I've seen worse.

SYLVIA: And them downstairs.

BERRY: Who are they? Nothing!

SYLVIA: (*Relentlessly*) And my job.

BERRY: Easy, ennit?

SYLVIA: Why should I stand on my feet with a bloody torch on a Saturday night and a – Gets on your wick.

He glares, and flings himself into a chair.

BERRY: Christ, you're a moaner. And you're getting worse.
She studies him as though about to say something of importance,
but then turns away into the kitchenette.
SYLVIA: The tea.
Momentarily alone, Berry scowls to himself. Then –
BERRY: (*Calls*) You showing off again? Sylvia? (*No reply*.) Sylvia!
 (*No reply*.)
He gets up, face darkening, and goes the few steps through to the
curtained-off kitchenette.
  Listen, you. When I shaggin' well ask you something, you'd
  better shaggin' well answer.
She carries on with what she is doing, her back to him. He plucks at
her shoulder.
  Hey. I'm talking to you.
SYLVIA: Do you want your supper or don't you?
BERRY: Sod the shaggin' supper!
SYLVIA: Suits me.
She has not turned. He grabs at her shoulder again, more roughly.
BERRY: Listen here – !
But she swings around fast, holding the saucepan lid, potentially as
a weapon.
 He blinks, steps back a fraction, and then hisses between his
teeth.
  You little tart. You cheap little –
He turns away, body stiff, hands clenching, leaving her to it.
 Sylvia puts the lid back on the saucepan. And smiles,
enigmatically.
SYLVIA: Yeh. I *must* be cheap. 'Cos I got no bleedin' money, have
 I?
She turns, smile gone, with a new look in her eyes.
  P'raps I'll start charging for it. What you think?
She puts out her tongue, and slowly moistens her lips,
provocatively.
 That night, into the small hours, and downstairs in the little
Fulham house, the Put-U-Up is down, the single overhead light is
switched off, and Francis stares up in the dimness at the ceiling,
eyes gleaming in the half-light.
 He sighs, restless. Then –
FRANCIS: (*Whispers*) 'I remember the wonderful moment – '
And what he actually remembers is Sylvia's quick look of appraisal

29

as he pulls back against the wall to allow her to pass.

(*Whispers*) ' – When before me first she stood . . .'
He falls silent again. But his breathing becomes heavier,
heavier . . .

Off, from above, an obscure female cry.

Francis stiffens, sits up, cocks an ear.

Silence.

Just as he is about to dismiss the sound, it comes again, louder, a
distant yelp. A muffled male shout as well.

Francis pads across to the light switch and, pyjama-clad, opens
the door into the hall, almost directly opposite the foot of the stairs,
in order to listen.

Up above, on the landing, Sylvia hurtles out of the room directly
above Francis' room, in her nightdress, distressed. Berry shouts
from inside the room.

BERRY: Come here! Come back, you bitch!

At his door, opening into the hall, Francis sucks in his breath in
indignant alarm, but not sure what to do.

Upstairs, on the landing, Sylvia is leaning against the wall by her
bedroom door, covering her face with her hands, beginning to
weep.

Berry does not come out. Then, from inside, in a different tone –
Oh, come on. Don't be so daft, Sylv – ?

Stealthy, vaguely excited, concerned, Francis creeps barefoot to
the bottom of the stairs, and tries to look up.

Berry has come out on to the landing above, in pyjamas. Sylvia
lowers her hands.

(*Quietly*) Sylvia. For Christ's sake.

SYLVIA: You – sodding – bully –

Her words come out in sobs.

BERRY: Shh! You'll wake up that mad bugger downstairs.

He reaches for her. She recoils.

SYLVIA: Hit me again, that's all. Hit me once more!

Francis listens at the bottom of the stairs, but is afraid of being
caught doing so.

BERRY: Aw, now – it wasn't that hard – He-ey Sylvia. Sylv, come
on, chick. Come on, I didn't mean it like that . . .

SYLVIA: You're a bully, Pete.

Berry is holding Sylvia now. She is not especially resisting.

BERRY: Baby. I'm sorry. I'm sorry.

30

SYLVIA: Then why do you do it? If you don't watch that bloody fist
    of yours, you'll kill me one d-
BERRY: Cover you with kisses.
SYLVIA: But why do you do it – ? Pete. Why?
BERRY: 'Cos I love you. That's why.
SYLVIA: Well, you got a funny way of showing –
He stops her speaking, with his mouth, fondling her, sexually.
    She half-pushes him away, but then yields.
BERRY: C'mon – c'mon –
SYLVIA: Oh, you bugger.
And he is carrying her back into the bedroom.
    Below, at the bottom of the stairs, Francis listens, fascinated,
appalled, excited by the tantalising sounds from immediately
above.
    Francis crunches up his face, at the erotic sounds. And then, the
shutting of their bedroom door.
    He stands still a moment. His expression changes –
FRANCIS: (*To himself*) I know that voice . . .
He listens. Silence. He shrugs and goes back to his room –
As he shuts the door, the shocked, incredulous realization hits, as
the fully-formed memory of Corporal Berry at the war office comes
to life again:
BERRY: Sol-dyah!
Francis leans his back against the door of his bedroom, digesting
astonishment.
Then he goes back to his bed, switching off the light, and stares up
at the ceiling.
    Faintly off, from above, the sound of creaking bedsprings.
    He screws up his face, in bewilderment, and in sexual anguish. A
moment and then the song 'The Green Door' creeps in almost
mockingly.
    Outside, in the darkened street, the middle-aged organist
Harold Atterbow, alone in his parked car, stares and stares
obsessively up at Sylvia's window, as though aware of what's
happening inside.
    The music still playing, the picture yields to that of two energetic
silhouettes in the bedroom directly above Francis. The Corporal
and his wife are still making the bedsprings creak, with an
increasing frenzy, and a rhythm not entirely unlike the continuing
music.

Down below, in his bed, Francis can hear and work out what is going on. Yearning and hunger envelope him. He pulls the sheet over his head, to shut out the bedspring creaks.

Outside, Atterbow's mysterious car at last drives off, its headlights sliding across the ceiling of Sylvia's bedroom.

And then, when there are no more pictures, 'The Man with the Golden Arm' by the Billy May Orchestra bounces and drives, fifties style, wordless, to the end.

Two

In the cinema, the newsreel is showing the 1956 Cannes Festival, catching some British stars signing autographs.

Upstairs in the dingy Fulham house, usherette Sylvia, in bed, in the morning, fantasizes, imagining herself doing the same, as she dunks a biscuit into her morning tea.

SYLVIA: (*to herself*) Sylvia Berry, Sylvia Berry. Best wishes – Sylvia Berry. (*She stretches, bare arms extending, smiling*) All my love, Sylvia.

The voice of the BBC Light Programme radio presenter is heard from the radio in the living-room.

BBC VOICE: Toby, the card says, pricks his ears and gives a little woof! woof! for this next recording by the Platters. It's all right. Toby is a dog. I hope.

'Only You' begins on the radio, sung by the Platters.

SYLVIA: (*Yells*) Turn it up! This is a good 'un!

Corporal Berry, shaving, still has half his face lathered. He is at the chunky, chipped, ceramic sink in the tiny kitchenette, curtained off from the small living-room. Last night's dinner plates, unwashed, yukkily unscraped, remain on the slatted, wooden draining board, along with the sticky shaving brush. The radio is loud, banging out the Platters.

Pete!

BERRY: (*Yells*) Turn it up yourself! (*Mutters to himself*) Lazy cow.

Sylvia, pouting, slams her cup down and scrambles out of bed in her baby doll nightie.

SYLVIA: (*To herself*) You bugger.

She scampers into the living-room. Here she gives a fierce glare towards Berry's back at the sink – the curtain is open – and turns up the Radio Rentals radio about as loud as it can go and glides back towards the adjoining bedroom.

In the flat below, Francis, too, is shaving at a similar but much cleaner sink – but he uses a bowl as well.

Here, too, the living-room radio, beyond the partly opened curtain, is switched to the Light Programme and the Platters.

And the words of the song – sexual longing with a fifties wa-wa-waa and proto-rock beat – bite into his mind, his

34

expression, as he scrapes away at his stubble. He thinks of the girl upstairs.

She lies in bed, listening to the music. A dream girl, of sorts.

Downstairs, Aunt Vickie puts sandwiches into Uncle Fred's bag. He is lacing up his boots.

AUNT VICKIE: One cheese and pickle. One corned beef.

UNCLE FRED: And? *And*?

AUNT VICKIE: (*Prompted*) And lucky to get it.

UNCLE FRED: (*With enthusiasm*) Lucky is the word!

He stands up and stamps one boot, another ritual – but then glares at the radio, and at – so to speak – the Platters.

Put it off. It's muck. Just muck.

She obeys, without a word.

But from the flat immediately overhead, the concluding bit of 'Only You' is thumping through loud and clear.

AUNT VICKIE: Her upstairs!

UNCLE FRED: It's a disgrace. It's – Get the broom. Give me the broom!

AUNT VICKIE: We could go to the council. We don't have to put up with this. And the bird don't like it neither.

UNCLE FRED: The broom. The broom!

Francis, still scraping with his razor, swivels his eyes to see Aunt Vickie, face thunderous, grab the broom from the corner by the back door into the yard and return to the living-room.

Aunt Vickie thump-thumps on the low ceiling with the broom.

Give it to 'em, gal!

'Only You', very loudly, comes to an end on the radio in the upstairs flat.

BBC VOICE: The time is just coming up to twenty minutes to eight. (*Voice changes tone.*) Time now for this morning's 'Lift Up Your Hearts'. The speaker is the Reverend Harold Warner, the vicar of St John's Church, Colebride.

CLERGYMAN: (*Unctuously*) Good morning. What kind of day do you think today is going to be? Which side of the bed did you get out on, as they say?

But during the latter part of the almost comically fawning clerical voice –

SYLVIA: (*Yells*) Switch it off!

She needn't have yelled. Berry is as offended by 'Lift Up Your

Hearts' as she is. Click! and the unctuous clergyman is cut off in mid-burble.

BERRY: Why not keep that sort of rubbish for Sundays. Gets
    right up your –

He breaks off, at last aware of the thump-bump made by the broom on the ceiling below.

SYLVIA: It's her downstairs again!

BERRY: The bitch.

Stamp! Stamp! with his foot on the floor, hard enough to make the cup on the table rattle in its saucer.

    I've had enough of this!

Below, Aunt Vickie goes Thump! Thump! with the broom, in response to the Thump! Thump! of the stamping foot.

    Corporal Berry goes Stamp! Stamp! in answer.

    Back below again, Francis rinses out his razor under the single cold tap, and it is clear that he is crunching up inside, astonished and distressed by the obvious enmity towards 'her upstairs'.

UNCLE FRED: All right. That's enough. That'll do, Vickie.

AUNT VICKIE: I could go on banging all day. Not that it'd do any
    good.

UNCLE FRED: But look at them marks. On the ceiling.

AUNT VICKIE: Pity they aren't on her backside.

UNCLE FRED: Now, then!

AUNT VICKIE: You're not here all day, every day. If it's not the
    wireless, it's the gramophone.

UNCLE FRED: I don't like violence, Vickie.

AUNT VICKIE: All depends!

UNCLE FRED: We weren't sent into the world for that, Vickie.
    We're not animals.

His voice has changed. In this frequent mode he is like another person, reeking with sanctimoniousness.

AUNT VICKIE: *She* is. A cow.

UNCLE FRED: Victoria!

There is a sudden, dangerous flash in his eyes – and the hint of a raised hand. She is instantly submissive.

AUNT VICKIE: Sorry, Fred.

The revealing expression passes quickly from his face, to let back in the humbug.

UNCLE FRED: We haven't got good neighbours, that's for sure.
    But that don't alter nothing, do it? We've got to live as the

Lord said we've got to. If we can.

AUNT VICKIE: That's a big if.

In the kitchenette, Francis can't believe what he is hearing, and clenches his eyelids shut, then grips the edge of the ceramic sink.

FRANCIS: (*Under his breath*) Cor – strike a light.

UNCLE FRED: And ifs and buts don't make no difference at the end of the day.

AUNT VICKIE: You're keeping an eye on the time, are you Fred?

UNCLE FRED: Ah soul.

AUNT VICKIE: (*Shocked*) Fred!

UNCLE FRED: What?

AUNT VICKIE: W-what – ?

UNCLE FRED: 'Ah soul, tossed on the billows – '

AUNT VICKIE: Oh, I thought you –

UNCLE FRED: – 'Afar from friendly land
Look up to 'im who 'olds thee
In the 'ollow of 'is 'and!'

Tiny pause.

AUNT VICKIE: It's quarter to, Fred.

UNCLE FRED: Time. Time. Times rules us all. And when I pack it in, what'll I get? A gold watch.

AUNT VICKIE: If you're lucky.

UNCLE FRED: Watchewmean? Lucky? What's luck got to do with it?

AUNT VICKIE: Might not be *gold*, that's all. Mean sods.

UNCLE FRED: Keep not your treasure in whatsit. All this greed and – I mean, it only rusts like the Good Book says –

AUNT VICKIE: Gold don't rust.

UNCLE FRED: (*Snarls*) Oh, you're such a bloody know-all.

AUNT VICKIE: Sorry, Fred. Expect you're right. (*Daring little edge*) You usually are.

He looks at her, then gathers up his sandwiches and half-pecks her on the cheek.

UNCLE FRED: Ta-ta then, my old pudding.

AUNT VICKIE: Ta-ta.

UNCLE FRED: I got a name.

AUNT VICKIE: Ta-ta, Fred.

UNCLE FRED: Frank!

Francis comes to the curtain which separates the kitchenette from the living-room, and he looks, small wonder, a little uneasy.

FRANCIS: Uncle Fred – ?

UNCLE FRED: I'm off now.

It sounds as though he is going on a long trip. Francis looks at him warily.

FRANCIS: Sorry – ?

UNCLE FRED: I said I'm off.

FRANCIS: (*Uneasily*) Right you are, then.

UNCLE FRED: Want to wish you luck.

FRANCIS: Yes – ah – thank you.

UNCLE FRED: You should be proud. Not every Tom, Dick and Harry gets to work at the war office.

FRANCIS: No. I – no, that's true.

UNCLE FRED: So all the best!

He extends his hand. Francis, a fraction late, shakes it. And then he shakes his wife's hand, too.

Above, sleepy Sylvia has snuggled back down in the bed. Berry appears in the doorway, then gets on to the bed.

BERRY: Thanks for my breakfast.

SYLVIA: Mmm.

BERRY: God almighty.

SYLVIA: Mmmwa– ?

BERRY: 'Ent you going to get up?

SYLVIA: What for?

BERRY: (*Fondling*) 'Cos you're my wife, that's what for!

SYLVIA: Stop it, Pete.

BERRY: Stop what?

SYLVIA: I'm tired.

BERRY: And so am I!

SYLVIA: Mmm.

And she snuggles back down, even more, eyes closed. He lurches off the bed and glares across the room.

BERRY: Dirt lazy. That's you.

No response. He clumps away, giving the door a hefty slam.

Sylvia – not so sleepy as she has pretended – lifts her head and stares at the slammed door.

SYLVIA: (*To herself, quietly*) Just you wait.

Meanwhile, Francis is about to leave. Aunt Vickie is embarrassed about her strange husband.

AUNT VICKIE: He came out of a pub on Sunday morning so drunk he could hardly stand up. Fell straight into the middle

38

of the bleed'n Salvation Army band, didn't he? They got
hold of him, Frank. They got their hands on him.

FRANCIS: Mum said he drank a lot.

AUNT VICKIE: I wish he still did! Won't touch it now. Not even
at Christmas. (*Hesitantly*) Do you have a drop, Frank?

FRANCIS: Oh, now and then –

AUNT VICKIE: Only don't let him smell it on you, will you?

He looks at her. She seems frightened. He frowns, concerned,
then touches her arm and smiles.

FRANCIS: Can't afford it anyway. Ta-ta, Aunt Vickie. See you.

AUNT VICKIE: I'm glad you're here, Frank.

He smiles, opens the door into the narrow passage leading past
the stairs to the street door, hears heavy feet descending on the
stairs, and quickly steps back, more than half-closing the door.

What's the matter – ?

FRANCIS: Shh!

Bad-mood Berry thumps down the stairs and along the dingy hall,
face like thunder, unaware of observation.

Francis, holding the narrowly ajar door, peers cautiously
through to see Berry slam the street door behind him, with an
awful bang.

AUNT VICKIE: He'll knock the whole bloody house down one
day! (*Then, at his expression*) What is it?

FRANCIS: I thought it was – I *knew* it was – he's the Corporal in
the – in my office at the war office. I mean, I have to work
with him! (*Growing horror*) And he *beats* her, Aunt Vickie.
That lovely, lovely girl –

AUNT VICKIE: What lovely girl?

Francis looks at her, goes to say something and then says
something else.

FRANCIS: I got to go. Better not be late on my first morning.

AUNT VICKIE: She's a tart, Frank.

FRANCIS: (*Hostile*) Yeh?

AUNT VICKIE: Oh Frank, Frank. There's been enough heartache
in this family.

FRANK: What do you mean?

AUNT VICKIE: Your mother married a Welshman and I married a
bloody maniac. Let's hope you can do better, eh?

Later in the morning, Sylvia sits alone on the edge of the bed

39

painting her toe-nails, and contemplating her legs with satisfaction.

Music glides in with a fifties style female chorus – 'The Story of My Life', as sung by Michael Holliday.

The music reintroduces the big room at the war office, where officers and men are again diligently stooped over their desks, nearly still-life figures in a tedious tableau.

Private Hopper lifts his gaze and appears to acknowledge the song, which continues.

And then Francis, too, lifts his head: but not so much in direct response to the music as in wistful reverie. An image returns to his mind.

SYLVIA: (*Flatly*) Kiss mine.

The girl fades from Francis' mind, as the song dies, and the pens scratch in the big room all around him.

Slightly louche Major Hedges – jacket off, showing his red braces – unfreezes from all the preceding immobilities, and lets out one of his long, mannered sighs.

Like someone enormously burdened, he looks around, and then drops his pen on to the chart spread before him.

Once more, comically on cue, he looks steadily and threateningly all around at Colonel Harry Bernwood, Major Johnny Church, Major Archie Carter, US Lt Colonel 'Truck' Trekker, Corporal Berry, Private Hopper and Private Francis.

It is Colonel Bernwood who reacts. He lifts his head from his own scratch-scratch labours, and sees that Hedges is about to do his malcontent turn once more.

BERNWOOD: Don't say it, Wallace. Please.

HEDGES: I'm sorry . . . ?

BERNWOOD: Just don't say it.

HEDGES: I was not proposing to, Harry. Whatever 'it' is. (*Deadly little pause*) Mind you. I contemplate it. Whatever 'it' might be. Cometh the hour, cometh the man.

But he picks up his pen again.

Hopper, the music-fantasist, now involved in a gradual handover of his duties as Russian Language Clerk to Francis, is showing the newcomer a half-sheet of paper.

The paper is charred at the edge, very crumpled, and badly stained. Hopper, smoothing it flatter, speaks with low-voiced, furtive disdain.

HOPPER: See – this is what I mean – this is why I say roll on.
You'll have to put up with it now. So put a peg on your nose,
Frank, old son. 'Cos this is the sort of shite we have to mess
with. And you can have it, mate. Welcome!

FRANCIS: Thanks.

Hopper looks at him, and sees that Francis' attention is
elsewhere. Francis has a baleful expression, eyes fixed across the
room.

HOPPER: What's the matter – ?

He follows the angle of Francis' gaze. It is directed at Corporal
Berry, who can be seen filing papers in the walk-in safe.
    Francis drags his attention back.

FRANCIS: Nasty little bugger.

HOPPER: What?

FRANCIS: Corporals.

HOPPER: Yeh. Well – (*Then*) What about them?

FRANCIS: What sort of bloke would ever want to be one?

HOPPER: Oh, there's lots of scope in civvy life if you've ever risen
as high as your actual two stripes.

FRANCIS: (*Disdainfully*) Like what?

HOPPER: Lavatory attendant. Or boot cleaner in a doss house.
Mind you, that's starting at the very top. Not every corporal
gets so far as that. (*Sniggers, then –*)Hey. Come on. We got to
get through this.

FRANCIS: Have we?

HOPPER: (*Sighs*) This is a letter. Right? One of theirs. Russian.

FRANCIS: I can see that!

HOPPER: Some poor bugger from our side hangs around near one
of their barracks – on the look out for scraps like this – he
hangs around, and then he creeps sl-ow-ly towards the shit
house on his hands and knees . . .

FRANCIS: Get off.

HOPPER: No, no – honest – the poor bloody sods don't have
proper toilet paper, or things like that . . .

Francis is looking at him with increasing distaste.

FRANCIS: What are you talking about?

HOPPER: The Russians.

FRANCIS: Propaganda.

Hopper looks around, anxiously, then mimics Francis' strong
Welsh accent.

41

HOPPER: Not so loud, Boyo.

FRANCIS: (*Whispers*) Well, it is. Lies, man.

HOPPER: Shhh.

FRANCIS: (*Whispers*) You know what I mean. It's the worker's
    state, that's why.

HOPPER: Well, whether it is or no, they wipe their backsides on
    the letters they get or the letters they don't send – or –
    something like that. And our man dives in after them.

Francis looks at the piece of paper in disgust, unsure about how
to respond.

FRANCIS: You're not having me on?

HOPPER: No. It's the truth.

FRANCIS: Are you telling me –

He stops, looks at the paper, swallows.

HOPPER: That's right. Our bloke creeps up behind the bucket
    when a bloody bolshevik has a shite (*Looks at* BERRY) A
    corporal, I should think. And he grabs the paper. Hot from
    the press.

FRANCIS: What? After he's – After it's been – *used*?

They look at each other, registering the full implication.

   Hopper lays the piece of paper he has been holding on to the
desk, with a sudden and comical decisiveness.

HOPPER: They fumigate it.

FRANCIS: Christ. I hope so.

Hopper looks around the big room with an extra boost of disgust.

HOPPER: You got to put your mind somewhere else on this job.
    You got to think of something else, or it'll drive you round
    the bloody bend.

FRANCIS: You sure this is – disinfected?

HOPPER: (*Not listening*) Just let your mind go. Just drift off.
    That's what I do.

FRANCIS: (*Queasily*) I mean, if they've wiped their bums on this –
    it's not right. It's not right at all.

HOPPER: What difference does one more little bit of shit make?
    The whole bloody job stinks anyway.

He picks up the offending piece of paper. His face changes. The
hard beat of 'Blueberry Hill' by Fats Domino begins and then
Hopper is suddenly 'singing' its words.

   Hedges, too, lifts his head, with a gleam in his eyes, and (in
Hopper's musical) takes up the lyrics.

Hopper – still in the midst of song – holds up the soiled paper, showing it to the others.

The music is by now completely dominant, so that, one by one, the others in the room take up sections of the Fats Domino lyric, pulling at an imaginary toilet chain or receiving rolls of lavatory paper into their in-trays, distributed by Corporal Berry in his normal manner.

The variously distributed 'vocal' continues until Hopper's mind switches it off and lets in the real conversation –

FRANCIS: Still. It's better than barracks.

HOPPER: (*Menacingly*) You'll see.

Francis looks at the paper, warily.

FRANCIS: What do we have to do with it?

HOPPER: Use it again. (*Sniggers*) What do you think! *Translate* it, nig-nog.

FRANCIS: But – it's a letter. I mean – it's, well, a *letter*.

HOPPER: Not a French one, neither. (*Looks at him.*) What you mean, it's a letter?

FRANCIS: It's – I mean, a letter is *private*.

Hopper stares, blinks.

HOPPER: Are you coco, or what?

FRANCIS: I got a conscience. I hope. I know what's right and what isn't.

HOPPER: Your feet won't touch the ground.

FRANCIS: Yes, but –

HOPPER: They'll have you on a charge in two minutes flat.

FRANCIS: Even so – (*Then*) Oh. All right, then.

Hopper looks at him with a gleam.

HOPPER: That was some struggle.

FRANCIS: There's no room for idealism in this world.

He says this seriously – and ludicrously. Hopper sniffs, and decides to ignore it.

HOPPER: Listen. Every time one of these *private* letters mentions a *place* you send the info to Room 123, two doors along. There's no girls in there neither. And every time it mentions a *person* – like, you know, the name of an officer or, better still, his CO, you send it upstairs to 223, and every time – (*Pauses: works his mouth*) Christ.

FRANCIS: What?

HOPPER: It's all bullshit.

43

FRANCIS: Is it?

HOPPER: This is the army, ennit? What do you think?

FRANCIS: (*Sighs*) Roll on.

HOPPER: (*Sighs*) Roll on.

They look at each other with the despair of conscripts.

A little later on the same otherwise bright day, as another song begins, Sylvia is looming in close to her oval make-up mirror, putting on lipstick.

Near, the Dansette portable gramophone, lid lifted, is the source of the new music: 'It's Almost Tomorrow' by the Dreamweavers.

Sylvia hums the start of the vocal, then stops in order to purse her shiningly lipsticked mouth at the mirror, narcissistic, studying herself from all angles, self-entranced.

But as the music bears in on her, her expression changes, becoming sullen, and the self-admiring kiss-kiss becomes a malcontent's pout.

Suddenly, violently, grasping the flexi-stem as though to strangle it, she pushes the mirror away, and glares around the dingy room.

SYLVIA: Bleed'n dump. (*Pause: her eyes harden*) I'm worth more than this.

Sylvia goes to her handbag, takes out her purse, and begins to count the coins on the table, while the music sings of love and tomorrow and love and yesterday and –

Three and tuppence ha'penny. Three and bloody tuppence ha'penny.

Back at the war office, in the sanctuary of the washrooms, Corporal Berry, whistling to the same tune, combs his hair, cocking his head in approval as he looks at himself in a large mirror set into expanses of white tile above a long row of washbasins in a vast stretch of space.

At his home in Fulham, though, Sylvia stops the record on her Dansette, clearly disgruntled.

Then, from below, she hears the street door shut. Her expression changes. She goes to the window to look out and sees Aunt Vickie, with shopping basket, leaving the house.

Sylvia's face shows a new thought. She turns from the window, thinking 'three and tuppence ha'penny.'

Meanwhile, at the war office, Francis and Hopper come out of the big room, into faded grandeur and seemingly endless lengths of wide, high corridor.

FRANCIS: My God. It's like being in some great tomb.

HOPPER: The main thing, Frank, is that you got to count each minute in this place as three minutes, it's so bloody boring.

FRANCIS: (*Glumly*) I suppose I'll get the hang of it. Eventually.

HOPPER: Six more weeks and three more days and I'm out of the calaboose!

They go into the washrooms, off the corridor.

FRANCIS: You lucky devil.

In the ceramically echoing, empty, white-tiled cavern they go to stand and unbutton themselves at the long row of urinals.

HOPPER: How long you got?

FRANCIS: Ten months two weeks and four days. Plus four hours.

HOPPER: What you going to do then?

FRANCIS: Get drunk.

HOPPER: Well, yeh. Who wouldn't. Christ. (*Turns away, buttoning himself.*) I meant, after your demob. Good job to go to, and that?

FRANCIS: Oxford. I'm – ah – actually – (*Slight twitch*) Going up to Oxford. You know, the university. Got a scholarship.

Hopper is impressed, but doesn't want to show it. He is washing his hands.

HOPPER: Yeh? Well. Takes all sorts.

FRANCIS: What are you going to do?

HOPPER: Drums.

FRANCIS: Beg pardon?

HOPPER: Music. I play the drums. Dance band.

FRANCIS: (*Also impressed*) Really? Caw – that's something!

HOPPER: Yeh. I can't wait. Mind you, I haven't got anything lined up, not yet.

FRANCIS: Still –

HOPPER: Oh, it'll happen, all right. Listen – that Oxford stuff . . .

FRANCIS: (*Cautiously*)Mmm?

HOPPER: I wouldn't mention it to Corporal Berry.

FRANCIS: What you mean?

HOPPER: He's as thick as shit in the neck of a bottle. And he hates anybody else who isn't.

FRANCIS: Poison. He's poison, that man!

45

But the poison, Corporal Berry, sitting on a lavatory, in a cubicle within the washrooms, his hand about to tear off paper from the roll, goes very still, hearing –

HOPPER: Blimey. He's got up your nose already, by the sound of it.

Beyond Berry's cubicle, Francis and Hopper are moving towards the door, across what feels like half an acre of tiled flooring, which gives their voices a peculiar resonance.

FRANCIS: Well, I had the shock of my life last night. And I don't know what to do about it.

HOPPER: What?

FRANCIS: He's living in the same place I am. Upstairs.

HOPPER: (*Laughs*) Too close for comfort.

FRANCIS: It's not just that. I –

He stops.

HOPPER: What?

FRANCIS: (*Sounding very Welsh*) Don't know whether to tell you or not.

HOPPER: Tell me what?

FRANCIS: It's about his wife, see.

HOPPER: (*Intrigued*) Come on, then.

FRANCIS: She's the most beautiful young woman I ever – Oh, I tell you, she's like a – like a –

He stops, embarrassed, as Hopper looks at him with an amused glint.

HOPPER: Bit of all right, is she?

FRANCIS: It's not that. It's – (*Suddenly*) He beats her! The bugger!

HOPPER: *What* – ?

FRANCIS: Last night. I heard it. I didn't know what to do. Oh, what a bully. Any man who can hit a lovely young –

He stops dead, as a decisive step sounds on the tiles, and he sees who it is.

BERRY: A word. I'd like a word.

HOPPER: (*Sotto voce*) Christ.

FRANCIS: (*Pathetically*) Listen, corporal. I –

But before he can finish quavering, Berry has moved very fast, hand outstretched, gripping Francis at the throat.

BERRY: (*Evenly*) You little shit.

In the same lethally efficient momentum, he slams Francis back against the washroom wall, by the exit door, with such force that he knocks the breath out of Francis' body.

FRANCIS: Phoooo – !

Thump! Thump! Berry bangs Francis' head against the wall, brutally.

HOPPER: (*Helplessly*) Hey – Corp – you'll kill him – No . . . !

Berry lets go, but thrusts his face close to Francis, eyes like stones.

BERRY: So. A snoop, are you? Come between a man and his wife, eh? Eh?

Francis is too dazed and winded to make much of a response.

FRANCIS: I –

BERRY: There's a pan full of shit back there – And you're just the bloke to deal with it – !

FRANCIS: (*Gasping*) Wha– ?

But Berry – again making a sudden, swift movement – grips Francis' arm, twists it up behind him, and frog-marches him towards the cubicle the corporal has just vacated.

BERRY: You tangle with me, my son, and you'll get more than you ever expected!

Hopper stays where he is, with revulsion on his face, unable to do anything to stop the vengeful corporal.

Berry forces Francis into the cubicle, where he has not pulled the dangling chain.

FRANCIS: (*Gasping*) Now look – now steady – What are you –

But a hand is on the back of his neck, ready to force his head down.

Outside the cubicle, hovering Hopper winces as he hears –

BERRY: Go on! Look at it! Look at it!

FRANCIS: No – ach – no – o –

BERRY: Go on! Take a closer look! Shit to shit!

Sound of Francis starting to heave. And then – mercifully – the creak of the ancient chain, and the sound of the lavatory flushing.

Meanwhile, back at the Fulham house, Sylvia stands still, half-way down the stairs, head cocked, listening, like someone nervously up to no good. A moment. Then she comes on down. Stops again.

SYLVIA: Hello? You there – ?

A look at the front door, and she moves again – rather like a thief in pantomime, Sylvia edges towards the living-room door of the downstairs flat.

Hello?

She curls her fingers, hesitates, then tap-taps on the door.
Inside the room, the budgerigar in its cage is the only occupant.
The door opens. Sylvia peers in, guiltily. She comes on in. The
bird makes a little ting! as it pecks at its bell.

   Shut up.
It looks, sounds, as though she has been here before. She quickly
pulls a chair from the table, opens a cupboard door, stands on the
chair. On the top shelf of the cupboard, above cups, plates,
various domestic muddle, is a tea-caddy. She takes one half a
crown out of the tin, gives it a rattle to check that it is fairly full,
decides to take another. She quickly replaces the chair at the
table, shuts the cupboard door. Sylvia purses her lips at the
budgerigar, making a little kiss-kiss sound, and goes to the door,
clenching the stolen silver tightly in her hand. The budgie tweets
or flutters or pecks at its little bell.

Across town, on the same day, in a Soho coffee bar (fifties style:
tin Coca Cola signs etc., but also the beginnings of later modes).
However, there is condensation on the big window, so that half of
it is steamed over.

   It is lunchtime. The big Italian coffee machine – latest craze –
gurgles and hisses.

   Francis and Hopper are at a small back table. Their frothy
coffees are in glass cups.

HOPPER: Still green about the gills, eh Frank?
He starts to laugh. Francis is offended, his accent becoming more
and more Welsh and sing-song in the extremities of his
indignation.
FRANCIS: I don't see it as funny. I don't think it's funny at all.
HOPPER: No. Not at the time. No.
But he can't stop laughing.
FRANCIS: Even this coffee is turning my insides – what's the
      matter with it? It's all frothy and – (*Reminded of something*)
      Yuk! No!
He pushes the cup away.
HOPPER: There's nothing wrong with the coffee, Frank. It's the
      new way, they force steam through it. Italian.
FRANCIS: Well, I don't like it.
HOPPER: Oh, it's all the style. Everything's changing.
FRANCIS: For the worse.

HOPPER: They have music here in the evenings. You can't get in
the place. Jam-packed.
FRANCIS: I'll get my own back one day, you see if I don't.
HOPPER: Put a string across the stair.
FRANCIS: What?
HOPPER: Or shut up about it.
FRANCIS: A string across the stair.
HOPPER: Break his bloody neck.
FRANCIS: (*Solemnly*) Oh, but I – no, I can't do that. There's a snag, see.
Hopper looks sidelong at him, almost warily.
HOPPER: Are you serious . . . ?
FRANCIS: It might not be him coming down the stairs. It could be
her.
HOPPER: Yes. It could.
Hopper cannot believe that Francis is being serious.
FRANCIS: And I wouldn't hurt a hair on her head.
This is said with such fervour, such obvious conviction, that
Hopper stares.
HOPPER: Were you expelled from the boy scouts, Frank?
FRANCIS: How did you know that?

Later, and a now familiar car crawls along the terraced houses of
the Fulham street, looking for the right number.
    In the car, a middle-aged man in spectacles, Harold Atterbow,
cinema organist and occasional broadcaster, looks at the house
numbers, and pulls on the hand brake.
    He sits a moment, drumming his hands on the steering-wheel,
like someone in doubt. Then – as organ music swells –
ATTERBOW: (*To himself*) Don't, Harold. Please, Harold. Don't do
it old mate.
He is in some sort of near-teeth-clenching inner conflict, out of
which the almost comic, very familiar music of a Compton theatre
organ plays Arthur Ketelbey's 'In a Persian Market Place'.
    Across the street, in the upstairs flat, Sylvia, tip of tongue out
in concentration, is painting her fingernails.
    'In a Persian Market Place' – theatre organ – swelling –
    In the downstairs flat, Aunt Vickie is standing on a chair to get
to the top shelf of the already purloined cupboard.
    At the side of the tea caddy there is a biscuit barrel, copper,
with a domed lid. She pulls off the top, rummages, and comes up

49

with a packet of five Woodbine cigarettes – two of which are already gone. She takes out one of the remaining three, clambers down, replaces the chair. With the air of one enjoying the ultimate but illicit luxury, Aunt Vickie gets a box of matches from the mantelpiece, kicks off her shoes, sits back in the easy-chair, lights the Woodbine and drags in smoke as though it were oxygen.

All the while, 'In a Persian Market Place' on the theatre organ.

Upstairs, Sylvia continues to varnish her long nails.

Aunt Vickie blows out smoke with a sigh of the deepest satisfaction.

'In a Persian Market Place' sinuously wavers on and on . . .

Outside, Harold Atterbow is still in his car, hands tight on the wheel, muscles tight on his face as 'In a Persian Market Place' strives towards a climax.

Aunt Vickie savours the cigarette, with seemingly excessive satisfaction.

'In a Persian Market Place' stops, suddenly, at a loud knock on the front door.

Aunt Vickie makes a disgruntled 'tut!' of a sound and pinches off the end of what is apparently an illicit cigarette.

Harold Atterbow on the doorstep has a fawning smile, which wavers into disappointment and then is quickly put back in place.

ATTERBOW: Good *after*noon –

AUNT VICKIE: (*Cautiously*) Good afternoon . . . ?

ATTERBOW: Are you by any chance her mother?

AUNT VICKIE: What?

ATTERBOW: Mrs Berry?

AUNT VICKIE: For God's sake!

So obviously and so quickly angry that he blinks and takes half a step back.

ATTERBOW: I'm sorry, but – this is –

AUNT VICKIE: *Two knocks!*

ATTERBOW: What – ?

AUNT VICKIE: Berry is the upstairs flat. Two knocks. I'm down. One knock.

And without ado she shuts the door.

Aunt Vickie, scowling, pads back along the narrow passage to resume her furtive cigarette. As she passes the stairs, she calls up –

Man from the VD clinic.

Outside, already unsure about what he was doing, Atterbow trails back to his car, demoralised. He opens his car door, hesitates, then squares his shoulders, adjusts his spectacles, and veritably *marches* back towards the front door.

Upstairs, Sylvia jerks like one who has been shot as two heavy knocks sound on the front door below. Her face says something like 'Is it the Rent Man, or . . .?', and she goes into the little bedroom, overlooking the street. She tries to peer down from the bedroom window. She can see the car, but the angle does not allow her to see who is on the doorstep.

At the front door, Atterbow, clearly nervous, and made more so by the delay, whistles 'In a Persian Market Place', softly, between his teeth. About to turn away, giving up – with a tinge of relief – he stops as the door is cautiously opened.

SYLVIA: Who is it?

Atterbow all but gives her a little bow.

ATTERBOW: I was just wondering if – I mean it happened to be on
    my way, and so –

He stops, embarrassed, aware of a helpless burble. She opens the door wider, looks at him – her face changes.

SYLVIA: Harold Atterbow!

Nervously, he actually does bow this time.

ATTERBOW: None other.

SYLVIA: But what are *you* doing here . . .

Her voice trails off. A knowing gleam comes into her eyes.

ATTERBOW: Ah, there you have it, there you have it, young lady.
    A combination of mere contingency vis-à-vis the street
    geography, so to speak, and actual – ah – impulse vis-à-vis
    my, my, my – *inclinations*.

SYLVIA: Pardon?

ATTERBOW: I was passing. Lost in wonder, so to speak. And I
    thought I would transport you to the Palace of dreams.

SYLVIA: (*Blankly*) Wha – ?

ATTERBOW: A lift. To the cinema.

SYLVIA: Oh. I – why?

ATTERBOW: I thought you'd find it helpful, and I – (*Shuffles*) Yes.
    I thought it would be jolly nice for me, too.

She looks at him. His eyes swivel away. She puts on a smile.

SYLVIA: Well that's very nice of you, Mr Atterbow.

ATTERBOW: Harold.

SYLVIA: Very thoughtful, Harold. (*Giggles*) Doesn't seem right me calling you by your first name. A famous organ player like you.

ATTERBOW: (*Simpers*) Famous? Oh – hardly that –

SYLVIA: You been on the wireless.

ATTERBOW: Occasionally. Occasionally.

SYLVIA: But I'm not quite ready yet, so if – ah –

ATTERBOW: Wait in the car – yes?

SYLVIA: Or . . .

ATTERBOW: (*Glows*) Yes?

SYLVIA: Yes, I shan't be long.

ATTERBOW: So I'll –

SYLVIA: Come up for a minute –

ATTERBOW: Yes?

SYLVIA: Well. All right then.

Aunt Vickie has her door ajar and is carefully listening.

Sylvia leads a beamingly flustered Atterbow through, and up the stairs.

Not much of a place to show anybody, Mr At– Harold. Bit muddled today an 'all. We can't wait to get somewhere else –

Aunt Vickie listens through the half-opened door.

AUNT VICKIE: (*To herself*) Nor me neither.

SYLVIA: (*Off, receding*) And we haven't got very good neighbours, I can tell you.

AUNT VICKIE: Bloody cow. (*Pause*) Cheeky little bugger.

Atterbow's eyes are fixed on Sylvia's legs as she leads the way up.

SYLVIA: I haven't had time to clean this morning, what with one thing and –

ATTERBOW: The other.

SYLVIA: What?

ATTERBOW: The other (*snigger*). Yes. Oh, take no mind. Take no mind. Really, my dear . . .

Sylvia smiles, aware of the sexual innuendo, and seemingly not at all averse to it. They go through into the living-room. The door shuts, with a distinct clap.

Back at the war office the officers are coming in, variously, and hanging their bowler hats on the ancient hat stands. Hedges tries to throw his to hit and stay on his peg – but fails.

TREKKER: You'll never do it, Wallace.

HEDGES: Oh, but I have.

TREKKER: I've never seen it.

CARTER: (*Coming in*) What's that?

TREKKER: Get his hat on the peg.

CARTER: With a throw? No.

HEDGES: But I have. Often. From the door, all the way across.

CARTER: Well, I wouldn't take *you* to the coconut shy, Wallace.

They go to their desks, as Bernwood comes bustling in, holding a
fat folder of papers.

BERNWOOD: Bit of a flap on upstairs –

HEDGES: When isn't there?

BERNWOOD: We shall know for sure this afternoon . . .

Agitated, he spreads the contents of the folder across his already
crowded desk.

CARTER: Know what? Harry!

BERNWOOD: Just a minute, Johnny. Give me a minute.

He stands unduly flustered and flutter-handed even by his own
standards.

Major Church – the Language Officer – comes through the
doorway, taking off his bowler hat.

CHURCH: I never cease to be amazed at how absolutely bloody
    punctual we are.

But then he stops, seeing the direction of each gaze (on
Bernwood) and feeling the slight tension in the room.

Am I missing something?

Hedges raises his eyebrows and puts a finger to his lips,
mischievously, speaking in a stage whisper.

HEDGES: 'Hush, hush, listen who dares – '

But Bernwood looks up sharply.

BERNWOOD: I'm very much afraid that this is not an occasion for
    your sort of levity, Wallace.

HEDGES: Oh, I say, dear old thing . . .

BERNWOOD: (*Interrupts*) It's the canal.

HEDGES: What canal?

BERNWOOD: (*Explodes*) I don't mean the Regent's Park canal,
    now do I? For heaven's sake!

HEDGES: All right. All right.

BERNWOOD: (*Almost a shout*) Suez!

Private Hopper is one move ahead, he has already been drawing little pyramids in pencil along the side of a translation he has been doing. He watches their reactions with interest, and some personal alarm.

CARTER: Come on, Harry. What is all this? What's going on?

BERNWOOD: Suez. Suez!

CARTER: You said that.

BERNWOOD: We have to get the new Battle Order out by midnight on Sunday. That's all I'm prepared to vouchsafe for the moment. We shall know more later.

HEDGES: *Midnight*? (*Utterly indignant*) *Sunday*?

CHURCH: Vouchsafe?

BERNWOOD: (*To* CHURCH) What?

CHURCH: What sort of word is that, Harry?

HEDGES: Look here. If there's some sort of flap on –

BERNWOOD: (*To* HEDGES, *wearily*) Wallace.

HEDGES: All I'm saying is –

BERNWOOD: Please. All of you. Please.

HEDGES: – all I'm saying – look here! – I mean, we're not Middle East, are we? We're not the fucking canal zone – so why do we have to –

BERNWOOD: Wallace!

Tiny pause.

HEDGES: I'm all ears. I think.

BERNWOOD: (*Sighs*) What pattern have we seen? What is it that is increasingly self-evident? What can we *deduce*?

Tiny pause.

TREKKER: South. Moving south.

BERNWOOD: Exactly!

He says this in an emphatic end-of-discussion-it's-all-so-obvious sort of voice, and bends back to his papers, with an anxious urgency.

Hedges looks across at Trekker, helplessly.

HEDGES: Truck? Enlighten me. For Christ's sake.

TREKKER: Get your head down, Wallace. We'd better get on with it, huh? (*To* CHURCH) I need some of these chickenshit captions translated if we're in this much of a hurry – OK?

CHURCH: (*Blinks*) Yes? Of course. Yes, I'll . . . Hopper? How are we . . .? (*At last noticing an absentee*) Hopper. Where's the new man? Where the hell *is* he?

He is tarrying on the Charing Cross Road at a second-hand
bookshop, with the books in untidy heaps and racks virtually
spilling out on to the pavement. Francis has opened one of the
books, and is reading with the total absorption of one unaware of
space or time or danger.

Inside the shop, a thin old man, Mr Shepherd, with badly
creased clothes, too-short trousers, cigarette ash down both lapels
and old food stains on his partly-buttoned waistcoat is both
amused and exasperated as he deals with Francis.

FRANCIS: 'Lord of one's self – ', eh? eh? Isn't that it? What he
says? 'Lord of one's self, uncumbered with a name'.

SHEPHERD: One of the few occasions he quoted correctly, I
believe.

FRANCIS: Uncumbered. Heavens, yes. Especially when you're
known by a *number*, as I am – What does he say? See if I can
remember –

He closes his eyes, lifts his head, ready to chant.

SHEPHERD: Oh, there's no need. No need for that. Please.

FRANCIS: (*Heedlessly*) 'To lose our – ' our – ah – one of his lists,
his lovely lists – our 'importunate, tormenting, everlasting
personal identity in the elements of nature – '

SHEPHERD: Yes, yes.

They are squeezed up between mustily towering stacks of books
in an overcrowded shop. Shepherd sits on a stool, smoking.

FRANCIS: And to be 'known by no other title than – '

SHEPHERD: The gentleman in the parlour!

Francis, who has been in full flight, is a little disappointed that
Shepherd can complete the quotation with such ease.

FRANCIS: Ah. Yes. So you know it.

SHEPHERD: Doesn't everyone?

FRANCIS: What?

But Shepherd takes pity on him.

SHEPHERD: All right. Perhaps our old friend Hazlitt has gone out
of fashion a little bit – and, yes, yes, I can see that you are –
well, enthusiastic.

FRANCIS: Oh, yes. As regards the *prose* writers, that is . . .

SHEPHERD: But I still can't knock a tanner off.

FRANCIS: No?

SHEPHERD: What you've got there is the nineteen hundred and
eleven edition, young man. And that was only the second

Everyman edition, after all.

FRANCIS: Still, it's not in a very good condition, not really –

SHEPHERD: A little foxing. And the price takes that into account.

FRANCIS: I'd give it a good home, you see. You can see that, surely?

SHEPHERD: My books are not orphans. Look here. We're only talking about half a crown –

FRANCIS: (*Sanctimoniously*) I think it's imp-or-tant to look after volumes like this, sir. I'd keep it next to my 'Eugene Onegin' – my Pushkin. I've got that in an old Russian –

He stops suddenly. The (boastful) mention of Pushkin has reminded him, belatedly, of where he is supposed to be.

Shepherd, sucking on his damp Gauloise, does not notice at first.

SHEPHERD: You can pay me a shilling this week, if you like, and I'll keep it on one side until –

He stops dead, aware at last of the extraordinary Jerry-Lewis-like change of expression on Francis' face: from the earlier wheedling supplication to what seems like a paralysing, half-crazed anguish.

FRANCIS: Oh sweet Jesu–

SHEPHERD: Well, it it's as bad as that, I'll –

He trails off, astonished, for Francis, all at once released from his nightmare paralysis, spins around, legs splaying and arms flailing, in order to run back to Whitehall. Indisputably awkward, he knocks several books flying in the narrow space as he plunges towards the street.

Hey – !

Too late. Francis, colliding with another would-be book buyer, is already out of sight.

The clock in the big room at the war office is now showing ten minutes past two o'clock.

Hopper covertly looks up at the clock with an oh-my-God-Frank incredulity. All around him there is diligent silence, except for the now familiar scratch-scratch of fountain pens.

Berry, finishing distributing some papers into each in-tray, leans over Hopper with a smirk and a whisper.

BERRY: They'll bloody roast the little sod.

HOPPER: Suppose so.

BERRY: He'll be on a charge!

Berry returns to his desk, with great satisfaction.

At the same time, in Whitehall: run-run-run, pant-pant-pant, tardy Francis charges along; just avoiding this or that collision, arms going like pistons.

FRANCIS: (*Gasp, choke*) Please God – Oh please – Please God – !

But the clock in the big room seems, now, to loom menacingly, like one of the clocks in 'High Noon'. Thirteen minutes past two o'clock.

Hopper is again looking at the clock. And he winces – unaware that his Language Officer, Major Church, is looking at him.

CHURCH: Not good enough is it, Hopper?

HOPPER: (*Quickly*) No, sir.

Church holds up a sheaf of papers.

CHURCH: I want all this put into reasonably comprehensible English by five o'clock.

HOPPER: Yes, sir.

He goes to get up.

CHURCH: No. Finish that first. How far you got?

HOPPER: Um. The fourth – (*Quickly*) – I mean the fifth page, sir.

CHURCH: Pull your bloody finger out.

HOPPER: Sah!

CHURCH: You're dealing with the bloody artillery, not the parish magazine.

HOPPER: Yes, sir. Sorry, sir.

Church's eyes fall back on to his own work. Hopper suppresses a sigh of extreme boredom, and looks up a word in his Russian dictionary.

He is diligent for a few seconds only before the boredom bites into his soul again. He writes one more word. Then – very much under his breath – he musters the opening line of Elvis Presley's 'Don't Be Cruel'. He sniggers, stops himself, writes a few more words, then covertly looks up at the oh-so-slow clock on the wall, which is looming ever more demandingly. The big hand judders forward to register one more minute.

Boo-boom-bop-bop! goes the introduction to 'Don't Be Cruel' – both comic *and* urgent . . .

And then Hopper's suffocating boredom releases him exuberantly and inspirationally into Elvis Presley and his 1956 recording of the song, allowing him to imagine himself as the glittered, pelvic-thrusting star, on top of the desk, which is now like a dazzlingly lit mini-stage.

But, in reality, Major Church is in a bad mood, and again

57

waving the sheaf of papers, and Hopper is able to convert this, too, into the urgent beat of Presley's 'Don't Be Cruel'.

All the officers put down their fountain pens, and begin to straddle their desks or their chairs with pelvic suggestiveness, making the Be-bop-wap-wapp! chorus of the hard-driving early rock 'n' roll number as Hopper continues to pluck at an Elvis-like guitar.

Meanwhile – as the music throbs on – a hot, bothered, and breathless Francis comes charging along what seems to be an endless, pillared and marbled corridor within the war office, on his too-late way to the big room.

In the big room, the Elvis recording stops for a moment. Sudden and total silence, and everything absolutely normal.

And yet a moment – a half second – of tension, as –

Crash! the door bangs open and Francis hurtles in, skids, throws up his arms both to save himself and in a helpless attempt at some sort of apology, totally loses his balance, and crashes down stunningly heavily on to the floor, right at Berry's desk.
BERRY: (*Hisses, sotto voce*) Get up, you piss-head.
Hopper looks down, aghast in the aghast silence, then switches what is undoubtedly a fantasist's gaze to Church, who has half-risen, and summons back the rock 'n' roll in the self-same movement, so that the officer, half-rising in officerly indignation, is caught or converted into a fragment of the Elvis vocal.

The music thrashes on at full pitch, and although the spread-eagled, hurt and deeply embarrassed Francis 'sings' his responses, the actions and the circumstances are otherwise what they really would have been.

During which, he clambers up from the floor, using Berry's desk as a prop, winces, and makes his way towards Major Church, standing stiffly to attention.

There is a driving wap-wap non-vocal beat for several seconds, in which there is a rapid exchange of intercutting, in rhythm, between Church's deliberately blank stare, Francis' helplessly apologetic twitch, Hopper's avid interest, Berry's clench-faced hostility, Trekker's incredulous amusement, Hedges' amiable delight and Carter's cold-eyed contempt.

The music ends, but there is no discontinuity in Church's facial expression, nor any break between the end of this 'singing' and his speaking –

58

CHURCH: I'll have you on a charge, Francis – that's what I'll do!
     Conduct prejudicial – !
FRANCIS: (*Miserably*) Yes sir.
CHURCH: You're given one hour and a quarter for your lunch,
     man. And that's generous! Generous!
FRANCIS: Sir, I –
CHURCH: Quiet!
FRANCIS: Sir.
CHURCH: Damn it all, Francis, there's a flap on here at the mo–
Bernwood lifts his head, offended.
BERNWOOD: Not a *flap*, Major Church.
CHURCH: No. Not a flap. Sorry. Misuse of – (*Snarls at* FRANCIS)
     Point is, we're bloody busy! And you chose to be late on
     parade on the very afternoon we're up to the eyeballs!
FRANCIS: Sir. I –
CHURCH: Be quiet!
FRANCIS: Sir.
Church picks up and brandishes the thick sheaf of papers yet
again.
CHURCH: All this – this! – has to be turned into English in a few
     hours – understand? Here! Get on with it! Now!
He virtually tosses the sheaf at Francis, who, ever-awkward,
makes a hash of catching them. The papers come loose from their
clip, and scatter.
     Everyone stops and watches as Francis gets down on his hands
and knees to gather them together again. Then –
HEDGES: You know what's going to happen next, don't you?
     (*Deadly little pause*) When he stands up he's going to bump
     his head on the underside of the desk.
A tiny pause, then everyone begins to laugh. Even Bernwood
leans back a little and has a titter.
     Bernwood's face adjusts instantly – the others take a little
longer – as a newcomer enters the room: Sanders of MI6, an
elegant, probably even slightly perfumed man with a bad limp
and a walking stick.
SANDERS: Good day, gentlemen. I'm glad to see that life still
     offers up its share of amusement.
BERNWOOD: Brigadier Sanders.
SANDERS: I rather wish I could exercise my less than elastic face
     muscles in the same carefree manner.

BERNWOOD: You have news?

Bernwood seems nervous, unable to relax, or share any would-be elegant chit-chat.

SANDERS: I always have news. My desk at MI6 is not at all unlike a nest in the mouth of a pillar box.

BERNWOOD: Yes. I meant –

SANDERS: Oh, don't be too eager for news, my dear. That's not a healthy desire, Harry. I would much prefer, myself, to sit at my ease in a calm pool of ignorance. Preferably under a coconut tree on a fragment of coral.

HEDGES: What? All on your own, Cecil?

Sanders picks up the faintest edge, the tiniest dig. He removes an imagined speck from the lapel of his beautiful suit, and looks across the room at Hedges, steadily.

SANDERS: Whom do you suggest that I should take, Major Hedges? One of these well-scrubbed young men, perhaps?

He indicates Hopper and the still paper-scrambling, floor-stooped Francis, with his walking stick.

HEDGES: Too well-scrubbed, surely?

Tiny silence. Church rushes in to close the awkward little gap.

CHURCH: Well, I wouldn't suggest *this* one, Colonel – (*Indicating* FRANCIS) Not unless you wanted the coconut to fall on your head when this one collides with the tree. In broad daylight.

Some renewed laughter, part of which is to cover Hedges' apparent lack of finesse.

Francis rises, flushed, the papers gathered back into his hand. Sanders examines him with interest.

SANDERS: Language Clerk. Is it?

CHURCH: (*Sighs*) It is.

Francis sits at his desk, next to Hopper, too obviously seething with resentment at the impersonal way he is being discussed.

SANDERS: He might have need for his Russian. More so tomorrow.

A small silence. A discernible tension.

BERNWOOD: Out with it, Cecil.

SANDERS: In the next day or so, Nasser is going to announce the – oh that phrase – (*Snorts*) the *nationalisation* of the canal.

VARIOUS: *What* – ?

SANDERS: Oh, it's the case, I'm afraid. No doubt about it.

BERNWOOD: But look here –

SANDERS: (*Smoothly*) Look here what?

Bernwood starts to splutter, absolutely affronted.

BERNWOOD: I never thought I'd see the day, that's all – such an
    utterly – I mean, it's getting that every little black or brown
    chap with a big mouth can – I'm just very very fed-up with the
    way things –

He subsides, suddenly, and looks around at the others, clearly
upset, and not trusting himself to keep strong emotions in check.

CARTER: Quite right, Harry.

HEDGES: (*To* SANDERS) We're going in, I take it?

Sanders spreads a hand, with the hint of a shrug.

SANDERS: Is there rot at the top? We'll soon find out.

CARTER: The people won't stand for it.

TREKKER: (*Mildly*) Which people, Archie?

HEDGES: Us!

Trekker looks at him, and sort of smiles. Sanders notices.

SANDERS: Yes. A lot depends on the responses of others.

CARTER: (*Coldly*) Oh? Like who?

Tiny pause.

TREKKER: (*Self-parody*) Hey, now. Don't all look at ol' Truck
    Trekker now. I'm just here to feed chickens.

BERNWOOD: (*Blankly*) What chickens?

Sanders snorts.

SANDERS: Harry. It's not chickens – or eagles, come to that. Settle
    your mind on bears instead.

BERNWOOD: Bears? (*Watch the penny drop.*) Yes. Indeed! The
    Soviets.

SANDERS: The point is –

CARTER: (*Snaps*) That they have been moving south for weeks now.

SANDERS: Exactly. (*Looks at his watch, ignoring the wall clock.*) I
    thought you fellows would be having a brew-up about now.

BERNWOOD: Bit early, Cecil.

SANDERS: Still –

HEDGES: (*Pleased*) Spot on, say I. Corporal!

BERRY: Sah!

HEDGES: What about the barely bloody drinkable?

BERRY: Sah! (*To* FRANCIS) Francis. Tea.

FRANCIS: Corporal!

He half-rises, confused. He doesn't quite know what he is
supposed to do.

61

CHURCH: (*Wearily*) Hopper.

HOPPER: Sah!

CHURCH: Better give him a hand.

HOPPER: Yes sir.

CHURCH: It's going to be a late night tonight.

BERNWOOD: 'Fraid so, 'fraid so.

That evening at the cinema, the big white organ rises slowly and majestically on its console out of the pit in a blaze of switching, flickering spotlight. A few bars of signature tune are being played as it rises, 'The Destiny Waltz'.

Atterbow is at the keys, swivelling half-around to nod and smile at the applause. He breaks from 'The Destiny Waltz' and speaks into his microphone.

ATTERBOW: Thank you, ladies and gentlemen. Thank you very much. I'd like to begin this evening with a jolly little piece called 'The Whistler and His Dog'. Let us take ourselves off to the green fields of dear old England. I want you to imagine the shepherd, his dog and his sheep! So – instead of clapping at the end, I want you all to go baa-aa-ah!

Some laughter, and Harold starts to play.

Sylvia, in her usherette garb, torch in hand, arms folded, leaning against the wall at the side of the aisle, watches and listens and then half-watches and half-listens as the organ music surges around her and then fades to let in her thoughts –

'The Whistler and His Dog' still slowly fading – and then disappearing – to release a literal, creamily perfect representation of the picture its notes have been suggesting.

A simple-minded and intermittently vulgar idyll: the blue sky, the gently sloping meadow, the perfectly English surroundings, the flock of woolly white sheep, the eager dog advancing half on its belly, ears pricked – and then – finding the shepherd. A vaguely familiar figure whose face cannot yet be seen properly, except that the man now defines himself in Sylvia's genuine recollection: confused, embarrassed, Francis all but presses himself against the wall to let Sylvia pass – on the first occasion they saw each other.

Sylvia, as 'The Whistler and His Dog' partially reasserts itself in the cinematic darkness, remembers Francis's face as she passed him in the hallway, and remembers the young man's obviously entranced question.

FRANCIS: Aunt Vickie – who was that?

The words fade as her gaze switches to Harold Atterbow at the great white spotlit organ as he thunders towards the slightly comical climax to 'The Whistler and His Dog'.

Harold's face is shining with sweat as the organ does a fair imitation of a shepherd's whistle-whistle and the sharp yap-yap-yap of the dog.

The organ music takes Sylvia's imagination back to her warped pastoral scenery, where the shepherd takes up the whistle for the real dog and the sheep.

Clearly now, the shepherd is Francis, looking confident, serene, handsome. But another, nastier memory inserts itself –

ATTERBOW: We could all do with an extra few bob, my dear – and there's no shame in that –

Displacing the uncertain idyll, Sylvia remembers Atterbow in her own living-room, his slightly moist face split by a sticky grin of half-lust and half-fear, as he holds up a pound note, his fingers stretching it out, almost in front of his face –

– and who's to say that there might not be more where this little fella came from. Eh? Eh?

Sylvia takes and rejects the image, a blank, almost desolate expression as in the flickering half-light of the auditorium, she half-leans, torch in hand, against the wall. Her gaze switches to Atterbow at the organ, with a sudden flare of contempt.

The console starts to descend back into the pit, in a spotlight blaze and a scatter of applause, as the organ interlude comes to an end.

Descending, Atterbow signs off with the sinuous opening bars of 'In a Persian Market Place', slightly parodied.

As he drops out of sight, the billowing notes hanging in the air, we are taken back to the war office, at night, with lights gleaming at the lower windows. Music continuing.

Inside the big room, 'In a Persian Market Place' fades away on the diligent figures, forced to work late, stooped over their desks.

Scratch-scratch-scratch of fountain pens.

Major Hedges seems as diligent as the rest, but then – suddenly – his patience gives out. He lets his pen drop with a clatter on to his desk.

HEDGES: Rectal orifices!

CARTER: (*Startled*) What?

63

HEDGES: Bum holes.

Bernwood lifts his head, wearily.

BERNWOOD: Wallace.

HEDGES: I know. I know.

BERNWOOD: We've got to get this bloody thing done.

HEDGES: I know. I know.

He sighs and picks up his pen again.

Scratch-scratch-scratch.

Francis is busily translating from the Russian. But then he looks covertly across at Corporal Berry, with hatred in his eyes.

A moment. He sighs. Then –

SYLVIA: (*In* FRANCIS' *head*) Hit me again, that's all. Hit me once more!

The young man, burdened, gets the overheard voice out of his head, and forces himself back to work. But the something-on-his-mind – the mythic Sylvia – will not leave him be. He looks sidelong at Hopper, as though wanting to communicate his ache. And Hopper looks sidelong back, as though wanting to understand. But Hopper, at least, has the magical ability to find the right way of putting such things –

Suddenly the Platters feed in 'My Prayer' with its fifties mix of syncopation and sanctimony.

Back at the cinema, Sylvia, in the flickering light of the screen and the projection beam, looks almost as though she is in the film herself – of which no sound can be heard, no images seen – Sylvia leans against the wall, torch in hand, a picture of apparently sweet loveliness: the girl in the song, as 'My Prayer' continues from the Platters.

Now, the glowing screen, huge beyond the darkened heads of the audience, is nothing but a gigantic projection of Sylvia's perhaps tawdry or banal and, probably, passing fantasy. Comic and yet oddly touching. During which the song continues, self-pitying, masturbatory, sweetly melancholic, with a strangely counter-emotion pre-or-verge-of rock beat –

And on the cinema screen – in Sylvia's mind – unlikely shepherd Francis, with his faithful Black Bob of a dog, strides home across vivid greenery and pretty wild flowers, apparently whistling.

At the door of the rose-clad, Hansel-and-Gretel-but-English little house, with latticed windows no bigger than an old family

bible, a demure young woman waits in a small flowered pinafore –
Sylvia, transmuted into the illustration on a biscuit-tin or a cheap
calendar. Her mind is not quite able to hold such an unlikely
transformation, for below the waist she wears stockings,
suspenders, high heels . . .

Shepherd Francis and happily barking Black Bob the border
collie come closer to the rose cottage as 'My Prayer' unctuously
continues. Half-shepherdess half-tart Sylvia rushes forward.
They embrace on the flagstones by the wind-up winch of the old
well, and the dog, approving, tries to jump up, tail-wagging. Oh,
what a kiss!

Usherette Sylvia, in the cinema, is half-blinking back her own
ludicrous images in the half-light, as the number has a
momentary break in a fifties-style diminuendo, and then the vocal
resumes.

The lyrics take us back to the big room at the war office – late
into the evening where five senior officers, a corporal, and two
privates are busily toiling at their desks, seemingly unaware of the
power of any fantasy except their own far worse one –

But there is no break in the music.

The vocal is momentarily interrupted, on the original
recording, by a clutch of descending piano notes, during which –
settle on Hopper, who can always summon up a song for his own
reasons.

He looks up, bored, inviting entertainment – and conjures up a
suitable *Ah-aa-aah*! chorus from the officers, in unison. Then
they lower their heads back to their desks as though nothing
untoward has happened, as the music beats on.

Click! The officers raise their heads again, and deliver up a
Platters chorus once more. And resume ordinariness, and work,
at once.

Private Francis, unaware, as he diligently translates, of any
fantasies being musically woven around him: one of which, for
sure, would meet the inchoate ache in his own heart. Except that,
borne by the continuing music, it comes once more from Sylvia
and her version of what is on the big screen at the cinema where
she works.

Shepherd Francis and shepherd's wife Sylvia at last, and
reluctantly, break from their long, long kiss: and even excited
Black Bob subsides. They look at each other. But because, after

all, this is only a passing daydream for Sylvia –

SHEPHERD FRANCIS: I've sold the sheep, my darling.

SHEPHERDESS SYLVIA: How much, my love?

He playfully dabs a finger on her cherry lips, and smiles.

SHEPHERD FRANCIS: Nine hundred and ninety thousand
    pounds, sweetheart.

SHEPHERDESS SYLVIA: Oh!

SHEPHERD FRANCIS: What's the matter?

She smiles bravely.

SHEPHERDESS SYLVIA: What a pity it wasn't a million.

'The Man with the Golden Arm' bounces us away from the idyll,
with a bright, hard, fifties insistence.

Three

The Union Jack flaps on Victoria Tower above the Houses of
Parliament. It is just before the 1956 summer recess. Big Ben
strikes three, merging into –
'ANTHONY EDEN': Her Majesty's Government is ever mindful of
the fact that this vital waterway is a –
A newspaper shows the same words, reported under the headline
'Think Again!'
  – is a main artery of world trade and a fundamental –
Widening to include the text and a picture of Anthony Eden –
 It is Private Hopper, in the big room at the war office, who is
reading the paper, his face showing concern and hostility.
  – fundamental interest in the defence and business of this
  nation. (*Rising tide of 'hear, hear!'*) Unilateral action by
  President Nasser puts in jeopardy not only –
Hopper's hostile eye is more and more arrowing in on what is to
him the danger man – pictured in the paper alongside the text.
  – only the efficient and proper use of an international –
As he reads, Hopper imagines the scene in the Commons, in his
own odd way –
'EDEN': – international waterway but also the proper conduct of –
What appears to be the same newspaper picture of Eden slides
away to reveal Colonel Bernwood who – in Hopper's hostile mind
– has become 'the man responsible for all threats to his demob' –
'EDEN'/BERNWOOD: – of international relationships as we
  understand them.
TORY MP/CARTER: Heah! Heah!
'EDEN'/BERNWOOD: It is time for the President of Egypt to pause
  for thought –
In the newspaper, the same words, under Hopper's gaze –
'ANTHONY EDEN': – There are some things he just cannot do!
  And so I say to Colonel Nasser –
Hopper, reading, shows more and more concern.
'EDEN': (*Over*) – And so I say to Colonel Nasser, take heed! You
  may imagine that you can do what you will, but –
Hopper is alone in the big room. It is the lunch hour. Hopper's
attentive reading changes into a smirk as Carl Perkins' 1956

version of 'Blue Suede Shoes' comes crashing in. And with it, the 'Eden'/Bernwood figure at the Despatch Box 'sings' and strums to the Perkins lyric, even while retaining the oratorical mannerisms of a spouting politician. Back in the otherwise empty big room at the war office, Hopper has transformed himself into a rock singer with a glitzy guitar, sobbing out the words of 'Blue Suede Shoes'.

And in the House of Commons, too, Hopper's imagined Anthony Eden lets rip with the classic rock warning.

The Mace itself is now a pair of blue suede shoes, and as honourable members jerk and sway, Hopper's mostly exposed 'dream girl' makes her way from back benches to front benches and even to the Table of the House.

Meanwhile, Private Francis uses his lunch hour to examine, carefully, a battered rack of second-hand books on the pavement outside a book-crowded jumble of a shop, dipping into a 'Shilling all this shelf' selection. The 'Blue Suede Shoes' lyric thunders on, from Carl Perkins.

And, in the Commons, 'Anthony Eden', too, is continuing to be an admonitory rocker, warning off the cat Nasser in a staccato sob.

Hopper, the master orchestrator – and fantasist – is still studying the threatening newspaper, but Carl Perkins is in his mouth, so to speak, still warning off anyone who might threaten his blue suede shoes.

In a London street beyond, a shabby old evening paper seller – '*News*, *Star*, *Standard*!' – and the wire-held placard:

> 'Nasser told:
> Hands off!'

'Blue Suede Shoes' continuing to beat.

As the lyric ends, back in the big room at the war office, Hopper quickly gets his feet off the desk as the door opens and someone enters: but it is only Francis, with a book.

HOPPER: Making sure this time.

FRANCIS: What?

Hopper nods at the clock on the wall, which shows twenty minutes to two.

Oh. Yes. Well. (*Then, eagerly*) Look at this. I got it for a bob!

HOPPER: What is it?

FRANCIS: (*Proudly*) 'The Bronze Horseman.'

HOPPER: What's that, then?

Francis stops dead still, stiffly incredulous.

FRANCIS: What do you mean 'What's that?' Don't you know?

HOPPER: Who's it by?

FRANCIS: (*More incredulously*) *What?*

HOPPER: (*Goads*) Well. If it's not by Mickey Spillane or Hank Jansen, I'm not interested.

FRANCIS: Pushkin!

HOPPER: Oh, yeh.

FRANCIS: One of his greatest poems!

Hopper holds up the newspaper.

HOPPER: You'd better clap your eyes on this bit of verse.

FRANCIS: What do you mean?

HOPPER: I mean, we'll never get out of the shagging army. Who cares about a bloody stretch of stinking water full of flies and stinking Arab shit.

FRANCIS: Oh. That.

HOPPER: 'Oh. That'. Look – I'm nearly done. I'm just a few weeks away from getting out.

FRANCIS: Yes. But nothing will happen.

HOPPER: You want to bet?

FRANCIS: (*Snorts*) Like what?

HOPPER: Like – like – stupid fat mums waving tear-sodden hankies from the dockside as you and me and Vera sodding Lynn sail off towards Wogland packed together like bleed'n sardines . . .

FRANCIS: Don't be daft, mun.

Hopper looks at him, studies him, almost with momentary hatred, as Francis opens 'The Bronze Horseman' and buries his head in it. A moment. Then –

HOPPER: They'll call me back as soon as I get out. The bastards.

But Francis is already lost in the lines of verse.

FRANCIS: (*Not listening*) Mmm.

Hopper restlessly paces, as new possibilities assail him.

HOPPER: (*Mostly to himself*) Just when I get used to a good lie-in and not shaving and – The bloody Russians will join in – he's their bloody ally – Third World War, that's what and – Oh. Christ. (*Bangs a folder down, hard.*) A future for arseholes. A world made for Corporal Berry.

At last Francis looks up, with a scowl.

FRANCIS: He hit her again last night.

HOPPER: What?

FRANCIS: Berry. I heard him. He gave her one hell of a crack.

Hopper, preoccupied with darker possibilities, stares at him.

HOPPER: What do you do, Frank? Got your ear tacked up on the
        ceiling or what?

FRANCIS: I creep out. And I listen at the bottom of the stairs –

He stops, realising what he has said, or what it sounds like.

HOPPER: Ooh. You sly little Welshman.

FRANCIS: No – it's not like that – Not like it sounds –

HOPPER: Creep up the stairs, do you?

FRANCIS: I – (*Then, too vigorously*) No! I do not!

HOPPER: Look through the keyhole?

FRANCIS: You got hold of the wrong end of the stick altogether –
        it's – Well, I don't know what to do about it, and that's the
        truth.

HOPPER: What can you do?

FRANCIS: Rescue her!

Another kind of rescuer has roughly similar ideas as, in the
particular Fulham Street, Harold Atterbow's car has just pulled up
outside Sylvia's house.

    In the car, Atterbow sits still, eyes dead, hands tight on the
steering wheel, willing himself not to look across at the top floor of
the little house where –

    In the bedroom of the upstairs flat, Sylvia seems to have been
standing side-on at the window. She tweaks the curtain just
sufficiently aside to be able to look out without being seen herself.
Her face is baleful, and yet melancholy. She sees Atterbow's car
below.

    Some small children are playing with a ball on the pavement.

    Sylvia lets the curtain fall back into place. She stands still for a
moment. Then she goes the few paces in the small room to sit on
the bed, expressionless, her hands laced, waiting, and not waiting.

SYLVIA: (*Softly, with infinite contempt*) You dirty sod.

At the same time, back at the big room in the war office, Hopper
and Francis still have the place to themselves: the clock showing
ten minutes to two.

HOPPER: What you've got to say to yourself, though, is what sort of
        woman would live with a prick like the corporal to start with?

FRANCIS: We don't know all the facts, do we? The circumstances.

HOPPER: (*Snorts*) Yeh – but he hasn't kidnapped her, has he?

FRANCIS: There's all sorts of ways a man can gain control of a
    woman. You and I both know that.

HOPPER: Well. Yes. That's – true.

They look at each other, two men of the world, unconsciously
comic.

FRANCIS: I mean – Svengali and Trilby. Mr Browning and
    Elizabeth Barrett. Oh, and – I tell you, man, the world of
    literature is full of it – look at poor Ophelia, and, and –

HOPPER: But have you ever talked to her?

Tiny pause. A mournful, long-vowelled, very Welsh answer.

FRANCIS: No-o-o.

Tiny pause. They look at each other.

HOPPER: Why don't you, then?

FRANCIS: Oh, mun – my tongue would stick to the roof of my
    mouth.

HOPPER: Oh, come on!

FRANCIS: You haven't seen her! She's the most beautiful creature
    that ever walked on this –

He stops, dead, as Corporal Berry comes busily in, whistling.

   Berry sees the way Francis stops, sees the way the two privates
look so swiftly and furtively at each other, and stops whistling,
immediately suspicious.

BERRY: What's this, then?

HOPPER: What's what, Corp?

BERRY: You two pansies. You look as though you're up to
    something.

HOPPER: What would that be, Corp?

BERRY: (*Snarls*) Corporal.

HOPPER: Sorry, Corp. I mean – Sorry, Corporal.

BERRY: You're a cheeky shagger, Hopper. You mind I don't put
    my prick in your ear and shag some respect into you.

Silence. Hopper looks at Francis, who keeps his eyes lowered.

   Ill-tempered, and suspecting that they were talking about him,
Berry unlocks his desk, pulls out a pile of papers, slams them
down on his desk. His ill-will is almost entirely due to his growing
suspicions of his pretty wife's infidelities.

    I hate this shaggin' job. And these shaggin' papers. And the
    shaggin' company I've got to shaggin' keep.

Silence. He glares at Hopper again.

72

What did you shaggin' say, soldier?

HOPPER: Nothing, Corporal.

BERRY: No. And you'd better shaggin' not, neither! (*Glares at* FRANCIS) Watchewdoin'?

FRANCIS: I – reading, Corporal.

BERRY: I can shaggin' see you're shaggin' reading! I askedchew *what*.

FRANCIS: Some p.p.po –

He is scared of Berry. His stammer comes back, immobilising him.

HOPPER: (*Half-maliciously*) Poetry.

BERRY: (*Furiously*) Did I ask you? Did I?

HOPPER: No, Corporal.

BERRY: (*Yells*) Then shut your shaggin' mouth!

But the almost inexplicable savagery of his rage seems to leave him suddenly, as Hopper's face tightens. Berry looks up at the clock. A degree of wistfulness creeps up on him, as he thinks of Sylvia.

> Christ. Here we go again. Listening to those twats. I wish I was dead.

Two faces look at him with slow, cautious interest.

> I should never have signed on. And if I'd known they'd put me in a shithouse like this – Oh God. Oh Christ.

Said with such unexpected desolation that Hopper and Francis turn their gaze off him, and look at each other. When they look back, Berry has put his head in his hands.

HOPPER: (*Cautiously*) What's the matter?

Silence. For one dreadful moment the two young men think that Berry is going to weep – or that perhaps he actually already is. But then Berry lowers his hands, sucks in his breath, visibly controls himself. He looks bleakly at both of them, and then settles on Francis.

BERRY: (*Flatly*) Poetry. You're reading poetry. Is that right?

FRANCIS: Yes.

Berry keeps his gaze on him, his face heavy with misery. A beat. When he speaks, it sounds almost friendly.

BERRY: (*Quietly*) Then you want your shaggin' head seen to, my son.

A few floors away, in the war office restaurant, at the end of lunch, Hedges puts a big white five pound note on the plate holding the bill.

BERNWOOD: That's very generous of you, Wallace.

CARTER: You do it too often, old chap.

CHURCH: (*Mumbles*) Much appreciated . . .

HEDGES: Christ. Don't go on. I'll spend my spondules as I see fit.
It's not affection, I assure you. There's no love lost.

They laugh. But Bernwood looks at his watch.

BERNWOOD: Well. I suppose we'd – ah –

HEDGES: Oh. Bum holes.

They sort of laugh.

BERNWOOD: I know. I know. It's – (*Suddenly*) I pray for this cup
to pass. You know, I can't even get a good night's sleep any
more. I see where their tanks are, where the infantry has –
(*Suddenly*) Let's have a bloody good brandy. On me.

He raises his hand, clicking his fingers, much to the surprise of
the others.

CARTER: It's two minutes to two.

HEDGES: Are you having a breakdown, Harry? Before our very
eyes?

Bernwood gives a very thin smile.

BERNWOOD: It's only a short toddle after all. A minute here and
there.

HEDGES: (*Mock horror*) I can hardly believe my ears. What is
going on? Harry! Speak to me!

BERNWOOD: We deserve a stiff one.

HEDGES: But we always *do*! Deserve a Remy, I mean.

Bernwood holds up four fingers to the distantly approaching
waitress, and half-mimes his order.

CHURCH: She looks as though she should be in an old folks'
home.

CARTER: They all do.

HEDGES: And what's to say they aren't already? (*Looks at*
BERNWOOD, *expression changing*) Now, now. Come on, old
thing. You're brooding.

It's true. For a microsecond Bernwood had looked almost vacant.
He pulls his attention back, and smiles even more thinly.

BERNWOOD: Yes. I suppose I am. But – (*Pause*) I dread what is
going to happen. Or, rather, what is *not* going to happen.

Compulsively, he looks at his watch. His face all but twitches.

HEDGES: Harry?

BERNWOOD: Oh, there'll be lots of United Nations this and
United Nations that and a conference and a peace initiative

74

and arbitration and – (*Almost shudders*) I can see the signs. I can see it already. (*Looks at them, virtually in turn*) Something has happened to us. As a people, I mean. And I never thought I'd live to see the day. Or, rather, the night. The long, long night. The darkness and the shame and then –

He stops, and clamps his teeth together.

CARTER: (*Bitterly*) I know what you're driving at.

HEDGES: (*To* CHURCH) Damned if I do! D'you, Johnny?

CHURCH: (*Slightly furtively*) Well. I –

CARTER: (*Snap*) We're not going in. That's what.

Small silence. They look at each other.

BERNWOOD: We're going to let that jumped-up little bugger get away with it.

Dreadful silence. Then Carter screwing his hands together, almost as upset as his CO –

CARTER: Dear God. Dear God Almighty! If we don't go in – If we don't fulfil our – (*Stops, his face changes.*) Now look here – ! (*Stops again*) Dear God. Dear God Al – (*Stops*) I don't know whether I – (*His eyes swivel, almost furtively*) Now look here. I'm going to say something I've never quite been able to – Look here. My father was a – a – The male parent – yes? – he was a – a – (*Has some difficulty*) he kept a – um – *shop* – you know . . .? Corner shop – I – um, no, no, no, he was a decent enough um – not something I've ever – um – (*Sudden rage*) I tell you this! That poor little old man would have, would have – Jesus Christ! – (*Slaps his fist into his palm*) Hit them! Go in! Hit them hard! Hard! (*Smacks again*) Fucking *hard*!

At about the same time, in the Fulham street, Harold Atterbow, out of his car at last, gives two precise knocks on the door knocker.

Hearing and knowing, Sylvia, still sitting expressionless on the bed, half-closes her eyes, and puts her arms around herself.

Atterbow's expectant expression at the front door begins to falter and he starts to whistle 'In a Persian Market Place' softly and nervously between his teeth.

Sylvia, sitting on the edge of the bed, holds herself very, very still, obviously tense. The ball sounds, below, bounce-bounce-bounce.

Atterbow lifts the knocker again, but then checks the movement, and quietly replaces it so that it does not thud. He walks, backwards, from the front doorstep to the edge of the pavement, where the small children are still bouncing and throwing the ball. He looks up and down the street, and then up at the window.

Inside, tense Sylvia begins to relax a little. She looks at the alarm clock beside the bed. Two o'clock. She makes a tiny 'tut!', gets up, goes to the window, stands side-on, and pulls the curtain aside a little to look down on the street below.

Atterbow's car is still drawn up in front of the house.

In the car, Atterbow sits as he sat before, his eyes dead, his hands too tightly on the steering-wheel.

Meanwhile, in the big room at the war office, Corporal Berry – husband of the prey – looks up at the clock on the wall. Five past two. He is worried by the absence of the officers.

BERRY: What's up? Wonder what's up?

HOPPER: I shouldn't complain.

BERRY: No. You're right, there. Still –

One of the telephones jangles.

    Which one's that?

HOPPER: It's the red one.

BERRY: Christ. The scrambler.

HOPPER: You'd better answer it.

BERRY: (*Nervously*) I'm not supposed to answer a scrambled phone, now am I?

HOPPER: Somebody'd better!

BERRY: Francis!

FRANCIS: (*Nervously*) Corporal?

BERRY: Answer that phone!

FRANCIS: B.but – I –

BERRY: Answer the shaggin' phone!

Jangle-jangle-jangle. Very reluctantly, with a look at Berry that is half-glare half-plea, Francis goes to the irritatingly jangling red phone on Bernwood's desk. He hovers for too long.

    Answer the shaggin' phone!

Francis gulps, obeys.

FRANCIS: (*On phone*) H.he . . . Hello? N.no – He's – No, he's out – Ah. One mo-ment . . . (*Covers the phone, looks desperately at the others*) Where are they, mun?

BERRY: We don't know.

HOPPER: Having a Jimmy Riddle.

FRANCIS: (*Solemnly, on phone*) He's having a Jimmy Riddle, sir.
    With the other officers.
Berry and Hopper look at each other in horror. Then – as Francis
continues – Hopper starts to laugh, increasingly helplessly. This,
in turn, infects Berry, who also starts to whoop.
BERRY: Jee-*sus*.
FRANCIS: (*On phone*) N-nun – no, I – N.no – Um. He's not here
    either – I – Fuffrancis, sir. No. Um – – Private, sir. I'm –
    (*Stands to attention*) Sah! (*Quavers*) Yessir one m.mum.mo –
    (*Covers phone, hisses at giggling pair*) Pup-pencil! Quick!
    Quick! (*On phone*) Yessir one m.mum. mo –
He signals desperately for pen or pencil to his now helplessly
giggling companions. Slow about it, and by now gasping for
breath, Hopper gives stiff and scared Francis a pencil. Francis, all
but tangled in the cable, drops the phone then grapples it back
into his hand.
    Yessir. I could you repeat that p.please – Yes. (*Writes*) Yes.
    (*Writes*) Yessir. Sorrysir. Thankyousir.
He puts the phone down as though it were wired to explode, and
then turns on the others.
    A fat lot of help! Thank you. Thank you very much!
But they are subsiding.
BERRY: Don't you shaggin' well know what a Jimmy Riddle is,
    you prick?
FRANCIS: (*Blinks*) What?
HOPPER: It's a piss. A piddle. Jimmy Riddle.
FRANCIS: Oh, God. I thought – I thought it was some sort of –
He retreats from the dangerous phone.
    Oh, I don't know what I thought, mun. He sound-ed so –
    so –
BERRY: Who was it?
FRANCIS: (*Awed*) It was the Foreign Office.
BERRY: Foreign Office?
HOPPER: Foreign Office?
FRANCIS: Foreign Office.
BERRY: Christ.
FRANCIS: My head went blank. It was for Major Hedges. The red
    braces.
But Hopper is suddenly gloomy.
HOPPER: Something's going on. And I'll bet you any money it's –

Oh shit. I just feel it. They're not going to let me go – (*To Francis*) What's the message?

FRANCIS: Am I supposed to tell you?

HOPPER: Why not? I'm only a Russian spy, enni?

FRANCIS: (*Reads*) Stormy Petrel.

BERRY: Code. It's in code.

HOPPER: What's a Stormy Petrel? A bird – ennit?

FRANCIS: One that flies ahead of the storm.

A tiny moment, while each of them chews over possible meanings. Then – in a rage of revelation.

HOPPER: See! You see! I told you!

BERRY: Told us what?

HOPPER: Not much of a code, is it? I mean, if I were some stupid moon-faced Russian peasant I'd soon work it out. It's a *warning*. Flying before the storm. The *battle*. That's pretty bloody obvious.

BERRY: Battle? What battle? (*Then – angrily, feeling obscurely, that his authority is demeaned*) Bollocks, Hopper. What do *you* know about it? There's more going on than you'll ever know, I can tell you that for a start.

'The Destiny Waltz' creeps under on the cinema organ, revealing Atterbow's car in the Fulham street.

And as the organ swells to full glories around him, Harold Atterbow remains like a dead man at the steering-wheel of the car still parked outside the dingy little terraced house. He is looking straight ahead through his windscreen, but at nothing. The ball bounces to and fro past his window, and occasionally against the car.

Across the street, in the upstairs flat, Sylvia checks the perfection of the gloss on her shining mouth in the mirror, dressed and high-heeled, ready to leave. Her eyes linger on their own reflection a moment, questioningly. No answer given by her own image, she goes to open the door to the landing and stairs. But then she hesitates – almost as though able to hear the organ music which has continued – turns back, her high heels clacking on the worn linoleum, to go into her bedroom, where she stands side-on at the window to look down again. She makes a small noise of disappointment and exasperation, because, below, the car is still there. And, on the organ, 'The Destiny Waltz' continues to swell.

Atterbow, in the car, sits and sits and waits – and waits. In some bleak part of his head, the cinema organ rises in a dazzle of spotlight on its console playing 'The Destiny Waltz'. But then – in some shift of the mind into dread and depression – the organ music suddenly stops, as he sits in the car, waiting, waiting . . . The spotlight slowly fading and, silent, the organ slowly descending back into the pit.

Directly across the street from the waiting Atterbow, Sylvia shuts the front door, does not look at the car, and hurries off towards the main road, her heels going tcha-tcha-tcha on the paving.

Atterbow comes out of his private horror and suddenly realises – as suddenly as the click of a light switch – that Sylvia is some yards away, her back to him, walking quite fast along the pavement.

ATTERBOW: (*Little, barely audible choke*) Oh, please.

He starts the car – not easily, for it whirrs and coughs – engages first gear and crawls along the edge of the pavement towards the departing young woman.

Sylvia, more than half expecting it already, more than half hoping not, becomes aware of the car gliding just behind her.

Atterbow, looking both helpless and desperate, keeps his eyes on her, yet seems not to dare to come up exactly alongside.

Sylvia suddenly stops, but does not turn around.

The car edges slowly and nervously level with her – in that odd way a vehicle shows the mind of its driver – and all but stops.

A strange little moment of stillness. His window is already wound down.

(*Eventually*) Sylvia.

SYLVIA: (*Tightly*) What do you want?

ATTERBOW: Sylvia. Please.

She still has not looked directly at him.

SYLVIA: I said – what do you want?

ATTERBOW: To talk.

SYLVIA: What about?

ATTERBOW: Sylvia. Please.

Now she turns, in a whirl of fury.

SYLVIA: Look – why the bleed'n hell don't you leave me alone.
    I'm already late because of you. Parked outside like a – I
    don't know what.

79

ATTERBOW: I'll drive you there.

He swings open the car door.

SYLVIA: No you bloody won't.

ATTERBOW: Don't be silly. Sylvia – get in. Please. Come on. Come
    on, there's a good girl.

She bites her lip. He repeats the invitation.

SYLVIA: (*In a small voice*) Oh Christ.

And she gets in.

Atterbow does not immediately drive off. They sit there for a
moment in silence, each looking straight ahead through the
windscreen. Then –

    I'm late. I shall lose my job.

He doesn't answer. She looks at him.

    Look. I'm not interested in you.

He looks at her, wretchedly yearning.

ATTERBOW: I know you're not. How could you be?

SYLVIA: You know what you are, don't you?

ATTERBOW: Yes, I do.

SYLVIA: Look. I rubbed you for a pound. That's because I was –
    because I was –

ATTERBOW: Short of a few bob. Yes.

SYLVIA: And I wish I hadn't done it. It made me feel – all sticky,
    and – it made me feel sick.

ATTERBOW: Yes. It would. Yes.

SYLVIA: (*Fiercely*) So what do you want! What are you doing!

He doesn't answer. He looks away, deep in misery. Her eyes glint.

    If I tell my Pete he'll break your dirty little neck.

ATTERBOW: Please don't.

SYLVIA: And if I tell your wife. The poor bitch.

ATTERBOW: Please. Please. Don't.

Silence. She studies him.

SYLVIA: (*Steadily*) It made me feel sick.

And she gets out of the car, her nose in the air.

This being the moment when the clock in the big room at the war
office is showing twenty minutes past two.

    Berry pulls his eyes from the clock, troubled in his corporal-like
way by any unexpected deviation from routine.

BERRY: This has only happened once before. And that was a year
    ago, and more.

80

HOPPER: I tell you. There's trouble. There's definitely something
      fishy going on.
BERRY: When they did it before they came back drunk.

Hopper and Francis look at him with genuine interest.

HOPPER/FRANCIS: Yeah?
BERRY: Pissed as newts.
HOPPER: Getaway.
BERRY: Practically arm in arm, they were. (*Works his face*) It was
      disgusting.

A few floors away in the war office restaurant, Bernwood,
Hedges, Carter and Church have persuaded themselves that they
deserve and, especially, need at least another brandy each: and it
may be the third.

Church, the Language Officer, is the one least in full-hearted
agreement with the prevailing sentiment.

CHURCH: The thing is – no, a mo, half a mo – If we go in on our
      own – and I'm not saying we shouldn't –
CARTER: (*Snaps*) I should hope not.

Cold-eyed Carter suspects procrastination. Church looks sidelong
at him, hinting at personal dislike and Englishly aware of the
'shopkeeper' confession.

CHURCH: If – if – You've heard of the conditional tense, Archie?
HEDGES: Oh, Christ. Don't talk about grammar.
CHURCH: (*Smiles*) If. Then what if the Soviets move?
CARTER: (*With contempt*) They already have. We've seen that.
      We're seeing it on our charts. Every day.
CHURCH: No – an ultimatum, I mean. If they give us an
      ultimatum.

Colonel Bernwood looks, somehow, not quite there, and it is
doubtful whether he is even listening.

His fingers are unconsciously picking brittle mosaics of over-
baked crust from the remains of a small, brick-hard bread roll,
making a mess on the immaculately starched and creased table
cloth. And oddly, faintly, stirring in the depths of his mind, so to
speak, a theatre organ begins to play 'In a Monastery Garden' by
Arthur Ketelbey.

At the same time –

HEDGES: Then I suggest that we get a bloody big bucket and
      spade and dig a bloody big hole in the nearest bit of empty
      ground.

CHURCH: (*Smiles*) Like the local cemetery.

CARTER: Tcha!

HEDGES: Or we call their bluff.

CARTER: Exactly!

CHURCH: If it were a bluff.

CARTER: (*Angrily*) If. If.

HEDGES: You've heard of the condit- what was it? The conditional tense, Archie.

He swills his brandy round in his glass, and drinks with great relish and his almost perpetual glint of amusement.

CARTER: I'm not saying these things are not possible. But what have we got the bomb *for*? (*Sniffs*) Anyway. What do you mean, on our own? Who said anything about that?

CHURCH: The French couldn't punch a hole in a paper bag.

CARTER: I'm not talking about the bloody frogs. I'd sooner go to war with my maiden aunt.

Church looks at him, goes to say something, doesn't and drinks instead.

CHURCH: This is very more-ish, I must say.

CARTER: The Americans. *Of course.*

Church looks at him with a faint smile.

CHURCH: Truck doesn't drink, we know. But it would be nice if he were here, wouldn't it?

CARTER: What?

CHURCH: Haven't you noticed? The *shop* has been left unattended. Mmm?

The remark is lobbed with malice aforethought at Carter and his earlier confession.

CARTER: (*Irritated*) What are you getting at?

CHURCH: Colonel Trekker is not much in the office, is he? Over the last few days.

CARTER: So?

HEDGES: No. That's right. He isn't.

CARTER: That's because his niece is in town. Over from wherever it is. Texas.

HEDGES: In boots. And a big hat. (*Sniffs*) I expect.

CARTER: This is balderdash.

CHURCH: Is it?

CARTER: You know it is!

CHURCH: Perhaps it is. Perhaps it isn't.

CARTER: We've never let them down. Why should they let us down?

Church doesn't answer, but he smiles again. This clearly irritates Carter.

HEDGES: I think I'll still look for a place to dig.

CARTER: Why do you smile like that, Johnny?

CHURCH: Like what?

Colonel Bernwood, lost, is still crumbling hard little bits from the cannon-ball bread roll, but, as 'In a Monastery Garden' thunders back in, now at almost full pitch, it is impossible to hear other voices.

A minute or so must have passed. Three faces are looking at Bernwood, puzzled.

HEDGES: Harry? What you think?

Clearly this is a repeated question.

CARTER: I'm saying that the Yanks are only too well aware of the – (*Stops, frowns*) Harry?

Bernwood becomes aware of being addressed. He drags himself back from a long way.

BERNWOOD: Don't hear them so much any more, do you? And that was something I rather enjoyed – (*Looks at his watch*) Good heavens above!

HEDGES: Harry.

BERNWOOD: The time.

HEDGES: Don't hear what?

BERNWOOD: Look here – what are we . . . We'd better get moving. God knows, there's flap enough going on. More than I – (*Looks at Hedges*) What was that, Wallace?

Hedges addresses him almost as one might a child.

HEDGES: Don't-hear-what so much, Harry? What do you mean? Where've you been, old thing?

Bernwood twitches, looks compulsively at his watch again with a fierce, swift dab of his eyes.

BERNWOOD: The Wurlitzers and whatnot. Like the one that used to be at the – Everything is – (*Looks at them, puzzled.*) Everything seems to be changing, don't you think? On the move. And – and – ah – (*Swift look at his watch*) Yes. That's what *we'd* better be. Come on, chaps. Skates on!

The big room, stuffily boring, is made worse by the bright

83

sunlight glancing across the desks and dappling the far, door-side wall.

Scratch-scratch-scratch go all the fountain pens, as ever.

Private Hopper is suffocating. Feeling the heat, he puts a finger in his collar to loosen it, longing to remove his tie. He translates half a line. His eyes glaze. He pulls himself together, and looks across at Francis, who is similarly glazed: but for a different reason. He is ever thinking of the girl upstairs.

Then Hopper's face changes. He remembers something – and hisses, stage whisper style, across to his companion at the next desk.

HOPPER: Psst! Frank. Hey – Frank. Wakey-wakey – !

FRANCIS: (*Surfacing*) What? Oh. Wha – ?

HOPPER: The message!

FRANCIS: What – ?

HOPPER: The phone message!

Francis stares at him. Then he slaps his forehead in an 'Oh God! I forgot!'

Francis half mimes a 'What shall I do?' to Hopper, who shrugs. But this small by-play attracts the attention of the nearest officer.

CHURCH: Auditioning. Are we, Francis?

FRANCIS: (*Startled*) Sir – ?

CHURCH: You're making more gestures than a bad actor in a Christmas melodrama.

FRANCIS: S.sorry, sir.

CHURCH: What the hell's the matter with you?

Francis half rises then half sits, agitated.

FRANCIS: Sir. I – There's a – Sir. When you were out – There was a message.

CHURCH: (*Frowns*) A message.

FRANCIS: On the telephone, sir. I answered the instrument.

CHURCH: The what?

FRANCIS: The red one, sir.

CHURCH: The scrambler?

FRANCIS: A communication for Major Hedges, sir.

CHURCH: A what? (*Exasperated*) Francis. You may be Welsh, but can't you try a little harder to speak in good, plain, decent English? Do you mean to sit there like a twitching cretin and tell me that two hours or more ago there was a call on the scrambler?

84

FRANCIS: Sir.

CHURCH: (*Glowers*) Did you write it down?

Francis is already looking with too obvious panic for the one small scrap of paper amongst the litter of his desk.

FRANCIS: I did indeed, sir.

CHURCH: (*Indignantly*) Don't you 'indeed' me, man!

FRANCIS: Sorry, sir?

CHURCH: (*Glowers*) Well?

With a gulp of relief, awkward Francis finds the bit of paper. Hopper, a few feet away, watches all this with a mixture of delight and horror.

FRANCIS: It's here, sir. I've got it.

CHURCH: I should bloody well hope so. Give it to whom it is
    meant.

FRANCIS: Yes, sir.

CHURCH: You bloody half-wit.

FRANCIS: Sorry, sir.

He gets up, awkwardly, all but knocking over his chair, increasingly self-conscious under the gaze of Church and, now, others. Francis, clearing his throat, goes across to Hedges.

    Major Hedges, jacket off, red braces glowing, seems the picture of absolute and perfect concentration, a Soviet tank disposition chart spread before him, pen poised like a hawk over the paper, as still as a statue.

    Francis stops, looks at him, shifts from one foot to the other, and – so deep is the Major's concentration – haplessly half-whispers his belated interruption.

      Excussse me, sir . . .

When nervous, his strong Welsh accent seems to be all sing-song sibilants.

    Hedges does not lift his head, nor make any other sort of acknowledgement.

    Francis, awkward and embarrassed, shifts from one foot to the other again, scratches the back of his leg, and tries again.

      Beg pardon, sir. But there was – I'm sorry, sir – there is a
      m.mum.message for you which I –

He stops, at the total lack of response. The dreadful thought occurs to him that Major Hedges has died – with his boots on, so to speak.

    Francis, not sure what to do, and by now too fascinated to

appeal for aid or advice from any of the others, comes another step closer, and peers.

    (*Awed whisper*) Major Hedges?

No response.

    Francis tentatively reaches out. And then, considerably less tentatively, grasps Hedges' upper arm. Hedges virtually leaps out of his chair, like one given an electric shock.

HEDGES: (*Gasp*) *Christ Almighty*!

Hedges half-standing, quivering. Francis stepping back in consternation.

    Everyone looking in astonishment at this momentary tableau.

    And everyone realising, at more or less the same time, that Hedges had somehow managed to disguise a deep sleep in the posture and the open eyes of deep concentration.

    Then Hedges, too, that half-a-fraction later, realises that everyone else realises.

    No, no, no, no.

FRANCIS: (*Still in shock*) S.sus sorry, sir – I –

HEDGES: No, no. I was not asleep!

Tiny one-two-three pause: and then a collective roar of laughter, in which even fretful and harassed Bernwood joins.

CHURCH: Of course you weren't, Wallace. Why do you think I
    sent my man over? He couldn't wake a sleeping kitten.

Some titters. Francis stops smiling. This place is a perpetual affront to his dignity.

HEDGES: I just felt this – something – on my arm. You know.
    When you're lost in thought. A sort of *tentacle*.

CARTER: (*Snorts*) Lost in thought? That's a new one for you,
    Wallace. You were fast asleep!

HEDGES: No, no. Lost in thought, Archie. Lost in thought, old
    bean. (*Focuses on* FRANCIS) You should be in the
    Commandos. Way you creep up on a fella. Had no idea. Well
    done.

FRANCIS: Sorry, sir. Th-thank you, sir.

HEDGES: What do you want? What are you after? My wallet is it?

Francis again shifts from foot to foot as he speaks.

FRANCIS: There is a message for you, sir. The Foreign Office.

HEDGES: (*Frowns*) Oh? When did this come?

CARTER: When you were asleep.

Some laughter, despite the edge in cold-eyed Carter's voice.

FRANCIS: (*Anxiously*) When you were out at dinner, sir.

HEDGES: Last night? Oh, but –

FRANCIS: Lunch. I meant lunch, sir. Luncheon.

HEDGES: (*Frowns*) Lunch?

Francis hangs his head, abjectly.

FRANCIS: I'm sorry, sir.

HEDGES: Well. So long as it's not urgent, eh? Like invading some
little country or other, eh? Like Sweden or something.

He is, essentially, an amiable and kindly man. And now that he is
properly awake he is looking at Francis with more than the
suspicion of an avuncular twinkle.

FRANCIS: I – I wrote it down, sir.

HEDGES: Good for you!

FRANCIS: (*Encouraged*) And then it sort of – s.s. suslipped my
mind, sir.

HEDGES: Well. What does it say?

FRANCIS: Pardon, sir?

HEDGES: The message. Who's it from? This chappie or chappess
at the FO. Well-known den of vice, Francis. (*Slight edge*)
Say who it was? Did he stroke she?

Francis looks at his scrap of paper.

FRANCIS: It was a Mr Philby, sir.

HEDGES: (*Encouragingly*) Jolly good. Keep going.

FRANCIS: He said – ah – (*Looks at paper again*) Stormy Petrel, sir.

Hedges is suddenly very alert. His whole face changes.

HEDGES: Time? Did he give a time?

Maddeningly, Francis looks at his scrap of paper yet again.

FRANCIS: Four o'clock, sir.

Hedges' eyes fly to the wall clock like an arrow. Thunk!
Twenty-five minutes past four.

HEDGES: (*Evenly*) You little shit. You miserable little pile of
poodle poop. You half-witted half-formed lump of
Caerphilly cheese. You – (*Sudden scream*) Look at the time!

FRANCIS: Twenty fuf.five past f.f.f. . . .

He stops, his jaw locked, his face collapsing, utterly demoralised.

HEDGES: Get out of my sight. Go on. Remove yourself.

FRANCIS: Yes sir.

Hedges' hand plunges to the telephone. Whirr-whirr-whirr on the
round dial. Never has he been so urgently busy.

HEDGES: (*On phone*) Telegraph? Sports desk, please. (*Waits*)

Bertie Cooper, please. (*Waits*) Bertie? Wallace here. Hedges.
Got the result in yet on the four o'clock, Newbury? Mm.
(*Waits*) Go on. Yes. All go? (*Face darkens*) The price?
Twenty to one. By God, yes. Nice for someone. No – not
me! Ta very much, Bertie. Toodle oo, old pip.

He puts the phone down.

All eyes are on Hedges, as he gives a deep, heart-rending sigh,
and tilts back in his chair, hands clasped behind his head.

Hopper, for sure, is no longer bored. Eyes alive, drinking in
everything. And ready to extemporise.

HEDGES: Well. It only goes to show. One must be philosophical
about these things.

He rights his chair, picks up his pen, and with apparent
insouciance, begins to write, to work, once more.

CHURCH: Wallace!

HEDGES: (*Busily, not looking up*) Mmmm?

CHURCH: Well – come on!

Hedges deigns to lift his head.

HEDGES: Come on, what? Oh. The gee-gees. Is that what you
mean?

CHURCH: (*Amused*) Wallace!

BERNWOOD: (*Lifting his head*) I really think we should get on, you
know. Time and tide – that sort of –

His voice trails off. His head drops back to his work. Nobody
takes any notice.

HEDGES: It was won by a filly. Ramona. First time in blinkers.

CARTER: What about Stormy whatsit?

HEDGES: (*Smirks*) Nowhere. (*Face changes*) Last time I trust
Philby. Supposed to be in the bloody know. Straight from
the horse's arse, eh?

Picks up his pen again, disgusted.

At his desk, Francis shows a mixture of relief and indignation.

Hopper looks across at the beleaguered Welshman with a
certain sardonic sympathy. He sees the change in Francis' face.
Francis reverts to thinking about the girl upstairs. He sighs,
lovelorn. Enter his thoughts –

Sylvia, in her nightdress, at the top of the stairs, in the little
Fulham house, leans down from a pool of near darkness into
light, and beckons gracefully with a bare arm. She is making the
gesture to Francis, at the foot of the stairs, in the narrow hallway.

At his desk in the big room, Francis is even more lovelorn. A pool of late afternoon sunlight suddenly opens out like a drawn curtain at a window on the wood and the papers on his desk.

Hopper looks at Francis looking at the oblong of bright light elongating across his desk, almost like a spotlight or even a heavenly radiance.

HOPPER: (*In a stage whisper*) Hey. Frank.

But Francis is lost in his own dreams, and does not seem to hear. He reaches out and puts his finger into the luminous, magical pool of sunlight like one trying to understand and to possess it.

Hopper smiles to himself. Music creeps in, under 'Raining in My Heart' by Buddy Holly and the Crickets. Francis sighs. But Hopper starts to 'sing', as Buddy Holly – and then he makes Francis do so, too, in a sardonic little twist of Hopper's mind.

Out of the song – where there is a cute little ploink! ploink! of instrumental rain, Sylvia, in her nightie, leans down, beckoning, still the most important image in Francis' thoughts.

Even so, Francis is made to continue the Holly lyric, lugubrious and hypnotic.

Bernwood, at work, looks anxious and distressed, almost as though edging towards some kind of breakdown, as the song continues, splashing instrumental tears.

Hopper makes half-mad Bernwood lift his furrowed brow, open his mouth, and take on the lyric.

The music surges on, without interruption, to reach the streets of Fulham, late in the day, where Corporal Berry is striding along, arms swinging, as though in uniform.

At the extended falling raindrops beat, between verses, his swinging, soldierly march seems to falter. He stands dead still, morose, like a man pondering things. And then he suddenly turns back, a dark oath at his lips.

BERRY: Shag it! Shag it all!

As Berry turns back towards the corner, Francis coincidentally turns the corner, sees him, and stops dead. Dismayed, Francis is not sure whether to stand still, walk on, or turn back, his body signalling alarm and uncertainty.

FRANCIS: (*Sotto voce*) Oh bugger.

And, suddenly, a malignant-looking Berry is thrusting his face at Francis.

BERRY: (*Arriving almost face to face*) Whatchew doing?

FRANCIS: Oh – hello, Corporal.

BERRY: Following me?

FRANCIS: Of course not – I –

BERRY: Don't want to walk with me? That right?

FRANCIS: Don't be silly –

BERRY: What's up with you, then? What's the matter?

FRANCIS: No, no – nothing – It's – well, we're a different rank, aren't we?

BERRY: We're what?

FRANCIS: I don't want to be presumptuous, see.

Berry looks at him, hard, to see whether there is the slightest element of satire or mockery. He decides there isn't.

BERRY: I don't stand on ceremony. Not after working hours, Frank.

FRANCIS: Right you are, Corporal.

His eyes flick uneasily from side to side, as though looking for some means of escape.

BERRY: Pete. It's Pete. After working hours, all right?

FRANCIS: Right.

BERRY: What's the matter?

FRANCIS: Sorry – ?

BERRY: You look as though you got an earwig up your arse. You got something against me or something?

FRANCIS: No. I – (*Then more determined*) I just don't like my head being pushed down the pan, thank you very much.

But Berry laughs – heartily – and slaps Francis on the shoulder. Berry seems to want company.

BERRY: Oh, that was nothing to cry about! A bit of good clean shit never hurt nobody. Tell you what – tell you what, Frank old lad – I'll buy you a drink.

FRANCIS: (*Reluctantly*) Oh. I –

BERRY: (*Darkening*) Turning me down?

FRANCIS: (*Uneasily*) No – it's just that – No, of course not . . .

Before Francis can muster together any acceptable sort of refusal, Berry once again half-punches him heartily on the shoulder, grinning wolfishly.

BERRY: Come on then, fella-me-lad! I'm not going to eat you, am I?

Elsewhere – no, not a place, but in a head – a cinema organ is rising out of the pit on its console, drenched with coloured light, playing 'In a Monastery Garden'.

But there is something not quite right about the angles, the setting – and the troubled face of Colonel Bernwood looms, the source of the image.

The organ is rising in his troubled head. Music swelling –

Bernwood receives the disturbing image, with a face too dark, too still. The oddity slowly reveals itself: the big room is empty except for Bernwood. And the lights are not on. At the large, old-fashioned windows, the thickening dusk outside presses gloomily against the glass, making the large space and all the unpeopled desks seem troubled and melancholy.

'In a Monastery Garden' continues on the organ, painting its own not dissimilar pictures.

Alone at his desk, face clenched against some unknown or obscure dread, Bernwood seems to gather himself together and push the organ music away from the centre of his head.

The music dies away to almost nothing. Then – very quietly, to himself –

BERNWOOD: No use worrying about it, old chap. No use at all.

Silence. No trace is left of the organ music.

Bernwood looks around the big room, with a slight air of surprise. Then he sighs deeply, gets up, gathers his bowler hat and his tightly furled umbrella from the near-antique hat stand, goes to the door, looks around the rapidly darkening cavern of a room once more, and goes out, shutting the door behind him.

Meanwhile, in the pub, Berry drains his pint and wipes the back of his hand across his mouth.

BERRY: Next one's on you, mate.

FRANCIS: Oh, but –

Francis is less than a quarter down his pint of brown and mild.

BERRY: But what?

Berry's eyes harden.

FRANCIS: I didn't really want a – And I certainly don't want *two*.

BERRY: But I do.

FRANCIS: Yes, but –

BERRY: You don't have a drink with a man and then duck out of
     your round.

FRANCIS: The thing is –

BERRY: I mean, I don't know what you lot do down in darkest
     shaggin' Wales. A lot of singing, I know. But up here, mate,
     a bloke is expected to pay his way.

FRANCIS: See, I'm a bit short.

BERRY: (*Nastily*) Oh, are you?

FRANCIS: Till payday.

BERRY: (*Morosely*) Who shaggin' isn't.

Francis looks at him. He doesn't want to be here.

FRANCIS: Here. You can have this.

He pours most of his pint into Berry's glass.

BERRY: Yeh – but that's brown and mild, ennit? Not my drink.

FRANCIS: Well, that's all you get.

Berry looks at him, sees a flash of something – just a hint – he had not suspected.

BERRY: Right. Have to do, then, won't it.

FRANCIS: I got to get going anyway. They don't like me late for my – (*Slightly hesitates over which word*) – tea.

BERRY: Who don't? The nutters?

FRANCIS: The what?

BERRY: Those two downstairs. (*Drinks, watching* FRANCIS) Off their heads. You know that, don't you?

FRANCIS: That's my aunt and uncle you're talking about.

BERRY: (*Sniggers*) Must run in the family.

Francis gets to his feet. He dislikes the company, and hates this squalid public bar, with its scatter of mostly old and seedy-looking Londoners.

FRANCIS: I'll – a – thanks for the drink, Corp. See you –

BERRY: You're shaggin' lucky to have some grub waiting for you. I'll give you that.

Francis, standing, looks down at him, wanting to go, but sensing that he might get some information about the loved one.

FRANCIS: Haven't you?

BERRY: The Missus don't get in until turned half past ten on a Tuesday and a Thursday. And the bloody weekends are shagged to buggery. That's the cinema business for you.

FRANCIS: The what?

BERRY: She's an usherette.

FRANCIS: Still – she gets to see some good films – and that. (*Clears his throat.*) W.where . . . ?

BERRY: What?

FRANCIS: Where is she an – Which cinema, I mean . . . ?

He sounds tense, and he shifts from foot to foot in his awkward fashion.

BERRY: The Gaumont. In the Broadway, you –
But then, belatedly, Berry picks up the tension and the intensity
of interest emanating from Francis.

    What's it to you?
FRANCIS: Oh – n.nothing – just –
BERRY: Just what?
FRANCIS: Just making conversation.

In a West End theatre, that same evening, the new production of
Chekhov's *The Seagull* has reached Act Two: 'A croquet lawn and
flower beds, with a view of the lake with bright sunlight reflected
in the water.'

  'Nina' and 'Trigorin': 'Young girl' and 'famous writer'.
'NINA': What a wonderful world you live in! How I envy you – if
    only you knew! . . . How different people's destinies are!
    Some just drag out their obscure, tedious existences, all very
    much like one another, and all unhappy –
In an expensive box, Lt Colonel Trekker, the absent American, is
watching the play with less than total enthusiasm.

  But next to him, as pretty as a picture, is his visiting young
niece, Lisa, very American, very enraptured.

    (*Continuous*) and there are others – like you for instance, one
    in a million – who are given an interesting life – a life that is
    radiant and full of significance. You are fortunate!
'TRIGORIN': I? (*Shrugs*) Hm! You talk about fame and happiness,
    and this radiant and interesting life, but to me –
Trekker is beginning to nod off, but jerks himself awake with a
start.

    – all these fine words of yours – you must forgive me – are
    just like so many delicious sweets which I never eat. You are
    very young and very kind.
'NINA': Your life is beautiful.
'TRIGORIN': But what is there beautiful about it? (*Looks at his
    pocket watch.*) I must go and do some writing presently.
    Forgive me, I haven't much time to spare . . . (*Laughs*)
    You've stepped on my favourite corn, as the saying goes, and
    here I am getting excited –
In the box, Lisa is utterly attentive and enraptured, not yet
noticing that her middle-aged uncle is having such difficulty in
keeping his eyes open.

– and a little bit angry, too. All the same, let's talk. Let's talk about my radiant and beautiful life. Well, where shall we begin? (*Thinks*) You know what it is to have a *fixed idea* – for instance when a man keeps on thinking about the same thing day and night, about – let us say, the moon. Well, I, too, have a kind of moon of my own. I'm obsessed day and night by one thought.

Trigorin's speech yields to Francis in the Fulham house. Suffocating. He sighs. He is on a hard-backed chair, with his newly purchased 'The Bronze Horseman' by Pushkin, but he cannot give his mind to it.

He is at the table with his book, inches from the irritating budgerigar. Aunt Vickie knitting in the half-armchair on one side of the fireplace. Uncle Fred, mouth open, asleep in the only real armchair opposite her.

There is no room to swing a cat – but every motive for wanting to do so, or to kill at least something.

Francis looks at the clock on the mantelpiece: twenty past ten. He shuts his book, an inner tension growing.

FRANCIS: Aunt Vickie – I think I'll . . .

AUNT VICKIE: (*Urgently*) Shhh!

She nods at the sleeping Uncle Fred, warningly.

FRANCIS: (*Whispers*) Sorry.

AUNT VICKIE: (*Whispers*) Then he says he doesn't sleep nights. I'll make the cocoa in a minute.

FRANCIS: (*Whispers*) I think I'll get some air.

AUNT VICKIE: (*Whispers*) At this time of night?

Francis stands up.

FRANCIS: A little stroll. I feel a bit – oh, I don't know.

He has forgotten to whisper. Uncle Fred's jaw suddenly clamps shut, loudly. Aunt Vickie and Francis watch him, anxiously.

Chomp-ggrumm-um-chop: he moves his mouth around, but does not open his eyes. Then the rhythm of his breathing steadies, back into a deeper sleep.

Aunt Vickie and Francis both let out their own breath: it was, for them, a moment of real tension. Francis would very much prefer that Fred did not wake and talk. Aunt Vickie would rather that he never woke at all – ever.

AUNT VICKIE: (*Whispers*) Don't trip over anything when you come in, Frank.

FRANCIS: (*Whispers*) Trip over? What do you – (*Sigh*) No. All
    right, Aunt Vickie.
At the theatre, as though Chekhov had not been interrupted:
'TRIGORIN': Well, I, too, have a kind of moon of my own. I'm
    obsessed day and night by one thought: I must write, I must
    write, I just want . . .
Lisa nods and beams and nods as though the character on stage
were describing her own life, her own feelings. She does not seem
to notice the half-snores next to her.
    . . . For some reason, as soon as I've finished one novel I feel
    I must start writing another, then another, then another . . .
Trekker's chin goes into his chest.
    . . . I write in a rush, without stopping, and can't do
    anything else. What is there radiant – or beautiful in that, I
    ask you? Oh, it's a fatuous life!
A sudden, enormous snore. Heads twitch.
    Here I am with you, I'm quite worked up, and yet not for a
    single moment do I forget –
Lisa is mortified by her uncle's trumpeting-elephant of a snore –
which has been repeated.
    She pushes him, almost violently, in the shock of her youthful
shame and humiliation.
LISA: (*Hisses*) Uncle Truck!
TREKKER: (*Startled, far too loudly*) What – ? What's that – !
LISA: *Sssh!*
OTHERS: Shh! Quiet!
TREKKER: Where am – – ? Oh. Oh. Sorry Lisa. I'm –
LISA: Sssh. Please. Oh, please.
He is silent, and bewildered, tries to focus on the stage, where –
'TRIGORIN': I look over there and I see a cloud shaped like a
    grand piano . . . At once I think I must put it into some story
    or other – the fact that a cloud looking like a grand piano has
    floated by. There's the scent of heliotrope in the air. I make
    a –
Lisa, recovering from shame, is almost instantly back into her
equally youthful entrancement. Eyes glowing, lips slightly
parted, she nods her personal agreement with Trigorin's
description of the joys/travails of a writer's life.
    – mental note: 'sickly scent . . . flower – the colour of a
    widow's dress . . . mention when describing a summer

evening' . . . I snatch at every word and sentence I utter, and every word you utter, too, and hurriedly lock them up in my literary pantry – in case they might come in useful!
And it's like that always, always . . . and I can't get any rest away from myself.

The next day, and in the war office, Bernwood, Hedges, Carter, Church, Berry, Hopper, Francis all at their desks. But, again, Trekker's desk is conspicuously empty of papers or person.

'TRIGORIN': (*Over*) I feel as though I'm devouring my own life, that for the sake of the honey I give to all and sundry, I'm despoiling my best flowers of their pollen, that I'm plucking the flowers themselves and trampling on their roots. Am I out of my mind?

During which, in a prowl around the big room looking at each diligent face – penultimately Hopper – end on, and settle on Francis as he translates. He has a dreamy, silly grin on his face, which he cannot control.

Hopper, the ever-observant, notices this marked change in his companion's demeanour and is a bit irritated by it.

Scratch-scratch-scratch of all the pens on all the paper.

HOPPER: (*In a stage whisper*) Hey! Frank.

Dreamy, dreaming Francis is too lost in his own world to hear.

Hopper *tuts* to himself, and tries again –

Pssst! Frank! Wakey-wakey.

FRANCIS: (*Surfacing*) What?

HOPPER: What you got to grin about?

FRANCIS: Nothing.

Francis, looking across at Berry, loses his dreamy smile.

And Hopper, following the direction of the glance, and seeing the change of expression, makes a swift deduction.

HOPPER: You talked to her.

FRANCIS: What – ?

HOPPER: (*Whispers*) Berry's wife.

Francis frowns, hesitates, then beams beatifically, unable to control his face muscles.

FRANCIS: (*Whispers*) Yeah. Last night.

Tiny pause. Hopper is obscurely peeved.

HOPPER: (*Hisses*) You dirty sod!

CHURCH: (*Barks*) Hopper! Stop whispering behind your hand

like an old tart in a pub doorway.

HOPPER: Sah!

But Francis' small, sly, secret smile is scarcely disturbed. He is thinking of his great encounter the previous night:

Click-tchick-chuck-click of Sylvia's high heels on the pavement of a summer night. She lilts into view.

Francis waits, full of tension, on the corner of the turn into the side-street.

FRANCIS: (*To self, rehearsing*) I know you have no reason to trust
me, but – good evening. I know you have no reason to – good
evening. I love you. (*Tiny pause*) Oh. Please. Please God.

And suddenly, too quickly, she is virtually alongside him, heels clacking.

Francis half-steps forward, with a gulp. But his nerve totally fails him, and he freezes.

Sylvia becomes aware of him, and almost breaks her stride – looks sidelong – but . . . continues on her way, making the turn into the narrower side street.

Click-tchick-chuck-click of departing high heels, into darkness.

Francis, feels, with bitter resignation, that he has blown it. His cheeks momentarily puff out with the expelled air of defeat and resignation.

But, further along, Sylvia, too, has a regret, though a far less fierce one. As she teeters along towards the Fulham house, her face shows some curiosity about what, or who, might be behind her. She slows a little, but does not turn her head.

Still tense but now almost despondent, Francis turns into the narrower street, on the same darkened route.

As each foot goes down, defeat drums in his ears.

(*Over*): Fool.

Bloody fool.

Fool!

Bloody bloo-dee fool!

Sylvia can hear steps behind her, and is not incurious, nor especially reluctant. Short of coming to an actual stop, there is not much else she can do.

Walking now just behind the deliberately slowing Sylvia, an increasingly desperate Francis, eyes fixed on the sway of her walk, mind fixed on the click-clack of her high heels, gropes in his inside jacket pocket – He pulls out his fountain pen. Hesitates because it cost ten shillings and more, then bravely throws it forward, in front of him, and at her heels.

    Excuse me –

She stops, half-smiles, half-turns.

SYLVIA: Pardon?

He swoops forward, picks up the pen – which is almost at her feet – and holds it up, like a trophy.

FRANCIS: I think you – Is this yours, by any chance?

SYLVIA: Mine – ?

FRANCIS: I mean – I think you d.dud. dropped it –

SYLVIA: Did I?

FRANCIS: Didn't you?

SYLVIA: It's a nice pen.

FRANCIS: I –

SYLVIA: Yes?

FRANCIS: I –

SYLVIA: What's the matter?

He looks at her. She smiles encouragingly. He draws himself up.

FRANCIS: (*Formally, ludicrously*) I know you have no reason to
    trust me, but – (*Stops dead*) Good evening. I know you have
    no reason to t.t.tut – –

SYLVIA: You're downstairs, entcha?

FRANCIS: Yes. I –

SYLVIA: Whatsyername then?

FRANCIS: Francis. My friends call me – (*Gulp*) Frank.

SYLVIA: Did you ever have any sheep?

Startled little silence.

FRANCIS: Pardon?

SYLVIA: Only, I thought – no, it don't matter.

FRANCIS: (*Suddenly gabbles*) I'm a national serviceman and I work
    in the same place as your – Corporal Berry – andandand I
    don't like the way he treats you andandand –

SYLVIA: Hey. Steady on.

FRANCIS: (*In another surge*) And I love you!

She laughs, looks at him, stops laughing.

SYLVIA: Look –

FRANCIS: But I do! I do!

She looks up and down the street. Then –

SYLVIA: Christalmighty.

FRANCIS: I beg your pardon.

SYLVIA: Look –

FRANCIS: I'm sorry.

SYLVIA: Um. Look – um –

FRANCIS: (*Eagerly*) Yes?

SYLVIA: Well – you can't come to the front door same time as me –

FRANCIS: No. I can't.

SYLVIA: – I go to the – They do dance lessons at the
     Hammersmith Palais on Sunday mornings –

FRANCIS: Oh, I'm no good at that. Two left feet, see.

SYLVIA: That's why they do lessons. Anyway.

FRANCIS: Yes.

SYLVIA: That's where I'll be.

FRANCIS: Oh. Th-thank you. Yes!

SYLVIA: Goodnight, then.

She gives him a look, then goes on towards the front door of the
particular house.

FRANCIS: Goodnight.

Click-clack-click of heels. He watches, a shadowed glow. At the
door, a slender dream, she looks back and half-raises her arm,
curling her fingers.

    A vision translated into the small, sly, secret smile of next day
Francis in the big room at the war office.

HEDGES: Corporal!

BERRY: Sah!

HEDGES: Time for the barely bloody drinkable.

BERRY: Sah! Francis!

Dreaming Francis does not respond. Everyone looks at him.

    Berry, with a licensed smirk, gets up, goes up behind Francis,
thrusts out his neck, and bellows –

    Wake yourself up you dozey littool man!

Francis jumps out of his skin – with a layer of guilt included.

    Beyond the room, along the approaching corridors, Colonel
'Truck' Trekker – missing for some time – brings his glow-glow
all-American niece Lisa to meet his questioning if not yet
estranged colleagues.

    Long, wide, marbled corridor, verging on the mausoleum: but
Lisa, Anglo-and-Europhile, is more than ready to be impressed.
She uses her highest register of praise.

LISA: Gosh, Uncle Truck – it's – gee it's like a – mooseum – !

TREKKER: You don't know how right you are.

In the big room, the usual fountain pen scratch-scratch-scratch –
and tea being made – and the door opens.

BERNWOOD: Ah. Truck. We were –

He stops, astonished by the presence of a young gel.

TREKKER: (*Drily*) Hi, folks. It's only us chickens. Thought I'd
show my niece where I sometimes hang my hat. Gentlemen
this is Lisa.

Hopper gapes at Lisa. Ping! A star explodes above his head. And
his eyes pop!

'The Man with the Golden Arm' takes us out, on the cusp of
yet another young man's dream . . .

IOI

Four

In the cinema where Sylvia works, the 1956 newsreel shows
Liberace's much-feted arrival in Britain, concluding with a view
of the Houses of Parliament at night.

BBC NEWSREADER: At the twenty-two nation meeting in London
of Suez Canal users, the American Secretary of State Mr
Dulles said he now saw every sign that military conflict could
be averted . . .

Listening to this final bulletin of the day, Colonel Bernwood cries
'No! No-o!' as he does a jigsaw puzzle in his sitting-room. He is
wired-up with tension.

Across London, Hopper lies morosely and half-undressed on
his bed, smoking, listening to the same news on the radio.

. . . This was after the majority at the conference supported
the American call for compensation for the canal company,
and international control of the Canal with an equitable
financial return for Egypt . . .

HOPPER: Yeh. They can have it, mate, and welcome!

But elsewhere, Bernwood, at home, is in obvious agitation, all but
grinding his teeth in anguish.

BBC NEWSREADER: . . . The United States, he added, would go to
any length to secure a peaceful settlement.

BERNWOOD: (*Screams*) *Judas!*

NEWSREADER: That is the end of the news.

Big Ben begins its sonorous chimes, for midnight.

Hopper, on his bed, drags in cigarette smoke, differently
troubled.

BBC NEWSREADER: The chimes of Big Ben for midnight bring
broadcasting to an end for today. Wherever you are, at rest
or at work, we wish you a peaceful night. Goodnight,
everybody. Goodnight.

God Save the Queen begins.

Bernwood, alone in the Highgate sitting-room, stands to
attention beside his wireless set.

Across town, as the ovational anthem almost finishes, Hopper
gets up, snaps off the radio, puts out his cigarette, keeps the butt,
and with a deep sigh of obscure longing, wanders aimlessly over

to the single window in the room – which, although small and high up in the house, is nothing like as dingy as where Francis lives.

From the high window, summer plane trees in a small night breeze shift their boughs, the foliage intermittently half-obscuring an elderly street lamp, making a dappling net of shadows on the pavement.

At the window, Hopper feels restless and melancholy, in a half-sweet sort of way, as though the scene outside is part of his head. His mind takes him swooping back to the source of these feelings –

TREKKER: Hi, folks. It's only us chickens. Thought I'd show –

Trekker is by the door of the big room at the war office, with lovely Lisa shy and smiling beside him.

– my niece where I sometimes hang my hat. Gentlemen – This is Lisa.

At his bedroom window, Hopper breathes a newly magical name.

HOPPER: (*Softly*) Lisa.

Further away, where Francis lodges, there are no trees in the street, and very little activity. But there is a solitary parked car, which seems familiar. Most of the windows along the street are dark. But – at ground level – there is a light on in Francis' bedroom.

As restless as Hopper, Francis, too, is stretched out on top of his Put-U-Up. Remembering a voice:

SYLVIA: I go to the – They do dance lessons at the Hammersmith
      Palais on Sunday mornings –

Francis accurately remembers the exchange, and accurately repeats his part in it.

FRANCIS: Oh, I'm no good at that. Two left feet, see.

SYLVIA: That's why – (*Continuous*) – they do lessons. Anyway.

FRANCIS: Yes.

SYLVIA: That's where I'll be.

Francis stares at the ceiling of his room, assailed by the words.

FRANCIS: (*Remembered*) Oh. Th-thank you. Yes!

SYLVIA: (*Remembered*) Goodnight, then.

A beat. He says again what he said – but now in a whisper.

FRANCIS: Goodnight.

At the same time, in the car parked opposite in the same night street, shadowed Harold Atterbow endures his obsession, looking up at the Fulham house.

Hopper, too, is awake and full of vague sexual yearnings, stretched out on top of his bed. He stubs out his cigarette, and sighs heavily.

Faintly, at first, an almost ethereal chorus creeps in, over, at the start of 'Unchained Melody' (Les Baxter, 1955), summoned up by Hopper but then transformed across a few square miles of dark streets to –

The Fulham house, where Francis sighs, eyes on the ceiling –

The chorus resumes, faintly, as Hopper, on his bed, reclaims it for himself.

The music yields to a soaring 'A-aaa-ah' of masturbating angels, and then, as though on the flash of his eyes to the corner of the room –

Hopper, as though by magic, plays guitar for the few seconds of its near-solo in the music, but then, in reality, and on his bed, Hopper blinks away the self-made image, and lets the lyric come to his lips.

The hungry words are as applicable to Francis, too, as he also broods and yearns on the Put-U-Up in the Fulham house, remembering Sylvia turning at the front door, curling her fingers.

As the song continues, in the other young man's room, Hopper is now standing in a puddle of wistfulness, looking down on to the dark street below, recalling Lisa smiling an hello at the war office.

The continuing music now picks out Atterbow sitting in the car in a long and desolate vigil, sucking in his breath as he looks across the street, and stung once more by the remembered image of Sylvia's coy wave back along the pavement, from the angle in which he saw and suffered it.

The simple lyric is again on Hopper's mouth as he stands at his bed-sit window. His expression changes as he looks out, but the song continues, his lips no longer moving.

As Lisa – summoned up by Hopper's empty yearning – steps half-in and half-out of a shifting lattice of shadow made on the pavement by the street lamp shining through foliage. She looks up as 'Unchained Melody' briefly continues with a final ludicrous flurry of 'A-aah's' and bells.

But Hopper is not at the window. He is stretched out on top of the bed, exactly as he was at the start of the song. He sighs deeply as the last note floats away. Silence.

In the same sort of silence, Francis is still on his Put-U-Up, hands clasped behind his neck, staring up at the ceiling which separates him from Sylvia. He sighs deeply. And whispers a single word.

FRANCIS: Sylvia.

But then, from above, a faint yet familiar rhythm of bedsprings being tested to destruction –

Upstairs, in the prevailing dark, the vigorous hump-like shape of Corporal Berry, vigorously humping.

Creak-Creak-Creak.

Below, Francis shows distress, distaste, misery, as the creaking sound seems to amplify a little in the inside of his head. He twists away.

And outside, Atterbow endures, eyes still fixed, pointlessly, on the house, with an obsessive's intensity, an obsessive's misery.

The pleading little chorus at the start of 'Unchained Melody' seeps in again.

Hopper, too, is wistful and aching as he lies on his bed. The music suddenly stops, at an impatient gesture from Hopper. He gets up, moodily, and goes to the window, looking out, and sees –

Just the shadows moving on the pavement. Lisa, of course, is not there. Hopper, staring out, seeing nothing, remembers instead the big room at the war office:

The circle of officer introductions for Lisa has been completed – and the three ORs – Hopper, Francis, Berry – standing to attention, are unsure whether they, too, rate an introduction.

Hopper is surreptitiously wiping his hand on the side of his trousers in nervous anticipation. But – with an airy wave –

TREKKER: Oh. And there are – These fellows are the clerks.

In his bed, Hopper mimics the American pronunciation of clerks bitterly.

HOPPER: Clirks. (*Sniffs*) Berks, more like.

Someone else, too, gives up as, in the narrow Fulham street, a car ignition wheezes and coughs. The car lights come on. Atterbow has abandoned his wretched vigil for one more night. Slowly, the car moves off. The headlights from Atterbow's car make a sliding rectangle of light on the cracked ceiling of Berry and Sylvia's room, below which, one sleeping figure, snoring – Berry. And the other lying very still, wide awake, her eyes glinting slightly in the half-darkness.

Bright day. Another day at the war office. Summer sun blazes against the pillars and windows.

In the big room, Colonel Trekker, US Army, back at his desk, is vigorously defending his corner.

TREKKER: OK – look at it from this angle – from September to January this year Nasser received via Czechoslovakia two hundred MIG-15 fighters and fifty Ilyushin bombers –

CARTER: (*Coldly*) We know this, Truck. We have these figures.

TREKKER: Three hundred medium and heavy tanks of the latest Soviet issue.

BERNWOOD: (*Sighs*) Truck –

TREKKER: (*Doggedly*) One hundred armoured SP guns.

HEDGES: Useless.

TREKKER: Two destroyers. Four minesweepers. All spares and back-ups. Radar. Guns. Small arms. The whole caboodle. Now these are no fly-swats. Are they?

BERNWOOD: But surely – look here – (*Incredulously*) It's not the position of the US that that that – – Good God alive, Truck.

TREKKER: All I'm saying, Harry –

CARTER: (*Snaps*) Forty-eight hours!

TREKKER: What – ?

CARTER: That's all it would take! Seventy-two at the most. And the whole bloody place is back in our hands.

TREKKER: I'm not going to dispute that, Archie. Give or take a month.

HEDGES: Well, then.

Trekker leans back, spreads his hands, feeling under some difficulty.

TREKKER: Look – I'm just – Hell, fellas, these are some of the questions my people – (*Changes tack*) OK. It's just two months ago that you had seventy thousand troops stationed on the Canal Zone. Now why were they shipped out? Huh? What's the *real* reason for that – ?

BERNWOOD: The treaty.

CARTER: A wretched deal. Total failure of political will. Utterly disgraceful. See a politician, and put a peg on your nose.

TREKKER: Maybe. Maybe. But – Well surely the thinking behind it – weren't all those men, all that equipment, effectively pinned down, hemmed in? I mean, without the cooperation of the Egyptians, they were –

CARTER: (*Cutting in*) No, no, no, no.

TREKKER: So – although, sure, the Canal can be taken with no great – sure, I agree – but what happens then?

Carter is rigidly postured, cold-eyed, and staring so fiercely at the American that it is almost comical.

CARTER: We sit there.

TREKKER: Being shot at.

BERNWOOD: (*Stiffly*) Isn't that what soldiering is about, Colonel Trekker?

Private Hopper's face shows that, no, as far as he is concerned soldiering is not about being shot at.

Trekker notes the coolness of tone and formality of expression from Bernwood. He rises, more than ready to go.

TREKKER: All those men tied down in a heap of sand and barbed wire, bitten half to death and running to the can every five minutes. Oh, boy. Wouldn't the reds just love it!

Trekker gathers up his less formal hat from the hat-stand.

CARTER: (*With an edge*) Leaving us already?

Trekker looks at him, steadily.

TREKKER: (*With precision*) Gooseberry fool.

CARTER: (*Blinks*) What – ?

Trekker gives him a slow smile, taking his time.

TREKKER: I'm taking my niece to lunch, Archie –

HOPPER: (*Thinks*) Where? *Where*?

TREKKER: – She's one heck of an Anglophile. I thought I'd test her out with one of your – puddings. Might make her think twice.

Hedges, who can't help it, laughs and puts his thumbs in his red braces, leaning back.

HEDGES: Just the thing for a young gel, Truck. Nice big lump of Spotted Dick.

Trekker leaves, with a satiric little bow. Hedges' smile switches off, and he looks at the others, who are not amused at all. Private Hopper is also not amused. How dare such a thought – says his face – sully such a precious creature.

A summer Sunday morning. Outside the Hammersmith Palais a few Teddy boys with DA hair styles, lounging in a group, do not think much is going on.

Inside, Victor Sylvester's strict-tempo 'By a Sleepy Lagoon'

(Coates), played through the loudspeakers.

On the sprung maple floor, a less-than-certain clutch of couples are essaying a waltz to the madeira-cake strains of the Sylvester recording. Slow-quick-quick-slow etc. Moving amongst them, adjusting here, correcting there, congratulating and admonishing, half a dozen female instructors.

Shy, out-of-place, and getting anxious about whether Sylvia is going to be there or not, Francis backs up against a decorative pillar, not wanting to get involved.

INSTRUCTOR: Come along, now! Let's see you on the floor!

The woman instructor startles him, because she has come up behind him, from the other side of the glitzy-glass column.

FRANCIS: Oh. I –

INSTRUCTOR: A waste of your half-crown, my boy.

She is very much the bossy type.

FRANCIS: In a – in a minute . . .

INSTRUCTOR: (*Briskly*) Shy. Aren't you!

FRANCIS: N.nun.n – Yes.

He tries to turn away. But she stands in front of him. 'By a Sleepy Lagoon' oozes on.

INSTRUCTOR: Hands round my waist.

FRANCIS: Oh, but –

INSTRUCTOR: Come along now!

FRANCIS: I'm no good at –

INSTRUCTOR: (*Briskly*) That's why you're here! Now. You know what this dance is, don't you?

FRANCIS: A – a quickstep . . . ?

His right hand already firmly gripped by this stout NCO of a woman, she nevertheless steps back in astonishment.

INSTRUCTOR: Waltz!

FRANCIS: What?

INSTRUCTOR: It's a waltz!

FRANCIS: Oh. Well – there you are.

INSTRUCTOR: Come along. On to the floor!

And she practically yanks him off his feet.

Meanwhile, on this Sunday morning, sprawled amongst the loose pages of the broadsheet *News of the World*, breakfast plate on the floor, Berry snores his head off.

Dressed to kill, Sylvia has left him to it, and is descending the stairs. She hesitates as the living-room door opens below, and

Uncle Fred and Aunt Vickie come along the narrow passage/hall to the street door. But Uncle Fred notices her.

UNCLE FRED: (*Loudly*) Watch your bag, Vickie.

AUNT VICKIE: What? (*Sees*) Oh. Yes. You're right.

SYLVIA: (*Calls down*) Kiss mine!

Uncle Fred and Aunt Vickie, tight faced, move on a few paces. But as he opens the front door, he turns and looks up at her.

UNCLE FRED: Off to church, are you?

Sylvia stays stock still on the stairs.

SYLVIA: Mind your own.

UNCLE FRED: Try it, my girl!

AUNT VICKIE: Come on, Fred. Please.

UNCLE FRED: (Looking up at SYLVIA) 'Hast thou no room within thy heart, Where Jesus may abide?'

SYLVIA: I'll look after my own heart, thanks very much.

UNCLE FRED: 'And canst thou say to Him, depart, Who for thee bled and died?'

AUNT VICKIE: Fred.

He looks up with a triumphant smirk that is almost a leer.

UNCLE FRED: You won't come to no good in this life neither!

SYLVIA: Bugger off!

Week night or Sunday morning, the sadly obsessive Atterbow keeps a discreet watch on the Fulham house. He stiffens. But it is only Uncle Fred and Aunt Vickie coming out.

Seconds later, Sylvia emerges. Put in a bad mood by Uncle Fred, she slams the door.

A little up ahead, Uncle Fred and Aunt Vickie look back at the sound, and exchange what are obviously indignant comments. She gives them a V-sign.

In the car, Harold Atterbow sucks in his breath, like a knife wound.

ATTERBOW: Oh. My lovely. My –

He stops himself, and twists a sad smile.

Sylvia teeters along in her high heels and tight skirt, keeping a cautious but resentment-filled distance from the couple in front. A very small, almost nervous peep! sounds behind her. She takes no notice. Crawling along very slowly, some way behind her, Atterbow makes another tentative peep! on his horn – and sees her turn to look. Sylvia stands still. The car stops. There are yards between them. A stand-off. Then –

SYLVIA: (*Yells*) What the bleed'n hell do you want!

Well up ahead, Uncle Fred and Aunt Vickie turn, and stop, and watch.

   In the car –

ATTERBOW: (*To self*) Oh sshh! Ssshh!

He goes rigid as he sees her walk the few yards back to him.

Sylvia leans in and bangs on the car window.

SYLVIA: Look! I'm warning you! If you don't stop following me
   around – !

He winds down the window, face contorting with stress and embarrassment.

ATTERBOW: Sylvia. Please.

SYLVIA: Please *what*?

ATTERBOW: Keep your voice down. Please. Please.

She looks at him steadily.

SYLVIA: I'll scream my head off if you don't leave me alone.

ATTERBOW: I – Sylvia – (*Pathetically*) I only thought you might
   want a lift somewhere.

SYLVIA: Yeh. I do.

ATTERBOW: (*Hopefully*) Oh! Right you are! Where to – ?

SYLVIA: The nearest police station.

ATTERBOW: Don't be like that. I beg you.

SYLVIA: (*Hard*) Lend us ten bob.

Sylvia's face, leaning in, is a mix of cunning and challenge. The bend of her body to the car only emphasises her physical attractions for the slightly damp browed Atterbow.

ATTERBOW: I – Yes. Perhaps.

SYLVIA: P'raps what?

ATTERBOW: If I – I – Well. What would *I* get?

Sylvia turns away and deliberates.

SYLVIA: A snog.

ATTERBOW: I – I – (*Swallows, then opens the door*) Get in!

Back at the Palais, a Victor Sylvester tango is coming through the loudspeakers.

   On the dance floor, a hapless and disgruntled Francis, made captive by the Amazonian instructor, is palpably unable to manage such a complicated and melodramatic set of movements. This, of course, becomes a comic routine. As Francis advances, robotically stiff, the other dancers are bumped and buffeted out of the way – or prudently remove themselves in advance. At the turn and swivel, parody tango, his splayed feet lose their balance on the sprung maple floor. Crash! down he goes: and in the effort to stay upright, Francis pulls the stentorian instructor down on top of him, in a heavy, near-obscene sprawl.

There are revelations of a more nubile order across the river, on Barnes Common, where on one of the side-paths, Atterbow's car is parked, in the midst of tufty grass and bushes. In the car, Sylvia's blank gaze looks out at the common, as Atterbow's head burrows and slurps at her exposed breast. She is chewing gum.

SYLVIA: (*Flatly*) Time's up.

Atterbow seems not to hear: at least, he continues what he is doing.

    I *said*. Time's up!

She hooks her fingers into his wispy scraps of hair and yanks his head up, fiercely, and painfully.

ATTERBOW: Ow – ! Ow-w-w – !

Sylvia adjusts her dress, still chewing gum.

SYLVIA: You've had what I said you could have.

ATTERBOW: But Sylvia – oh, Sylvia – Why are you so –

SYLVIA: (*Cutting in*) Harold. Stop it.

ATTERBOW: We could have such a nice time, Sylvia, if you'd only –

SYLVIA: (*Cutting in*) Drive me to the Palais.

ATTERBOW: What?

SYLVIA: In the Broadway. I got to see a bloke.

ATTERBOW: What?

SYLVIA: Are you deaf, or something?

ATTERBOW: Yes. I am, my dear. Deaf to all reason. And blind to their consequences.

SYLVIA: (*Nastily*) Funny. I thought you was just dumb.

ATTERBOW: A man can only take so much, you know.

SYLVIA: Come on. Start the bleeding car, willya!

Atterbow tries comedy, with a pseudo-Gallic shrug.

ATTERBOW: And where does my fine lady wish her iciness to be deposited? The *Palais de Danse, oui*?

She actually smiles, and touches his face. But he grabs too urgently at her fingers.

    Voulez-vous danser avec moi?

Sylvia jerks her head away.

SYLVIA: I'm going to be late, fanks very much!

At the Palais, a manager in a bow-tie is at the microphone on the stage.

MANAGER: Ladies and Gentlemen. It is now twelve noon. I'm
    pleased to tell you that the bar is now open for those of you
    who wish to congratulate yourselves on the steps you have
    made this Sunday morning. I will also say that the bar is also
    open for those who wish to commiserate with themselves on
    – well, not quite making the progress they wanted. And – ah
    – in *that* respect – (*Looks all around, smirking*) there is a drink
    on the management for one particular gentleman, who has
    shown us all just how dramatic a tango can be!

Francis half-smiles half-scowls and jerks with embarrassment, trapped between fluted pillars.

    Dance band musicians are coming on to the stage behind the manager as he finishes his announcements.

    This is also the time when we give you the chance to try out
    what you've learned in the first hour with a real, live dance
    band. And a chance, too, for musicians new to the profession
    to set their own steps on the ladder to the stars. Please
    welcome the Colin Copper dance sextet!

Some polite applause. The dance sextet begins to play a rather insipid and certainly orthodox 'Try a Little Tenderness'.

    A closer look at the Sextet and there, previously unobserved, is Hopper – at the drums. The expression on his face shows that he does not like playing in this style.

    Suddenly the music changes – and the dancers falter.

    In the midst of the sickly syncopation, Hopper has let go on the drums with an almost manic frenzy, to universal consternation. But it is soon clear from the surprise and the musical responses of his fellow players that they did not expect such an adventurous deviation – and mostly do not approve.

    At the frenzied drumming, the dancers stop, startled, even aghast.

    The manager who had been at the microphone, frowning, crosses back towards the stage.

    Francis, picking up on all this in the midst of his hangdog disappointment, follows the irritated manager with his eyes – and then, astonished, at last realises that his war office colleague is playing in the band.

Sensing danger, Hopper slips back into the expected tempo, to the relief of the other five musicians, who had all but given up on supporting his beat.

Outside, Atterbow's car pulls up at the Palais. Sylvia already has her hand on the door handle, before the car has completely stopped.

Atterbow watches her go across the road. He still has her bra. He holds it, in helpless lust.

ATTERBOW: I dreamt she walks the streets in her . . .

He stops, abandoning the words of the old 'Maidenform' bra ad, and looks at Sylvia's disappearing figure as she enters the Palais.

> (*To self*) Oh, you bitch.
>
> You –
>
> You shaggable,
>
> *Shaggable* little tart.

Inside the Palais, Francis and Hopper are standing at the bar, with half-pints.

HOPPER: (*Enraged*) Bloody nonsense. Bloody bloody ridiculous! I
    mean – listen to it!

Across the floor, beyond the pillars, the sextet – now a demoralised quintet – is trying to smooch out what is audibly a less than full-toned 'So Tired . . . of Waiting for You', minus the necessary prop of the drums.

Francis, making desultory circles with the bottom of his glass in the wet on top of the bar, is fed-up for other reasons, his gaze still switching vainly about.

FRANCIS: I been looking forward to this morning with all my –
    And look how it's turned out. Me flat on my back and you
    sacked before you even started!

HOPPER: You can't play a tune like that without the bloody
    drums. Where's the rhythm? Where's the throb? Where's
    the heartache?

FRANCIS: (*Melodramatically*) Here, mun. Right here.

He taps his chest. But indignant Hopper is not interested in that.

HOPPER: Sounds as thin as an old lady's widdle – bloody
    disgrace, that's what – And if they don't give me my two
    quid I shall see my solicitor.

Something in this catches Francis' morose attention.

FRANCIS: You got a solicitor?

Hopper squares his shoulders and looks at him. Of course he hasn't.

Coming in, beyond them, Sylvia looks carefully all around the floor, with more eagerness, perhaps, than might be expected.

Some of the anticipatory light diminishes in her eyes, as the draggy and extra-thin 'So Tired' staggers towards an end of sorts, with ragged ensemble. But a voice comes at her shoulder, from just behind her.

MAN AT PALAIS: Are you looking for somebody?

She turns, with an appraising half-frown, like one too used to being approached, but never completely uninterested.

SYLVIA: Why?

The man – ten years or so older than she – has lots of Brylcreem and plenty of sauce. Plus the sort of sahth London accent that has tried to filter itself through Mickey Spillane and/or American 'B' Movies.

MAN AT PALAIS: 'Cos if it's a bloke – (*Looks hard at her.*) Well,
      I'd like to shake that guy by the – neck. Hey?

She laughs.

The diminished band tries to bounce into 'I'm Beginning to See the Light', as Hopper holds forth.

HOPPER: You just got to look around, entcha? I mean, you can't
      put your finger on it, but – it's there, definitely there.

FRANCIS: (*Dubiously*) What is?

HOPPER: Change!

Francis sips at his half-pint, and pulls a face.

FRANCIS: Well. Nothing tastes the same, I'll tell you that.

HOPPER: I'm not just talking about the music, Frank.

FRANCIS: No. I know you're not.

HOPPER: There's something in the – well, in the air – in the – I
      mean, that git down there dressed like a shaggin' penguin is
      – people like that don't know what's going on. It's the same
      in the office. Ennit?

A beat. 'I'm Beginning to See the Light' surges, almost too much on the nose. The two young men look at each other.

FRANCIS: (*Heavily*) Yes. It is.

HOPPER: But it's not just the army – it's – oh, more than that –
      (*Struggles for the thought, the words.*) I mean – we're all in
      uniform, even those who aren't. In Britain, I mean. On

114

parade. All in different ranks and (*Gives up*) Oh. Shit. Do
you want another?

FRANCIS: You got any money?

HOPPER: (*Gloomily*) Oh. Shit.

FRANCIS: I've had to buy a pen. Lost my –

HOPPER: (*Cutting in, freshly indignant*) Two quid I'm owed by
that smarmy sod down there! And if I don't get at least half
of – What's the matter?

Because Francis' face and whole stance has suddenly changed.
Hopper turns to see what has caused it. Sylvia! But with the bold
young man, who is laughing about something she has said.

FRANCIS: (*To himself*) Oh God.

HOPPER: Why? Is that . . . ? (*He looks at her again*) Bit of all right,
Frank.

But he is clearly surprised, expecting someone less tarty, and
maybe less overpoweringly attractive. Francis, ashen, eyes fixed
on Sylvia, does not speak.

Sylvia, in mid-laugh, sees him – and stops laughing. Yards
away from the two young men, she says something to her
companion, leaves him, and walks straight over. The man doesn't
like it.

FRANCIS: H.hel – –

His tongue is stuck.

SYLVIA: I didn't think you were here. I looked around.

FRANCIS: I – yes. I'm here.

SYLVIA: (*Laughs*) I can see that, can't I?

But Francis is in a paroxysm of shy awkwardness, narrowly
avoiding knocking his glass over. Hopper stares at them both,
fascinated.

FRANCIS: I d.didn't – I didn't think you were coming either.

SYLVIA: Said I would.

Her gaze falls on Hopper, who lowers his eyes.

FRANCIS: Oh, this is – this is – m.m.m. –

SYLVIA: (*To* FRANCIS) Spit it out.

But this is said without a trace of derision. She seems flattered by
his all too evident awe and shyness. Francis gets out the words
that had stuck in a rush, and is suddenly released from his only
very intermittent impediment.

FRANCIS: Mick Hopper. He works at the war office too.

HOPPER: For a few days more. Hello.

SYLVIA: Hello, Mick. (*Slight frown*) So you –

HOPPER: Yeh. With your um –

FRANCIS: Husband.

This came out too quickly. There is a small silence. Hopper feels uneasy.

HOPPER: (*Half-laughs*) I've heard a lot about you already.

SYLVIA: Yeh. But who from?

Her attempted joke – designed to allay a slightly awkward moment – is unfortunately met by one of Francis' most nakedly earnest declarations. He doesn't seem to know the rules.

FRANCIS: Me. From me. Because I sit there at my desk thinking
about you all day long, and the thoughts can't be held in. It's
impossible.

Tiny pause.

HOPPER: Well. I'd better be –

Sylvia, recovering, and ignoring Hopper, turns on Francis, oddly angry.

SYLVIA: What you talking about! Are you trying to take the
mickey or what?

FRANCIS: No. No!

HOPPER: (*Sardonically*) Christ, no.

SYLVIA: (*To* HOPPER) You keep out of it!

HOPPER: Sorry. Sorry.

Strangely, she is on the point of tears, and her eyes glisten: but the anger is still there, too. Francis ploughs on, obtuse and sanctified.

FRANCIS: You mustn't think I don't mean what I say, Sylvia.
(*With a strong Welsh accent*) It's like this, you see. There is a
re-dempt-ive pow-er in love which transforms the –

Crack! She smacks him straight round the mouth in a fury.

SYLVIA: Don't you talk to me like that!

MAN AT PALAIS: (*Arriving*) Somebody interferin' with you,
chick?

Francis, his hand at his finger-marked cheek, is hopelessly enraged: not at her, but at such an intervener.

FRANCIS: You f.fuf.f- –

Everyone is, of course, staring. Hopper is still trying to digest his comical incredulity. The 'fuck off' stays tongue locked on the 'f'.

MAN AT PALAIS: Get it out, pal. And then I'll take your teef-aht.

SYLVIA: Leave him alone!

MAN AT PALAIS: Wha- ?

Francis gives up on the 'f', releasing another torrent, equally ludicrous.

FRANCIS: (*To* MAN) I would no more interfere with this young
　　lady than I would hurt a little bird in the cup of my hand.

MAN AT PALAIS: Wha- - ?

SYLVIA: (*Fiercely*) You heard him!

MAN AT PALAIS: (*To* SYLVIA) Now look –

SYLVIA: Piss off.

He grabs her arm, indignantly.

MAN AT PALAIS: You was in some sort of –

FRANCIS: Don't you touch her!

HOPPER: (*Mutters*) Steady, Frank –

The man lets go of Sylvia's arm but only to push Francis away, hard, with the flat of his hand on Francis' chest.

SYLVIA: (*To* MAN) When I want you to poke your nose in, I'll ask
　　thanks very –

MAN AT PALAIS: Silly cow.

A bit embarrassed, he goes to turn away, but Francis, recovering from his rapid backward momentum, launches himself forward again, all flailing arms.

FRANCIS: Watch what you call her you ignorant lout – !

Wham! Francis goes backward again, at considerably greater speed, from a crisply delivered and very hard punch.

　　Mayhem. The staggering Francis cannonades, knocking over several glasses and almost a few of the interested spectators. At the same time, Sylvia smacks out at her would-be protector, the man, who holds her off at the wrist. Hopper puts up his fists in total confusion – and the manager with a heavy-type assistant comes rushing towards it all.

MANAGER: Right! Out. Out! All of you!

MAN AT PALAIS: I'm not going to be called a lout by –

SYLVIA: (*Screeching*) Why not? That's what you are!

Francis blinks up from the floor, the back of his head against the bar, utterly stunned.

MANAGER: I said out!

ASSISTANT: (*To* HOPPER) Come on. Out you go, cowboy.

For spreadeagled Francis, all the noise in which other voices join blurs and distorts as his head sings and his eyes threaten to cross.

　　But then a lovely face looms. All noise dies. Lovely lips purse, and lovely lips kiss. The birds sing. Sylvia has bent down, inexplicably affectionate, as the last notes tinkle of the extended 'I'm Beginning to See the Light', unconsciously ironic. The notes just extend to the parked car, now on the other side of the road, strategically placed. Relentless, obsessive, Atterbow sits like a waxwork behind the wheel, eyes clamped on the Palais. A while, then he sees Francis and Sylvia come out, together. They stand and talk for a moment. Atterbow watches, even more intently. He switches on the ignition, ready to follow, to observe. Francis and Sylvia are walking away together, up ahead . . .

Across Hammersmith Bridge, on the southern side of the Thames, where the park winds, trees enfold, grass and bushes encroach.

Francis and Sylvia are sitting a little apart on a bench, facing the river.

FRANCIS: I've never touched a girl. Not once. Though I've thought about it, mind.

She looks sidelong at him, half-wary, half-amused, or incredulous.

SYLVIA: What – *never* – ?

FRANCIS: Well I –

SYLVIA: (*Disappointed*) Oh. You have.

He looks straight ahead, at the river, rather than at her. He seems ashamed of something, but is also being a little shy.

FRANCIS: I want to tell you the truth. That's important, see.

SYLVIA: Oh, they all say that.

FRANCIS: All?

He looks at her, with a quick dab of a glance, then flicks his eyes away again, back to the river. She doesn't answer. He waits, then begins again.

I *have* wanted to touch. Very very much. And once – (*He stops*) At the pictures.

SYLVIA: What? What do you mean?

FRANCIS: I'd keep moving my seat, see. So I could – I could sit next to a g.g. –

The crucial word, dream word, sticks.

SYLVIA: I know the type.

She gives a little laugh, but then sees how very serious he is. But her laugh lets out a string of words – and as ever when he is emotional or on-the-spot, his Welsh accent becomes more and more sing-song.

118

FRANCIS: It's horrible. It's terrible. Like some monster takes over, driving you on. And everything you hope you are, everything you try to be, is suddenly nothing. You're just a degenerate. Out of con-trol!

SYLVIA: Christ. What have you done?

FRANCIS: (*Mournfully*) Touched a girl's knee.

SYLVIA: What – ?

Then she laughs, really laughs. He turns and looks at her.

FRANCIS: Oh, it's not fun-ny. It's not funny at all, bach.

She stops laughing, and, suddenly, puts her hand on top of his. He jerks, but then lets it stay there, but half-looking down at her hand on top of his as he speaks.

SYLVIA: What a lot of fuss, though –

FRANCIS: Ah, but you haven't heard me out. You don't know the half of it. See, I'd moved my seat twice already that day, so I knew what I was doing. Or the devil in me did. (*Looks at her*) Aberystwyth. The big cinema there. Don't suppose you know it?

She keeps a straight face. He begins to manoeuvre.

SYLVIA: No.

FRANCIS: Time and again I'd move and – and I'd – oh, God, I don't like to say this, but – and I'd sort of let my hand sort of accidentally on purpose, like hang down or – all the time I'd be looking at the screen, not really hearing a word of – then I'd – (*Swallows*) Make contact!

SYLVIA: Oo. You dirty devil!

FRANCIS: And then she'd jump and I'd jump and say sorry and go red and – and – (*Abjectly*) Move away as soon as I could you know. Go to the gents. Or leave altogether. But on this day – this one particular day of shame and infamy –

SYLVIA: And what?

FRANCIS: Infamy.

Something about his face, his tone, makes her hold her tongue. A moment. He continues his narrative, but half-describes Sylvia, using the tale to touch her.

This girl, see. Pretty. Little tilt of the nose, and – oh, hair like a cornfield in the summer sun. As sweet as an apple on the – I moved next to her, see. And I was all aflutter, and – I let my hand sort of *creep* and – When I touched the side of her hand on the arm of the seat between us – well, I jumped away and – (*Sucks in his breath*) But she didn't.

SYLVIA: (*Satirically*) Oo. The cow. (*As he looks at her*) Sorry.

FRANCIS: She didn't. She just kept looking at the picture. And –
so I sort of – – put my – the tips of my fingers back towards
her. They touched her wrist. And do you know what?

SYLVIA: The steam engine.

FRANCIS: What?

SYLVIA: Oh, for God's sake. What. Watt.

He looks at her, puzzled, then as abruptly as though he were
leaving her, he gets up, and goes towards the river.

Sylvia is looking at him with stirrings of real feeling.

But also looking – at both of them – is Atterbow, half-crouched
behind a bush, getting creepier by the minute.

Francis picks up a stone, momentarily broods, then hurls it
into the water, turns, and goes yearningly back to her – again
using his story to prompt his own hand on her.

FRANCIS: I didn't jump away. I kept my fingers there, on her
del-i-cate little wrist – oh! – And I gradually sort of – curled
my hand and – All this took a long time, mind. I was
frightened the film was going to end and the lights come on –

Atterbow, stooped, strains to watch and listen.

But she – no, she didn't pull her hand away . . .

Francis sucks in his breath again, as though reliving the great
moment of passion.

In fact – in fact – she put her other hand across and – a bit
like you did just now – and thank you very much, thank you!
– and this girl, she placed her hand on top of mine and – then
I – Well, I was getting excite-ed, see – And I said 'oh', all soft
and full of – yes, awe is the right word – like when Pushkin
met – (*Stops himself*) And then I noticed.

A little pause. She stares at him.

SYLVIA: Noticed what?

FRANCIS: She had an iron on her leg.

SYLVIA: (*Puzzled*) A what?

FRANCIS: A brace. An iron brace. You know – what polio victims
wear – and – oh the poor thing. The poor little thing. She – I
said 'Excuse me, I've got to go to the gents.' That's all we
said. The only words. I left my seat – clack! Up it tilted – and
I – (*Looks at her*) I went straight out.

She looks at him, increasingly touched, increasingly tender.

SYLVIA: Does your eye hurt?

FRANCIS: (*Blinks*) What?

SYLVIA: It's getting puffy. Going to be a shiner.

It is his turn to stare at her in consternation.

FRANCIS: But – what I'm saying is – What I'm –

She touches his face, carefully, just above the 'puffy' eye.

SYLVIA: You're nice.

FRANCIS: Oh. But –

SYLVIA: Fancy making a fuss about a thing like that.

FRANCIS: I – I'm not proud of –

SYLVIA: Shhh.

Her fingers stroke his cheek. He gulps, looks at her, and manages to hold the gaze.

FRANCIS: Sylvia . . . ?

SYLVIA: So you haven't even kissed a girl, then? Proper, I mean. A proper kiss.

FRANCIS: (*Barely audibly*) No.

SYLVIA: You daft ha'peth.

FRANCIS: (*Barely audibly*) Yes.

SYLVIA: Well, do it then.

FRANCIS: W-what – ?

She cups his face, and kisses his lips – then pulls back a little, examining him.

SYLVIA: Is it nice?

FRANCIS: (*Gasps, trembles*) Wonderful. But –

SYLVIA: But what?

FRANCIS: But – we shouldn't – I mean – Oh dear God. Why did you m.mum.m – I mean – corporal, I mean your hus – *him*. (*Then*) – Ouch – !

SYLVIA: What is it – ?

FRANCIS: My eye. Don't half hurt.

They look at each other. She becomes a little scared of her own feelings.

SYLVIA: (*Quietly*) What do you want?

FRANCIS: I'd like to jump in the bloody river.

Atterbow, peering, stooping behind the bush, and knowing his wretchedness, straightens in alarm at the crunch of feet close behind him. A man walking gives him a sidelong look of suspicion. Atterbow half-smiles, half-nods, observably embarrassed. Crunch-crunch the man goes on, veering towards

121

the bench, but looking back at Atterbow in a giveaway manner. Atterbow watches anxiously, but then the shame and the indignity rise in his throat. He edges away, backwards, terrified of exposure. Once in the clear, going back towards Hammersmith Bridge, he starts to run. As he runs – faster, faster, and panting – 'In a Persian Market Place' swells on the theatre organ.

The music takes us on to another summer's day, and the big room at the war office. 'In a Persian Market Place' continues as an anxious looking Bernwood, at his big desk in the big room at the war office, listens – listens – listens on the telephone.

Or could it be the organ that he hears, in some other part of himself?

The organ music fades out as Bernwood is at last able to get a word in on the telephone – with all other officers immediately interested. But Trekker, the American, is again not there.

BERNWOOD: (*On phone*) But General – my in-tray – you should see it, sir. A veritable Niagara, cascading over the – Yes. Yes. Of course. All hands to the pumps. I understand . . . But – ah – but – ah – Well, if I could leave *one* clerk here. Otherwise we're – Yes? Good! Thank you. Goodbye, sir.

He puts the phone down, troubled, and speaks generally, to all in the room.

Spot of bother. And it's a damned – Corporal.

BERRY: Sah!

BERNWOOD: You'll have to leave us for the rest of this week.

BERRY: Sah!

BERNWOOD: (*Irritated*) Wait a minute. Wait a minute. Don't just bellow like that until I've finished and you've understood what I've said.

BEERY: Sah!

Tiny pause. In which a faint snigger can be heard: Hedges, inevitably.

BERNWOOD: (*To* BERRY) Upstairs needs you and another clerk with full security clearance – um – ah – Is this your last week, Hopper?

HOPPER: No, sir. Next week.

BERNWOOD: Well, then, ah – ah – ah –

But he seems to drift off, almost into vacancy. The rest of the room stares.

As Bernwood's eyes glaze and jaw sags, in a small rehearsal for complete nervous exhaustion – the sly, sinuous, opening notes of 'In a Persian Market Place' on the theatre organ.

HEDGES: Harry? Old chap?

Bernwood comes back from a long way away, and the music dies.

BERNWOOD: Operation Musketeer!

He barks out the two words, almost like one on parade. There is a small, startled silence. Then Carter puts his pen down, eyes hard.

CARTER: So we're going in.

Said with quiet intensity, and immense satisfaction.

BERNWOOD: (*Agitated*) Are we? Are we? We cannot say that for sure, Johnny. I can't put my hand on my heart and tell you we're *definitely* going in. But I tell you this – I tell you this – (*Stands up*) I'd rather *cut* my heart out if we don't.

Extraordinarily agitated, he paces up and down between the scattered desks, and especially around Trekker's unoccupied space, as though the man who is not here is indeed here.

They're all gathering upstairs from tomorrow. Musketeer. Musketeer. That's what they're calling it. But what troubles me – I don't mind saying this one little bit – what makes *me* wonder how really, truly, really, really *serious* they are about it – Wallace – ?

HEDGES: Old thing?

BERNWOOD: You were there – a long time.

HEDGES: Egypt? Not half.

BERNWOOD: Where would *you* land?

HEDGES: (*Crisply*) Alex.

BERNWOOD: Precisely! Alexandria.

HEDGES: If you want to knock them out, that is. The whole Egyptian army, and what-have-you. Desert Road starts there. (*Uses side of hand.*) Chop! Straight through to Cairo.

BERNWOOD: Precisely!

Hopper is worried. He doesn't want to hear this sort of thing. And what did Bernwood's question mean? Are they going to try to keep him – ?

CARTER: (*Suspiciously*) What have you heard, Harry? What's going on?

BERNWOOD: Port Said.

CARTER/HEDGES/CHURCH: *What* – ?

Bernwood nods, sententiously.

BERNWOOD: I'm very much afraid from what Donald tells me that the objective being laid down is simply and solely that of getting hold of the Canal itself, and not knocking out all the Egyptians.

HEDGES: But, look here, you can't land at – Bloody hell, Harry. Are you sure?

BERNWOOD: As sure as God made little apples.

HEDGES: The beaches are too shallow. I can tell you that as a matter of absobloodylute fact. Far too shallow! Like a bookshelf.

CARTER: And then there's that damned causeway.

BERNWOOD: Damned what?

CARTER: From the beach. It's twenty miles long –

HEDGES: More like thirty.

CARTER: And only about four hundred yards wide.

HEDGES: Less than that.

CARTER: What?

HEDGES: In places.

Carter doesn't like being interrupted, and Hedges knows it.

CARTER: (*To* BERNWOOD) There's two bridges to get you on to it.

HEDGES: One.

CARTER: (*Snaps*) Two!

HEDGES: Ah, yes. But only one will take tanks.

Carter glares, but cannot dispute the point.

CARTER: It's a nightmare, whichever way you look at it.

HEDGES: There's only one place for a landing, Harry. Alex!

BERNWOOD: (*Almost a scream*) It's not going to be Alexandria!

Silence. Everyone can see the near hysteria. But Bernwood just manages to pull himself back from the door of the cuckoo house – although, still on his feet, his limbs twitch and tremble.

HEDGES: Well. We've established one thing.

CARTER: (*Snaps*) And what's that?

HEDGES: (*Smirks*) It's not going to be Alexandria.

BERNWOOD: (*Screams*) Wallace!

HEDGES: Now, now, old pip –

But this final provocation has sent Bernwood spinning around the loop. He picks up a random file – from the nearest desk – and advances on Hedges like one demented.

BERNWOOD: (*Sobs*) You bugger. You bugger. Oh, you bugger!

Hedges half-stands in alarm.

HEDGES: Harry – ?

Bernwood, momentarily crazed, eyes burning, lifts the heavy box file, about to bring it crashing down on Hedges.

Hopper's face is alive with malicious glee, ready to editorialise, musically.

The box file is poised. Hopper's fantasist mind takes over, as it half-descends – crash in the music. 'I See the Moon' by the Stargazers, big hit of a year or so earlier, a dreadful half-mad comic song. And suddenly, all in the office are 'singing' it, ludicrous in voice, posture and activity.

Bernwood's lunacy is now choreographed, with music, into a crazed 'Arabian' fantasy, with belly dancers, Ali Baba pots, a pantomime camel and hundreds of party balloons. At the windows, Hopper's fantasized 'dream girl' floats past on a magic carpet. 'Arab brigands' threaten with scimitars, some of the yashmak belly dancers turn out to be hideous, or male, and the camel defecates amply enough to provide Hopper, Francis and Berry with ammunition to sling at the officers. Hopper remains the orchestrator, the impresario, gleefully beating out the lyrics with lunatic abandon, happily turning his superiors into wobble-voiced loons.

And then, abruptly exactly as they were before the music began: Bernwood, enraged, with the box file, Hedges half rising from his seat.

HEDGES: Steady. Steady.

Bernwood takes sudden, bewildered control of himself. He lowers the threatening file, and looks at it in surprise.

BERNWOOD: Whose is this – ?

FRANCIS: (*Nervously*) M.mine, sir –

BERNWOOD: Then for goodness sake keep it where it's supposed to be kept!

He kicks the last, stray balloon out of the way, putting the file back on Francis' desk with an irritated and dismissive thump.

FRANCIS: S.sorry, sir.

All eyes upon him (puzzled, concerned, or half-amused), twitchy and shamefaced Bernwood returns to his desk, fiddles with his papers a bit, lowers his head to work, then looks up again, vague, puzzled –

BERNWOOD: I was – ah – Yes. I was saying something. Ah – Ah, yes . . . (*Revelation*) Operation Musketeer. That's the – A name not to be divulged, needless to say. They're using the big conference room over the bank holiday and – ah – all next week. (*Looks around*) Colonel Trekker is very conveniently not here.

CARTER: (*Edgy*) Which is jolly significant!

BERNWOOD: Anyway this – pay attention, you clerks! – Operation Musketeer – that's the Suez – ah – ah – All reference to it and all documentation is category British Eyes Only. Understood?

BERRY/HOPPER/FRANCIS: Sah!

BERNWOOD: (*Vaguely*) There was something – there was some – yes – upstairs needs – Corporal!

BERRY: Sah!

BERNWOOD: You'll have to leave us.

BERRY: Sir?

BERNWOOD: Upstairs needs you and another clerk with full security clearance – um – ah – you're not with us much longer, are you, Hopper?

Hopper answers as though he has not done so before.

HOPPER: No, sir.

BERNWOOD: Well, then – ah – ah – (*Narrowly avoids drifting again.*) Then it'll have to be the other – the other one – (*Looks at* FRANCIS) – What's your – ah –

FRANCIS: Francis, sir. Francis F.

BERNWOOD: Yes. You, better be you, F. You're to go with Corporal Berry. Help with the – ah – Understood?

Francis has no idea what he is talking about.

FRANCIS: Y.yessir.

Bernwood lowers his head back to his work, with an abstracted sigh.

Observed by an amused Church, Francis looks at Berry, helplessly. Berry frowns, equally at a loss.

BERNWOOD: (*Suddenly*) Johnny. You're to have observer status at the Planning Conference on behalf of this office.

CARTER: What? Not allowed to muscle in?

BERNWOOD: Only as – ah – No. 'Fraid not. They might need us later. If the Soviet Battle Order changes in any significant –

CARTER: But it already has!

BERNWOOD: (*Crisply*) Quite. Quite!

Carter tut-tuts real annoyance at Bernwood's oddity.

CARTER: Harry. For God's sake.

BERNWOOD: What is it – ?

Carter glares at him, then shakes his head.

CARTER: Get a grip, old chap.

Bernwood puts his pen down.

BERNWOOD: I –

Silence. Bernwood is as though made of stone. They stare at him.
Then Hedges gets up, goes across to him, puts his hands on
Bernwood's desk, leaning in, peering intently.

HEDGES: Harry.

A moment. And it's too long.

BERNWOOD: There's too much at stake, Wallace.

HEDGES: Harry –

BERNWOOD: If we don't go in, at the right place, in the right
    manner, and with all the punch it needs, we're done for as a
    nation and as a people. We might just as well roll over with
    our legs in the air like a – (*Stops, stares at* HEDGES.) Wallace?

HEDGES: Cup of tea, old thing?

Bernwood passes his hand across his face.

BERNWOOD: Overdoing it. Aren't I?

HEDGES: A bit.

BERNWOOD: Keep an eye on – – Yes. Thank you Wallace. I'm –
    Yes, I'm all right now.

HEDGES: Corporal. Time for a spot of the old undrinkable.

BERRY: Sah! Francis. Tea!

FRANCIS: Corporal!

But as he springs up –

BERNWOOD: (*Angrily*) Corporal. What are you doing?

BERRY: Sir? I –

BERNWOOD: I told you and whatshisname there – F! – to report
    for duty elsewhere. (*Furiously*) I will not tolerate this
    insubordination! What in the name of blazes –

HEDGES: (*Interrupts*) Harry, I don't think –

BERNWOOD: Just a minute, Wallace! Please! Corporal. I gave you
    an order.

BERRY: Sir. Permission to speak, sir.

BERNWOOD: (*Roars*) Not granted!

Bernwood is literally quivering with rage, and obviously near to a
complete nervous breakdown. As he rises, spluttering, Hedges
puts a hand on his arm, firmly.

HEDGES: Harry.

BERNWOOD: Keep out of this –

HEDGES: Harry!

The grip, the tone, strong enough this time. Bernwood stops, blinks, looks at Hedges.

BERNWOOD: Wallace?

HEDGES: I think there's a small failure on the old intercom here.

BERNWOOD: What – ?

HEDGES: The corporal is not being insubordinate. Though I'd no doubt he'd like to be, given half a chance. Eh, Berry?

BERRY: Yessir. I mean, no sir!

Bernwood has lost the wild spurt of anger, and now looks confused and much older all of a sudden.

BERNWOOD: But I – didn't I?

HEDGES: (*Gently*) No.

BERNWOOD: Oh.

HEDGES: Berry and Francis understand that they are to give clerical help at the planning conflab next week.

BERNWOOD: Yes. All next week.

HEDGES: But they haven't yet been told where they – Harry. Are they wanted now? Or what? (*As* BERNWOOD *stares at him.*) Harry?

BERNWOOD: Cancel dressing-down, Berry.

BERRY: Sah!

BERNWOOD: Delete last remarks.

BERRY: Yes, sir.

BERNWOOD: Present yourself and Private – Francis, there – to Brigadier Dittonson's office. That's room ah – room – (*Finds the note he has scribbled.*) Room 369. Straight away!

BERRY: Sah!

FRANCIS: Sah!

BERNWOOD: (*To* HEDGES) Going to be a bit shorthanded, Wallace. Fetch and carry for ourselves.

HEDGES: Never mind, never mind.

But he is watching Berry and Francis, each rather flustered, leave the room. His eyes fall on Hopper. He approaches him, suavely.

Hopper.

HOPPER: Sir?

HEDGES: Any pretty gels in the typing pool these days?

HOPPER: Not really, sir.

HEDGES: Well, so long as none of them has a moustache, eh? Why

don't you go along there for – ah – (*Looks at the wall clock.*)
Let's say be back in exactly fifteen minutes, shall we? Cast
your eye. The random thigh, what? You never know.

HOPPER: Yessir.

Hopper feels awkward in the silence as they wait for him to go.
The door shuts. A beat –

BERNWOOD: All right. All right. A poor show, yes?

CARTER: Yes.

HEDGES: In front of the men, old thing.

BERNWOOD: Oh, I don't think that –

CHURCH: They're good lads, on the whole. They understand the
pressures, I would think.

CARTER: (*Snaps*) That's hardly the point.

BERNWOOD: If I could just get a decent night's sleep.

HEDGES: I think we should toddle along to Uncle Nick's for a
little tot.

CHURCH: At this time?

HEDGES: Oh, you can get a drink there any time. If you're with
me.

BERNWOOD: A drink? Oh, but –

HEDGES: And a little chat.

BERNWOOD: What about?

Meaningful little silence.

HEDGES: Hopper can hold the fort.

BERNWOOD: But a *drink* – at this hour –

HEDGES: Lubricates the – I think we all need one, Harry. And –
the little chat, mmm?

Bernwood looks at him, puzzled, hurt, worried.

Upstairs, in the ornate conference room at the war office, there is
a long wide table with twenty four placings. Some side tables. An
enormous map of Eastern Mediterranean Egypt occupying
virtually all of one wall.

A young staff captain, in uniform, is addressing the (basically
National Service) military clerks, who stand in a tight huddle
between the huge, polished boardroom table and the wall map.

CAPTAIN: Some of you chaps have worked in this room before on
general staff matters. But as you can see we've had to
supplement your numbers with clerks from the various MI
sections. Now – you've all got clearance. You don't need any

reminding, I hope, of the hell on earth which will await you if
you open your mouths about anything whatsoever that goes
on in this little room. You'll have your balls cut off – but only
after they've been fried in hot camel's piss.
Some uneasy laughter, picking out Private Francis, tightly
surrounded by laughing faces – he alone does not smile. His
thoughts are too troubled, and elsewhere –
(*Off*) This will be a joint services planning conference under
the name Operation Musketeer. It will begin at nine o'clock in
the morning. Two of you to each top table placing and the rest
on general – –
As the captain's voice fades, go with Francis' wayward thoughts,
back to the day before, and the Sunday afternoon tow-path at
Hammersmith, where:
Sylvia and Francis look at each other. She becomes a little
scared.
SYLVIA: (*Quietly*) What do you want?
A beat.
FRANCIS: I'd like to jump in the bloody river.
They become conscious of the man walking, and the slightly odd
way he looks back over his shoulder – at the lurking Atterbow,
though they don't know this.
The man crunches past, with a curious glance at them.
(*Agitated*) Does he know you?
SYLVIA: No. (*Looks at his scared face.*) What's the matter – ?
FRANCIS: I – Oh, Sylvia. Oh, my lovely. This is not – I lie awake
right under your room thinking about – about you and I can
hear –
He stops. She looks at him, then touches his face again.
SYLVIA: What? Hear what?
FRANCIS: The bed creak-ing.
She half laughs, a bit embarrassed.
SYLVIA: Well – Pete likes it – He's a piggy. Hey. What you – Hey.
What you got tears in your – (*Astonished*) Blimey. Your dead
serious, entcha?
He half turns his head away, trying to hide his emotion. The level
of her incredulity is going up and up. And she is more pleased by
his responses than she had bargained for.
FRANCIS: (*Mumbles*) Sorry.
SYLVIA: Don't be sorry, love. Christ! Only I – well, I just thought

you wanted a shag, that's all.

He sucks in his breath, in a thrill of fear and wonder, and turns to look at her, tears in his eyes, voice barely able to squeeze up the dry and tightening lining of his throat.

FRANCIS: Oh. But I do-o-o.

The very opening chords of Gene Vincent's 'Be-Bop-A-Lula' (1956) crash in – bouncing back to the big room at the war office.

And as the 1956 rock smashes out, discover Hopper alone in the big room, enjoying himself. He picks up the number, with an appropriately frenzied glee, using a file as a 'guitar'. As the tempo quickens – Hopper deliciously fantasises – rewriting the Hammersmith Palais débâcle:

On stage at the Palais now, triumphant this time, Hopper leads the BlueCaps in full pelt, as he 'sings' 'Be-Bop-A-Lula'. The dance floor is now full of bopping teenagers, fifties style, full of joy.

Back in the reality of the war office, as Gene Vincent suddenly pants with apparent lust and excitement before releasing himself into the next sequence, while the BlueCaps scream and the beat becomes even more physical, Hopper squeezes out the image of Lisa as she first came into this room with her uncle, as sweet as . . .

An image of delight which allows Hopper in an ecstasy of wishful thinking to return to imagined triumphs at the Palais, leading the Vincent BlueCaps group. The boppers on the dance floor – in an old filmic tradition – have stopped dancing in order to gather together in admiration in front of the band.

The band now goes berserk, in a hard, driving proto-rock celebration, to the delight of the young crowd pressing ever closer to their idol, Hopper. Especially, a bright-eyed, adoring Lisa. Hopper in full fantasy in the big room at the war office, using pen, file, paper, anything to beat out the surging non-vocal continuation of 'Be-Bop-A-Lula'.   And as he swings around, facing the door –

The discreetly absent American Lt Colonel Trekker is standing in the doorway, staring at the gyrating, frenzied Hopper.

Music out, abruptly, on the tide of Hopper's shock and embarrassment.

TREKKER: Ants in your pants, Hopper?

HOPPER: (*Gulps*) Sir. I – I – ah –

Trekker ambles across to his desk, amused.

TREKKER: Maybe you should take a cold shower, huh?

HOPPER: Yessir.

TREKKER: Where is everybody?

HOPPER: They – ah – sir. They will return shortly.

TREKKER: I see.

Trekker takes stuff out of his drawer – unlocking it with a key he carries on a little chain – and lays it out on his desk.

Still embarrassed, Hopper extra-diligently bends over a document he is translating.

A moment. Scratch-scratch. Then –

Hopper.

HOPPER: Sah!

TREKKER: (*Winces*) Does everyone in this man's army yell when they're spoken to – ?

HOPPER: Sorry, sir.

TREKKER: I'm going to ask a favour of you, Hopper.

HOPPER: Sir?

TREKKER: My niece. The young lady I brought in here the other day.

HOPPER: (*Quivers*) Sir – ?

TREKKER: She's going to be very disappointed in me this evening. I've just heard that I have to be with our – I have to be at the embassy. Trouble is, I've promised to escort Lisa to the theatre. (*Looks across at Hopper, closely*.) You busy tonight, Hopper?

Hopper half-stands, hardly daring to hope.

HOPPER: I – no, sir. No, sir. Definitely not!

TREKKER: Come over here.

HOPPER: (*Eagerly*) Yessir!

Trekker is writing on a memo pad.

TREKKER: Tell you the truth, Hopper, I'm glad to miss this thing anyhow – She's seen it already. Beats me why anybody – Still. That's what she wants.

HOPPER: Sir?

Trekker tears off the note, gives it to Hopper.

TREKKER: This is the address. I'll call her – say who you are – (*Takes out his wallet.*) Be there at – oh – quarter of seven, maybe before, if you can – Here's the tickets, OK?

HOPPER: Yessir!

TREKKER: And – ah – yes. You might need this. Put her in a cab.
  A little drink, maybe.
Trekker gives him a wad of pound notes.
HOPPER: Oh, but, sir, I –
TREKKER: Don't be stupid.
HOPPER: No, sir. Thank you, sir!
He goes back to his desk, like one in a dream. Trekker resumes work.
  As his great good fortune sinks in, a look of bemused wonder glows in Hopper's eyes.
  (*Whispers, to himself*) Be bop a lula.
'The Man with the Golden Arm' crashes us out of the episode.

Five

Children are at play on the pavement in front of the close-packed terraced houses of the Fulham street.

Inside one particular house, it is the evening meal – sausage and mash – on the tight table with the caged budgerigar. Uncle Fred, Aunt Vickie, Francis.

Silence – except for the awful sounds of diligent eating.

Aunt Vickie darts glances at Uncle Fred, as though she were frightened of him. Francis slices into the fat sausage, abstracted, cutting into his heart. He sighs, as the fork journeys to his half-reluctant mouth.

UNCLE FRED: (*Suddenly*) 'Twill not be long!

Francis stops dead, the forkful of greasy sausage halfway between his plate and his face. Aunt Vickie's eyes flash alarm.

AUNT VICKIE: Fred?

UNCLE FRED: (*To* FRANCIS) Lots of sighs.

FRANCIS: Pardon?

UNCLE FRED: Sighing a lot, Frank.

FRANCIS: Sorry. Am I?

UNCLE FRED: 'Twill not be long –

FRANCIS: Pardon?

UNCLE FRED: Our journey here.

Tiny pause.

FRANCIS: I'm just – No – I've – ah – I've always been fond of
      sausage. It's one of my –

His voice trails off as Uncle Fred, mouth full, lifts his hand like one who has been grievously misunderstood.

In tension and horror – with swift, covert glances at each other, Francis and Aunt Vickie watch him swallow the lump of sausage preparatory to addressing them.

UNCLE FRED: 'Twill not be long – our journey here, each broken
      sigh and falling tear will soon be gone; – '

FRANCIS: Well – Yes. I –

UNCLE FRED: ' – and all will be a cloudless sky, a waveless sea.'

Francis, realising that an evangelical hymn is being laid on him, puts the bit of sausage back on to his plate, with a determined air.

FRANCIS: Uncle Fred.

UNCLE FRED: One of my favourites!

Francis' nerve fails him.

FRANCIS: Oh . . . is it?

UNCLE FRED: Nice chorus.

FRANCIS: Well –

UNCLE FRED: (*Suddenly bellows; sings*)
    'Roll on – dark stream! –
  We dread not thy foam.'

Tiny pause. Francis feels desperately, desperately miserable.
Uncle Fred fills his mouth again. Chew-chew-chomp, then –

UNCLE FRED: It's nice to have somebody here to talk to, Frank.
    After all this time.

AUNT VICKIE: Thanks very much.

Uncle Fred takes absolutely no notice, his gaze far too resolutely
fixed on Francis.

UNCLE FRED: Only, you were sighing.

FRANCIS: Was I?

UNCLE FRED: Not 'alf!

FRANCIS: I – well. I wasn't aware that I was.

UNCLE FRED: Wasn't what?

AUNT VICKIE: It's the way he talks, Fred.

UNCLE FRED: Aware? Aware? Wasn't aware?

AUNT VICKIE: Fred.

UNCLE FRED: Does that mean you didn't know you were doing it?

Francis puts his knife and fork down.

FRANCIS: That was very nice, thank you, Aunt Vickie.

AUNT VICKIE: But you haven't finished.

FRANCIS: I've had enough. Thank you very much. It was nice.

But there is a strange, dangerous light in Uncle Fred's eyes.

UNCLE FRED: All them sighs. And then you don't clear your plate.

FRANCIS: Sorry.

UNCLE FRED: Sorry? Sorry? What abaht?

Tiny pause. Francis considers his options.

FRANCIS: It's a nice evening, isn't it? Think I'll go for a little
    walk . . .

He watches, astonished, and a little scared, as Uncle Fred savagely
drives his fork down into the remains of the sausage on Francis'
plate, and holds it up under Francis' nose, his teeth all but grinding
in some manic inner disturbance.

UNCLE FRED: Waste not. Want not!

Francis stares at the lump of sausage held so menacingly in front of his face. For half a moment it seems that Uncle Fred is going to force feed him. Francis switches his gaze to stare down his disturbing uncle . . .

FRANCIS: Eat it then.

UNCLE FRED: What?

FRANCIS: Eat it!

Aunt Vickie stiffens with an odd kind of fear.

AUNT VICKIE: (*Faintly*) Frank –I

But Francis keeps an implacable stare. Uncle Fred blinks, and almost timidly puts the forkful of sausage into his own mouth.

Chew-chomp-chew. He works his jaws. They watch him. He swallows, then –

UNCLE FRED: It's a nice enough evening. You're right there, Frank. (*Pause*) 'Twill not be long. 'Twill not be long. (*Voice changes*) I bloody well hope not.

Theatre curtains swish open to Act One of *The Seagull* by Chekhov, in the production which has so engaged Lisa, the young American.

The set on stage is of the park on a Russian estate, where a 'stage' is being erected, with sounds of hammering etc.

'Masha' and 'Medvedenko', returning from a walk, enter –

'MEDVEDENKO': Why do you always wear black?

'MASHA': I'm in mourning for my life. I'm unhappy.

'MEDVEDENKO': But why? I can't understand it. You're in good health. Your father isn't rich, but he's comfortably off. My life is much harder than yours.

In the audience, attentive faces, eyes on stage.

Except – Hopper, all aglow with a young man's wonder, eyes on Lisa, beside him.

I only get twenty three roubles a month, and from that my superannuation is deducted. Yet I don't wear mourning.

'MASHA': It isn't money that matters. Even a pauper can be happy.

Hopper at last turns his face but not his thoughts to the stage.

'MEDVEDENKO': Yes, in theory he can be, but in practice it works out like this.

Bang! – without any break – he becomes the agent of Hopper's mind, and 'sings' (i.e. lip-syncs) 'I'm in Love Again', by Fats Domino (1956).

Hopper, in the audience, permits himself a secret little grin of a fantasist's delight as 'Medvedenko' continues to be Fats Domino.

Besides Hopper, Lisa is prettily attentive to the presumed Chekhov.

His head in a whirl, full of music and entrancement, Hopper looks sidelong at the pretty girl, and takes up the continuing Fats lyric.

On stage 'Medvedenko' and 'Masha', as though in the Chekhov, are continuing the lyric.

But then, for the attentive, reverent audience and stage, the music begins to fade, letting in Chekhov again:

'NINA': For the sake of being happy like that – of being a writer or
     an actress – I would put up with unfriendliness from my
     family, with poverty and disappointment –

For wide-eyed Lisa in the audience, these words are her words, these wishes are her wishes.

     – with living in a garret and having nothing to eat but rye
     bread. I would gladly suffer dissatisfaction with myself in the
     knowledge of my own imperfections, but in return I would
     demand fame – real, resounding fame . . . (*covers her face*) My
     head's going round! Ugh!

Outside the Fulham house on the same summer's night, streaking dark blue glimmers, Francis comes out of the front door, shoulders drooped, not at all happy. He steps back to look at the upstairs window. There is no light on. He stands still a moment, then turns and walks on along the terraced row, slowly.

'TRIGORIN': (*Over*) It's a beautiful place! But – what is this?

'NINA': (*Over*) A seagull. Konstantin Gavrilovich killed it.

On stage, in the theatre, far and close to Francis, so to speak –

'TRIGORIN': What a beautiful bird! Really, I don't feel like going
     away –

He makes a note.

'NINA': What are you writing?

Francis' left foot goes down, right foot goes down, broodingly heavy, in a silent and empty side-street.

'TRIGORIN': (*Over*) Just making a few notes . . . An idea suddenly
     came into my head. A subject –

At the theatre, rapt Lisa, and Hopper glancing at her, pleased to be so near.

     – for a short story: a young girl, like you, has lived beside a

lake from childhood. She loves the lake as a seagull does, and
she's happy and free as a seagull. But a man chances to come
along, sees her, and having nothing better to do, destroys her,
just like this seagull here.

A small silence. 'Arkadina' appears in the window.

'ARKADINA': Boris Aleksevich, where are you?

'TRIGORIN': I'm coming!

Goes, then looks back at 'Nina'. To 'Arkadina' at the window –
What is it?

'ARKADINA': We're staying.

'Trigorin' goes into the house.

 'Nina' advances to the footlights. Alone, she thinks a bit, glows –
then –

'NINA': It's a dream!

The curtain (end of Act Two) starts to close.

 Francis is now standing at the corner where he had stood while
waiting so nervously for Sylvia. His face tight with another sort of
anxiety.

 In the theatre, the curtain completes its closing, as the applause
rises – Lisa is too enraptured to clap, eyes still fixed on the now
curtained proscenium arch. It is an interval, and people begin to
rise, in a hum. Hopper looks at her. Everyone around them is
moving. But she is still in an entranced immobility. He clears his
throat.

HOPPER: Do you – shall we have a drink, or – ? (*At her non-response*)
We've got fifteen minutes, so I –

She turns and looks at him, glowing.

LISA: Isn't it wond-er-ful – ! Isn't it all just so – Wonderful!

HOPPER: (*Not too sure*) Well. Yes.

LISA: (*Astonished*) You don't think so.

HOPPER: No, no. It's pretty good.

Meanwhile, on the street corner, Francis a very still figure in the
increasing darkness. His face shows deep gloom and remorse, of
what used to be thought of as Russian proportions.

FRANCIS: (*Thinks*) You're a monster, Francis. A monster. (*Pause.
Speaks out loud*) There's no doubt about it.

Footsteps. Francis shakes himself out of brooding immobility, and
looks up. Coming towards him is Sylvia, on her way home from the
cinema. Her heels go click-click-click on the pavement. She stops

in front of him. They look at each other, without speaking. And then she does speak, straight into it, with no preliminaries.

SYLVIA: All afternoon. All evening. All through the bloody picture three times and the newsreel and everything. All that time I been thinking. And thinking. I thought you'd be here. I knew you'd be standing here. (*Looks at him*) Do you want your pen back?

FRANCIS: What?

SYLVIA: I got it safe. I don't do no writing. It was yours, wasn't it?

FRANCIS: Yes.

SYLVIA: You're daft, entcha?

FRANCIS: Yes.

Each of his responses is like a dry croak.

SYLVIA: Don't you have nuffink to do with me.

But he reaches for her. Upset, she evades his grasp.

You hear me?

FRANCIS: Sylvia.

SYLVIA: Don't say my name like that. It makes me feel – I go all funny inside and I – (*Decisively*) No. I'd bugger you up, wouldn't I? See. You don't say no. You know I'm right. I'm not for you. But – I wish to Christ I was.

She gives him a swift search of a look, then a tight little smile, and turns abruptly away before he can see her tears.

He stays where he is, but rocking a little in distress on the balls of his feet, listening to the click-clack-click of her departing heels.

Sylvia approaches the house in the narrow ill-lit side-street of dingy terraced houses. A sudden blaze of headlamps makes her stop, and put her hands to her eyes, startled, blinded.

Back on the corner where the side-street joins the wider road, Francis is dead still again, no longer rocking slightly on the balls of his feet – and clearly feeling very sad. Then, as though he cannot let this be, he begins to run, turning into the side-street towards the comparatively distant and illuminated Sylvia.

FRANCIS: (*Calling*) Sylvia – wait! Sylvia!

In his parked car, Atterbow is drunk. He has his window down, and the car has been parked on the skew so that its headlights can glare along the pavement.

ATTERBOW: (*Tipsily, calling*) Come on – Sylvia duckie – come here – come on – ! Please!

Sylvia, lets out an angry yelp and runs towards the car. And, approaching fast, Francis continues to call to her.

SYLVIA: This is the last time I'm telling you – ! Just leave me alone
    you dirty old sod!

But the car door opens, and Atterbow, dangerously drunk, half
rolls out, grabbing at her.

ATTERBOW: Sylvia – lishen – lishento –

As he clutches, he loses his balance, ending up hugging her legs as
he thumps down on to his knees, tufts of hair standing on end and
spectacles awry. Sylvia gives a little yelp, and smacks him hard
around the side of the head, just as Francis arrives.

SYLVIA: Let go! You bugger! Let go of me – !

FRANCIS: (*Astounded*) What's going on – ? Who is – (*To*
    ATTERBOW) Hey. Stop that! What do you think you're . . .

Atterbow is weeping, and clutching, still on his knees.

ATTERBOW: (*Sob*) Oh you cruel you cruel – How can you be so –
    Sylvia my love listen listen . . .

Sylvia, stepping back, and kneeing herself free, lets Atterbow go
further down on to his hands and knees.

SYLVIA: (*To* FRANCIS) He's been pestering me. Following me.
    Tooting. Calling. Knocking on the door.

FRANCIS: He's as drunk as a – Who is he?

ATTERBOW: (*Meanwhile*) Bow! Wow! Bow! Wow! Wow!

Totally gone, on his hands and knees like a child pretending to be a
dog, he is barking and scrabbling about on the pavement, giggling.

SYLVIA: There's no bloody end to it. Look at him! Look!

Francis tries to lift Atterbow to his feet.

FRANCIS: Come on. Get up. Get up.

Atterbow's drunken, giggling bow-wows are turning into
drunken, mauling weeping, as he half-rises, clutching at Francis.

ATTERBOW: I love her and I'd – I'd – give up every – I'd – You
    don't know – Nobody – (*Sob*) Nobody – what it's like –

SYLVIA: Shut up!

FRANCIS: (*To* ATTERBOW) You're drunk. You'd better go home.
    And leave her alone, you hear?

The three are all the while illuminated like figures on stage by the
headlights of the askew car.

ATTERBOW: Home? Home? Got no home! (*Sob*) Home is where –
    home is where the heart is . . . Sylvia! Sylvia!

SYLVIA: (*Hisses*) Piss off!

FRANCIS: What are we going to do with him – – ?

141

Because Atterbow is draped all over Francis, and if Francis lets go he will surely fall flat on the pavement.

SYLVIA: Kick his head in.

But Atterbow, face thrust drunkenly into Francis', is changing his expression.

ATTERBOW: On the towpath!

FRANCIS: (*Startled*) What?

ATTERBOW: You! It was you! With her!

He steps back and swings at Francis, in wild and dangerous lunges.

FRANCIS: Hey. Hey!

SYLVIA: Clock him one, Frank.

Not wanting to hit a drunk, Francis tries to pinion his arms instead, while Atterbow shouts obscenities.

Along the dingy row of houses, people are starting to come to their doors, and to pull aside their curtains, to see what all the noise is.

ATTERBOW: (*Yelling, barely coherently*) You – dirty – little – shagging – little – taking her away from – On the towpath! On the – (*Scream*) In the bushes!

FRANCIS: Oh, Christ.

SYLVIA: (*Enraged*) Peeping Tom! Peeping Tom!

She starts to smack out and claw at Atterbow.

A NEIGHBOUR: (*Shouts*) What's all the noise! Hoy! Haven't you got a home to go to!

FRANCIS: Sylvia – No!

Because she is hitting at Atterbow in an increasing frenzy – and Francis is worried about all the fuss, and the exposure.

But, with yelps and countercries of pain, Sylvia is beating Atterbow back to the skewed car, the door of which still hangs open, engine still running, headlamps still beaming, making a grotesque chiaroscuro of the figures on the narrow pavement.

SYLVIA: (*Yells*) Get in the car!

ATTERBOW: Yes – Yes – sorry – Yes –

SYLVIA: (*Screams*) Get in the bloody car!

Cringing now, Atterbow gets into his car, but then gives her another bark. She rushes up to him, kicking out, yelling –

Get away, you bugger! Get away from here!

Sylvia slams the door shut with as much force as she can manage, much to the ire of the protesting neighbour a few doors along.

NEIGHBOUR: Stop that bloody noise!

Sylvia puts up two fingers, her eyes flashing.

Francis is standing aghast. The thought at last reaches his book-fuddled mind that perhaps, after all, she is not the ideal love from Pushkin or any of the Romantic poets.

SYLVIA: (*Coming up to him*) He plays the organ. And he's even been on the bloody wireless! But *I'm* not playing his bloody organ. Not no more, I'm not.

Francis looks hard at her.

FRANCIS: What d'you mean, *no more?*

In the car, the drunk, hurt, humiliated Atterbow sucks in his breath, inflamed by the sight of the two of them on the pavement some yards in front of him.

ATTERBOW: You – you – You've asked for – !

Beyond the car –

FRANCIS: (*Shocked*) But Sylvia – if you lead people on then you – *look out!*

Facing him, her back is to the car, which is hurtling up on to the pavement, with homicidal intent. Sylvia – reacting too slowly – is knocked off her feet by Francis' lunge at her.

It is a hairbreadth escape. They end up on the ground, against a house window, coiled.

The car, half on the pavement, half on the road, buckets along in a wildly veering, drunken acceleration, scattering the onlookers and interested bystanders, its tyres screaming.

Atterbow's head lolls back as the car hurtles along street and pavement, out of control. He has passed out. Walls and lamp-posts spin by, narrowly missed, or grazed.

The musty pub at the end of the street – and on the opposite corner to where Francis had waited for Sylvia – releases Corporal Berry into the night. Berry's face opens in terror. Atterbow's car, beyond any control, almost on two-pavement-side wheels, and swerving blindly, is careering straight at him.

Back up the street, Francis helping up a shaken Sylvia –

SYLVIA: He's mad – ! He's gone mad, the bugg—

Sound of crash, at the end of the street. They look at each other, startled. The hideous reverberation is followed by the worse sound of a man screaming.

Francis and Sylvia and the others on the pavement begin to run towards the source of the awful screaming.

Atterbow's car has half-concertina'd against the side wall of the pub, below or into the frosted-glass windows.

Pinned under the wheels, screaming, is Berry. But the sound stops.

Pub customers, still running out, drag a semi-comatose but burbling Atterbow from the driving seat, while others try to lift the car off the now unconscious Berry.

Francis, arriving, is just able to see who it is under the wheels, through the throng of would-be helpers.

A MAN: (*To* FRANCIS) Reckon he's a goner, mate.

FRANCIS: Have they – have they phoned for an ambulance – ?

SECOND MAN: Yes, from the pub. Well, that's what they were doing – (*Sniffs, with odd morbid satisfaction.*) Hearse'd be more like.

SYLVIA: (*Arriving, out of breath*) What's happ –

Francis grabs her quickly by the arm.

FRANCIS: Sylvia. Don't go near the – I mean. Wait! It's –

She stares at him, then seems to realise all at once, and rushes towards the front of the car. When she sees –

SYLVIA: Pete – !

Half-way between a choke and a cry, she makes a noise, and pushes through to him.

HELPER: No – no – stand back – keep back –

SYLVIA: It's my husband. My husband!

She goes down on her knees to touch or cradle his head. Francis stands a little off, stricken with complex feelings and guilt. Then he makes himself go forward, and put his hand on weeping Sylvia's shoulder. She does not look up at him.

Atterbow, all this time, has his back to the pub wall, legs stretched out on the pavement, nose streaming blood, eyes rolling in near-vacancy.

Unaware, after the theatre, Hopper has taken Lisa to his favoured coffee bar. Beyond the hissing Italian machine and the crowd of predominantly young people, Hopper and Lisa drink froth from glass cups. Rather to Hopper's dismay, she is still over-aglow with the play they have just seen. A red-banded Penguin Classic is, alas, open on the table – the 1954 *The Seagull and Other Plays*, translated by Elisaveta Fen – and she is quoting with total admiration from the few pages of introduction.

LISA: (*Reads*) 'Life must be exactly as it is, and people as they are. Not on stilts.'

144

HOPPER: Not on what?

LISA: Stilts.

He looks at her with a certain glint – he is no Francis, in awe of
literature or its practitioners.

HOPPER: Why should they be on stilts? Never met anybody like
      that myself.

LISA: Chekhov meant that – (*Slightly unsure laugh*) Hey.

HOPPER: On the other hand, if you're a dwarf it might make a lot of
      sense.

The glow dies in her eyes. She looks at him with the beginnings of
disdain.

LISA: Come on. What are you saying here? You know what it – He
      wanted to cut out all the phoney and the –

HOPPER: (*Quickly*) Yeh. Yeh. Got you.

LISA: And he's right!

She turns her eyes back to the Penguin. He sips cappuccino, wipes
froth from his lips with the back of his hand, looks at her, wishing
she would look up from the book.

HOPPER: Except for the circus.

She looks up. But with a slight frown.

LISA: What?

HOPPER: I mean, if you – I mean, stilts. Could be useful.

LISA: You're being literal minded.

HOPPER: That's my trouble.

But we know that it isn't.

   Lisa looks at him, looks at the page, hesitates, then reads a bit
more, just when he is hoping that enough has been said on the
matter.

LISA: (*Reads*) 'A play should be written in which people arrive, go
      away, have dinner, talk about the weather, and play cards.'

HOPPER: And sing.

LISA: No – you don't sit in a room and – Listen. You don't
      understand.

HOPPER: No?

LISA: No!

Her attention goes back to the book, where she flips a few pages to
find something else. He feels frustrated – and a little demeaned by
the glimpse of something close to scorn.

HOPPER: I mean, people can have dinner and talk about the
      weather or whatever this bloke says and all the time they can

145

hear a tune, right? People can sing even when they've got their mouths shut. *I* do. And I'll bet you do, too.

LISA: No. I don't.

HOPPER: And I don't see why they shouldn't put stilts on, neither. Or funny noses. If they want to. (*Looks at her*) As well as – Well. What about kissing, and that.

She shuts the book, and gazes at him, steadily, intimidatingly.

LISA: What?

HOPPER: Just a thought.

A beat. He averts his eyes, momentarily. Then looks at her, and grins, shyly. But her expression does not soften.

LISA: You know – that's the second time I've seen *The Seagull* since I came here. First off, my uncle falls asleep and snores. And now –

HOPPER: (*Quickly*) Sorry. Sorry.

LISA: Why didn't you like it?

HOPPER: I didn't say I didn't.

LISA: (*Directly*) You were looking at me more than the stage.

HOPPER: (*Embarrassed*) Oh, I wouldn't say – (*Then*) Well. You're very – very – um –

LISA: Very what?

Trouble is, she is not smiling. But Hopper intends to be valiant, and we can see him making himself so.

HOPPER: What I'm trying to say is – yes, you're right – but I'm sorry you noticed. I mean you were so – you looked so wonderful – as you watched the play and – Well, you know the lines, and everything. Your lips were moving as the actors said the – And my eyes have a sort of life of their own. Perhaps I should wear blinkers. You know, like the horses. But I was really glad you were enjoying it so much. But I didn't want to spoil it for you, or anything.

LISA: You didn't.

She gets up, much to his dismay.

HOPPER: Oh! Have I offended you?

LISA: No. And thank you for being my – escort.

HOPPER: But – don't you want another cup of – or . . .

LISA: (*Too crisply*) No thank you.

HOPPER: Listen. I think you're right about Ch- um – Chekhov. I see what you mean. About the stilts, and that . . . Hey, don't go now. I brought you in here because – look, in about ten

minutes they have music in here – you know, try-outs for
young –
LISA: Oh, you can stay. That's OK.
HOPPER: No, no. I – your uncle said I was to put you in a taxi and
make sure you –
LISA: I'm not a child.
She is already on her way to the door, threading her way across
crowded space, and drawing male eyes. Hopper cannot quite keep
alongside her, and has the slightly frantic air of someone who
knows that he has messed things up but doesn't quite know why.

There is a thick press of young people by the door, as though
something is about to happen. Lisa has to go sideways to make
progress, and the scarlet-edged Penguin Russian Classic in her
hand seems out of place.
LISA: Excuse me – Excuse –
HOPPER: (*Further back*) Lisa: – I mean – Miss Trekker!
Some fellows look at him with amusement. He cannot quite get to
her. There is a sudden escalation of hustle, bustle and hubbub.
CRIES: Here he is! Here he comes!
A young singer, with shining studs on leather, and a glitzy guitar
strapped upon himself, is coming in with a phalanx of admirers and
some screams. On the pavement outside, a throng of the young are
trying to get in, in a rush that seems to have come into being from
nowhere. The coffee bar singer is clearly very popular. Lisa puffs
out her cheeks as she pushes her way on to the pavement.

Hopper, in the press inside the coffee bar, realises that she has
gone. He is hurt and incredulous. But there is applause all around
him, as he gives up trying to push his way out.

The applause rising as the coffee bar singer springheels up on to
a specially kept table by the Italian machine, and strikes a few
chords. Pressed in tightly, as the guitar twangs, Hopper turns.
And –

– he is singing Sanford Clark's 1956 hit 'The Fool', easily
turning himself into the coffee bar singer. Magically it is Hopper,
studded and glitzy-guitar laden, who is on the table, above a sea of
admiring young faces.

And in this exuberance, reaching out to the dark Soho street, in
Hopper's mind, at least, pretty Lisa stops, dead, as the Sanford
Clark song continues, sobbing of love's failures and follies. During
which, this imagined Lisa bites her lower lip, considering things,

weighs the Penguin *The Seagull* in her hands, then tosses it away, into the road.

On the table in the coffee bar – and 'seeing' all this above the enthusiastic throng, Hopper is again Sanford Clark to the life.

Hopper-imagined Lisa peers through the steamed-up window, brought back by the vocal. Inside, Hopper, again the singer on the table, twanging his glitzy guitar in plangent rhythm, and 'singing' rhythmic self-pity. Imagined Lisa pushes her way in, through the tight press, as the original recording continues. Reaching the end of the number, as the singer on the table, with bejewelled tears glistening on his cheeks.

Hopper's expression changes, as the shoulder-to-shoulder crowd pulls back to make an aisle of space between themselves for Lisa to walk towards the table upon which Hopper performs. She nears, and comes up on to the table, with a lilt of a smile and opening arms. Hopper and Lisa kiss, adoringly, after looking long and deep, on the dying chord, into each other's eyes. Tumultuous applause for the fantasy. And then –

Tumultuous applause in the place as it really is. Whistles, foot-stamps. The enthusiasm is for the coffee bar singer, not for Hopper. He makes a heart shape with his fingers on the steamed-up window.

More desolately, a few miles away across west London: ring-ring, ring-ring, the pre-ooh-ah ambulance pulls away from the wreck of Atterbow's car and the crowd still gathered around it.

A policeman bends over the sprawled, conscious but befuddled Atterbow, with a second ambulance backing-up.

POLICEMAN: What do you mean, you got no home?

Tears well up amongst the blood on Atterbow's face.

ATTERBOW: The heart. It's – Home is where – oh. Christ in heaven.

In the receding ambulance, jolting and juddering along, with fugitive gleams of city light passing across its darkened windows, Berry lies covered with a blanket, either unconscious or dead, attended by ambulancemen.

Sylvia, ashen and silent, mascara streaks down her face, holds Berry's hand, protruding from the blanket.

Francis, looking half dead himself, sits hunched beside her on the narrow bench, his body rocking a little with the movement of the ambulance.

Nobody speaks. Then –

SYLVIA: (*Flatly*) He's not going to make it. I know he isn't.

She turns her head slightly, to look Francis full in the face. Oddly questioning, and challengingly. He holds her look for a bare moment, then looks down at his hands.

The next day, in the long summer, the war office almost shines in the light. But in the particular big room it is again scratch-scratch-scratch of fountain pens. Bernwood, Hedges, Carter, Church and Hopper. No Berry, no Francis, no Trekker.

HEDGES: Hopper.

HOPPER: Sir?

HEDGES: Isn't it time for the barely bloody?

Hopper looks harassed. His desk is awash with paper of various kinds.

HOPPER: I – yessir.

CHURCH: He's a bit snowed under, Wallace.

HEDGES: So am I!

Bernwood lifts his head, looking as troubled as ever.

BERNWOOD: I don't want anything to delay or hinder this new directive. It's bloody unreasonable. I would have thought 3P were better equipped to – (*To* CHURCH) How are we doing?

CHURCH: (*Peeved*) It's never been part of our brief to keep tabs on Russian and East European so-called 'volunteers'. I've lost a language clerk to the conference, and we've got to trawl through a mountain of paper even to get any sort of base figure.

CARTER: But it's obvious that the wogs will let those bloody reds man the equipment. The Soviet equipment. We should always have had that in mind. When I go into that conference room tomorrow, that's what they'll ask me. Thank God I'm not called today. We should have those numbers! No doubt about it.

CHURCH: Well, you've never said so before. I'm not a miracle worker. (*Sharply*) What are you doing, Hopper?

HOPPER: The coffee, sir. I –

CHURCH: Sit down and get on with your work. This language section cannot do *everything*. We're not running a cafeteria.

HOPPER: (*Resuming seat*) Sir.

HEDGES: But what about the barely bloody – ?

149

CHURCH: Wallace. They want something to chew on at the
conference, and they want it today. How many Russian
advisers – volunteers – artillery experts – demolition men –
CARTER: Exactly the detail they'll be asking me. I know I'm only
down as observer but – Oh, they'll want to know.
BERNWOOD: We've been caught napping. This office has been
caught on the hop. No doubt about it.

His whole body seems to be clenching with a gnawing anxiety.

HEDGES: Yes, but it's eleven o'clock.

A beat.

CARTER: Wallace!

HEDGES: What's that, old bean?

CARTER: (*Snaps*) It's not eleven o'clock. It is one minute to twelve.

A beat.

HEDGES: Righty-oh. My old throat's as dry as a bone, that's all. I'll
think of it as training for a long war in the desert. Which – if
we *don't* land at Alexandria –

The door opens. Everyone looks up.

   Unshaven, red-eyed, unkempt, Francis stands for a moment in
the doorway. And then without a word, like an automaton, he
shuffles towards his desk.

   Everyone looks at Francis, for a moment too surprised to speak.
Then –

BERNWOOD: You! You, man. What do you think you are doing?

Francis automatically taking a file or folder from one of the drawers
in his desk, looks up, bleary-eyed, sounding very Welsh.

FRANCIS: My duty, sir.

CHURCH: Francis. You're not supposed to be here – (*Rising tone*)
Why are you unshaven? What the hell do you think –

FRANCIS: Corporal Berry, sir.

CHURCH: (*Roars*) What about him!

FRANCIS: He's dead, sir.

Startled little pause.

BERNWOOD: He's what?

FRANCIS: His mor-tal soul has passed from amongst us, sir.

And then to everyone's astonishment, Francis covers his face with
his hands and begins to weep, as openly as a child. But (alas) it *is*
funny . . .

CHURCH: (*Uncertainly*) Look here, Francis –

BERNWOOD: What's going on? What's going on?

But cold-eyed Carter has had enough of this. He is suddenly in front of Francis' desk.

CARTER: Att-en-tion!

The snapped command jerks Francis to his feet.

FRANCIS: Sah!

CARTER: You're a soldier, soldier!

FRANCIS: Sah!

CARTER: Stop snivelling! At once!

FRANCIS: Sah!

CARTER: And explain yourself properly, if you don't want to be put on a charge!

FRANCIS: Sah!

He sways a little, like one about to fall over.

CARTER: Well?

FRANCIS: He – the corporal, sir – He passed away at 0700 hours this morning, sir.

On Hopper's face, very briefly, an unmistakable 'thank Christ for that!', then a swift adjustment to something more proper.

I was with him all night, sir. And his – his w.wife, sir. At the West London Hospital in Hammersmith, sir.

CHURCH: (*Astounded*) What?

FRANCIS: (*Helplessly*) Off the Broadway, sir. In Hammersmith Road, next to –

CARTER: Pull yourself together, man! We don't want to know where the damned – What happened? How did he – ?

FRANCIS: A car knocked him down, sir. At twenty-two ten last night. He – A mad organist, sir. Harold Atterbow.

Bernwood is instantly on to this apparently weird statement.

BERNWOOD: Atterbow? Harold Atterbow? The Wurlitzer Man?

Carter makes a gesture with his hand, looks at Church and goes back to his desk, muttering.

CARTER: Deal with it. Deal with it.

BERNWOOD: 'In a Monastery Garden'.

CHURCH: What – ?

BERNWOOD: And – 'A Persian Market Place'

HEDGES: (*To* BERNWOOD) Harry, what are you talking about . . . ?

BERNWOOD: He's the one who – Oh, yes. Oh, yes. I was particularly fond of 'The Whistling Shepherd and His Dog' . . . (*Becomes aware, twitches*) Look here, Hopper – I mean, Francis – what has all this beautiful music – what in God's

name has Harold Atterbow to do with Corporal – um –
        Berry – ?

Hedges has so far had great difficulty holding in first his incredulity
and then his laughter.

HEDGES: I had a – a certain regard for Corporal Berry – yes, I did –
        but – (*Makes a peculiar noise*) But any moment now I'm afraid
        I'm going to – (*Another strange noise*) I'm going to –

He doesn't have to say laugh: the strange noise in his throat surges
out, at first like a sob, but then into a loud and increasingly helpless
guffaw.

    The others look at him, appalled. But as he tries to get words out
through the laughter they are (except Francis) less and less able to
keep straight, let alone solemn, faces.

        Hoo! Hoo! Hoo – ! – I mean – Hoo! Hoo! the Whistling
        Wurlitzer – Hah! Haah! Wurlitzer and – Ha! Hoo! Hoo! Ha!

BERNWOOD: (*Frowns*) No, no. 'The Whistling Shepherd'.

CHURCH: (*Face collapsing*) And his dog.

Hedges, who has been trying to rein back his laughter, almost
bursts.

HEDGES: Haa! Hoo-hoo-hoo – Oh, Christ – Hoo Hoo Ha ha
        Haaaah!

Unexpectedly, cold eyes still cold –

CARTER: Hee hee hee!

An odd, repressed little whinny, like a nervous horse. Hedges,
totally unable to speak by now, points at him, freshly fuelled into
whooping paroxysmic laughter, in which all, except Francis,
unavoidably join in.

    As the laughter at last ebbs –

FRANCIS: Both his legs were broken, and his pelvis. His spleen was
        ruptured, and his rib had punctured his lung.

The last giggle and smirk has suddenly ended. Francis is still on his
feet, as Carter had commanded.

CHURCH: (*Quietly*) Sit yourself down, lad.

FRANCIS: Thank you, sir. (*As he sits*) He took a long time to die,
        see. And I had to stay with him.

BERNWOOD: Oh, dear. Oh, dear. I – Of course I shall write to his –
        this comes at quite the wrong time. We're all – naturally –

He shifts papers about on his desk, confused and troubled. Church
looks at him, then at Francis –

CHURCH: Have you been to the conference room?

FRANCIS: Sir?

CHURCH: That is where you are supposed to be. In uniform.

Francis jerks to his feet in alarm.

FRANCIS: Oh good heavens, sir, I – I f.f.f. –

Church is quickly scribbling a note.

CHURCH: You'd better take yourself up there. Don't want the redcaps knocking on your door, do we?

FRANCIS: (*Alarmed*) N.nun.no, sir.

Church tears off the note.

CHURCH: Here. Take this to whichever officer is in charge of the support clericals up there.

FRANCIS: Thank you, sir. Very much.

They watch him go to the door, where, as he goes out, he turns and looks across at Bernwood.

He tried to kill me, too, sir. The mad organist.

He shuts the door. A beat.

BERNWOOD: I'm – ah – I'm (*Pulls himself together*) Hopper. Make the barely bloody, for God's sake. Before I start walking up and down in a Persian Market Place.

HEDGES: In a what, Harry?

Bernwood looks at him with a sort of mournful prescience.

BERNWOOD: In a room with white walls. Wearing a jacket that is done up at the back.

'The Whistler and His Dog' flows in on the theatre organ, with its own order of comment.

At the same time, in the upstairs flat of the Fulham house, Sylvia lies on top of the bed, numbed and exhausted, her shoes kicked off.

'In a Persian Market Place' swells, over, and then slowly fades as, not too sure of herself, Aunt Vickie carries a tray with a boiled egg and a cup of tea, up the stairs.

AUNT VICKIE: (*Calls, tentatively*) Hello – ?

Sylvia lies still. Blank. She does not respond to the not very firm knock on the outer door.

(*Off*) Hello? Anybody home – I mean, Sylvia? You there?

A door opens, closes, near. She does not respond.

Aunt Vickie has come into the adjoining living-room, from the landing. She looks around the little room, and cannot hide a spasm of distaste at the untidiness and the uncleared plates on the table. But –

AUNT VICKIE: Sylvia? You there?

153

In the bedroom, Sylvia still does not respond. There is a tap-tap on the bedroom door.

SYLVIA: (*Mutters*) Piss off.

Aunt Vickie comes in with the tray. She stops, looks across at the bed, unsure.

AUNT VICKIE: I don't want to barge in on you – but I heard the terrible news –

SYLVIA: What do you want?

AUNT VICKIE: I've brought you a nice cup of tea. And I suppose you've had nothing to eat, have you? (*At her silence*) I've – well, I've boiled an egg with some bread and butter, and –

Sylvia lifts her head, then props herself up on an elbow.

SYLVIA: I couldn't eat nothing.

AUNT VICKIE: It's only the one egg. And a little one, and all. You got to eat something.

SYLVIA: Why?

AUNT VICKIE: To keep yourself going –

SYLVIA: No, I mean, why are you doing this?

AUNT VICKIE: We're neighbours, after all.

SYLVIA: Christ.

AUNT VICKIE: Bygones is bygones when something like this hits you. Here. Come on. Sit up. Have the cup of tea anyway – while it's hot.

Sylvia looks at her, evenly, seems about to reject it, then –

SYLVIA: Ta.

AUNT VICKIE: It's a terrible thing to have happened.

Sylvia sips.

SYLVIA: Yeh.

AUNT VICKIE: My Fred and me heard all the noise. But he wouldn't let me go out. I couldn't have done nothing, though, could I?

Sylvia sips.

SYLVIA: No. Not a bloody thing.

AUNT VICKIE: Try and eat. A little bit of egg. Shall I take the top off?

Sylvia sips, looks at her.

SYLVIA: He used to hit me about.

Aunt Vickie is taking the top off the egg.

AUNT VICKIE: I know.

SYLVIA: But he was – he was –

She cannot finish as her throat tightens.

AUNT VICKIE: Here. Have some egg. Come on.

SYLVIA: No.

Sylvia puts a hand to her face, and turns her head away in a spasm of grief.

The egg yolk dribbles off the spoon as Aunt Vickie's attention goes to the slender droop and distress of the young woman.

AUNT VICKIE: Oh, dear. I'm sorry I've dropped some of the yolk on the sheet –

Sylvia turns away her eyes full of tears.

SYLVIA: They're dirty anyway.

AUNT VICKIE: All the same –

SYLVIA: Everything in here is. Dirty. Rotten. Horrible!

AUNT VICKIE: Well, you don't want to bother yourself with that now –

SYLVIA: (*Savagely*) And so am I!

AUNT VICKIE: (*Blinks*) What?

Sylvia gets up, in one swift swirl, and moves to the close-curtained window in a rage of guilt, grief and self-contempt.

SYLVIA: It should have been me under that car. I should have been the one. It was me he was after. I didn't treat him right –

AUNT VICKIE: Who?

SYLVIA: Pete! I didn't do right.

AUNT VICKIE: That's not the way to – It's no use blaming yourself. Not at a time like this.

Sylvia turns from the window, looks at her, face hardening.

SYLVIA: What do you know about it?

AUNT VICKIE: Sylvia.

SYLVIA: Don't Sylvia me, you cow.

AUNT VICKIE: (*Splutters*) Oh – you – you –

SYLVIA: We never had a chance, Pete and me, with you two down below.

Aunt Vickie tries to control herself.

AUNT VICKIE: Do you want this egg, or don't you?

SYLVIA: Banging on the ceiling and mouthing me on the stairs. We had no privacy. Pete said – Pete used to say – he –

But the use of the past tense catches at her. She starts to cry again.

Aunt Vickie holds off. But Sylvia weeps pathetically. Aunt Vickie suddenly puts her arms around her, moved.

AUNT VICKIE: Let it out. That's it – let it out.

Sylvia is about to push her away, but then yields, crying hard.

SYLVIA: (*Sobs*) Oh – what shall I do-o-o – ?

AUNT VICKIE: You'll keep going, that's what you'll do. Because in the end – in the end, that's what we all have to do. It all comes down on the woman in the end. But there's always a – things have a way of working out. You've got to look after yourself, Sylvia. It's your own life now, love, and – (*Sucks in her breath.*) I'll tell you something. May God strike me dead.

The change in tone is so marked that Sylvia stops weeping, and pulls back a little in order to look at her.

SYLVIA: What – ?

AUNT VICKIE: I wish it had been my Fred under that car.

In an ante-room at the war office, the main conference room, where refreshments can be made, stationery stored, maps rolled, supplies stacked. Francis, stretched out on two chairs, fast asleep.

A few bored soldiers – Intelligence Corps and RASC clerks – read *Reveille* and the *Daily Mirror*, smoking, sipping tea from mugs.

Just beyond, a general is booming in the immediately adjoining conference room, apparently summing up the morning's session.

GENERAL: (*Off*) On the fifth day of the battle – day five in the folders but day six counting from the – day six on the charts – the assumption is that the great concentration of the Egyptian army will have been largely defeated to the north and to the west of Cairo –

In the conference room, the uniformed, red-tabbed general is holding forth, with a long pointer and a gigantic map of Egypt.

– And then we shall turn directly east and on day, by day eight – or day nine on the other tabulation – the Canal will be effectively in our hands –

While Francis sleeps in the ante-room, the voice continues to boom.

(*Off*) It is reassuringly apparent from this morning's session that there are to date no significant inter-service disputes –

SOLDIER: (*Reading*) That Diana Dors.

SECOND SOLDIER: What about her?

SOLDIER: Bet she's a good shag.

SECOND SOLDIER: And I'll bet you never find out.

GENERAL: (. . . *Off, continuous*) But there is no disguising the

156

central issue at this time. Leaving aside the movement of the
Tenth Armoured Division from Libya.

The first soldier puts down the weekly *Reveille*, yawns, stretches.

SOLDIER: Oh. You never know. It's the size of the dick that
counts.

Beyond, in the conference room:

GENERAL: (*Continuous*) – Which, it has to be said, is not the
strength it should be, with just the one artillery regiment, two
tank regiments and one – only one – battalion of infantry – but
leaving aside this, ah, ah, denuded and no doubt already *fly
blown* Tenth Armoured – (*Ripple of sycophantic amusement*) –
We have at Task Force disposal the Third Infantry, Third
Royal Marine Commando and the Sixteenth Parachute
Brigade at base here in blighty, and at full muster – all of
which, however, have to be assembled and transported.

BRIGADIER: And the frogs.

The General looks over the top of his glasses.

GENERAL: I think we should avoid that type of – ah –

BRIGADIER: (*Bad accent*) *Je m'excuse.*

Some titters.

In the ante-room, Francis stirs, with a deep groan, and looks
around, bleary-eyed, unsure for the moment where he is. The
voice, off, booms in his head for a moment.

GENERAL: (*Off*) But, yes, indeed, currently the French
contribution, which will represent one third of the strike
force, is the Seventh Division M-m-*Mécanique Rapide* and the
Tenth Division *Parachutiste*, both now in Algeria.

FRANCIS: Is there any tea left?

Nobody answers, continuing to read the papers. He gets up and
goes to the stewing urn, pouring himself a mugful.

GENERAL: (*Off, continuous*) Any such listing – which will almost
certainly be added to, on both sides – brings to the fore the
crucial question, which is – Time-scale for movement. You
have before you the considered interservice estimates. The
Task Force Commanders' summary is inescapable. The
movement will take six weeks – by which I mean six weeks
from whatever day is chosen as M-1, or first day of
movement . . .

The voice-over is made even more irritating and boomingly
resonant by the acoustics of the conference room, a little like a

voice speaking near-gibberish at the edge of a dream.

At the tea urn, Francis still seems like one trying to wake up. The voice, beyond, booms on and on . . .

SECOND SOLDIER: Have a good kip, did you? Taffy?

FRANCIS: I haven't had a wink, mun.

They laugh, derisively.

SOLDIER: No, but you had a bloody good snore. In Welsh, an' all.

FRANCIS: I mean, I was awake in my sleep. I could hear that voice all the time. I could even see myself asleep. I wonder what that means?

SECOND SOLDIER: Means you're round the twist, mate.

Francis sips the tea, thoughtfully.

FRANCIS: (*Almost to himself*) Yes. Perhaps I am.

A hospital. Day. 'The Destiny Waltz' surges, on the theatre organ.

A detective inspector and a uniformed policeman, holding his helmet under his arm, are being escorted by a nurse towards a small doorless side-room at the end of the corridor and the head of a big open ward.

'The Destiny Waltz' playing, on the organ.

In a side-room off a ward, Harold Atterbow sits up in bed against a pile of pillows on his back rest, with stitches on his face and an arm in plaster from wrist to elbow. He looks surprisingly cheerful, but not like one listening to the organ music, which fades as the two policemen enter.

INSPECTOR: Thank you, nurse. (*Looks at* ATTERBOW) Mr Harold Atterbow. Is that so?

ATTERBOW: Almost so.

INSPECTOR: I'm sorry?

ATTERBOW: Henry Arthur Harold Atterbow. But I abandoned the first two names in my youth.

The inspector moves the one chair in this small space nearer to the bed, sits down, while the policeman stands, helmet under arm, at the foot of the bed.

INSPECTOR: I see. Bit of a mouthful, was it?

ATTERBOW: No, the initials. H-A-H-A. Ha-Ha! I didn't ever want to be a comedian.

INSPECTOR: Organist.

ATTERBOW: Former organist. Ex-organist. Thank goodness.

The inspector takes out his notebook.

158

INSPECTOR: I'll put down organist, though. If that's all right, Mr
    Atterbow.
ATTERBOW: Perfectly all right by me, whatever I'm called.
INSPECTOR: What are you smiling for?
ATTERBOW: I don't know. Life's little ironies. The passing of its
    passions.
INSPECTOR: Only I wouldn't have thought you had too much to
    laugh about at the moment.
Atterbow looks at the policeman at the end of his bed.
ATTERBOW: Ah. But you're not me, are you?
INSPECTOR: No. That's true.
ATTERBOW: I was addressing the chap with the helmet.
INSPECTOR: No. He's not you, neither.
ATTERBOW: Double negative.
INSPECTOR: What?
ATTERBOW: Oh, take no heed, take no heed. I'm just having a
    quiet chuckle to myself. The console will rise no more from
    the pit.
The inspector is puzzled by Atterbow's demeanour, and getting
irritated.
INSPECTOR: I'm afraid I don't follow you, sir.
ATTERBOW: (*Beam*) No more selections from Snow White.
INSPECTOR: Ah. That.
ATTERBOW: 'Some Day My Prince Will Come'. 'Whistle While
    You Work'. 'The Dwarf's Yodel Song'. Bugger me. Bugger me.
INSPECTOR: Well. If we could just –
ATTERBOW: 'With a Smile and a Song' and – and – oh, my dear
    sweet Lord – (*Giggles, oddly manic*) I've always had my
    suspicions about those bloody dwarfs. Snow White must have
    been quite a fruity little peach, don't you think? Perhaps she
    was a bit – you know – What do you think?
The inspector stares, offended.
INSPECTOR: I don't understand your attitude, if I may say so, sir.
ATTERBOW: Never mind. Not all lies within our grasp.
INSPECTOR: I haven't paid you this little visit to bandy words with
    you, sir –
Atterbow laughs, interrupting him with a gesture of his good arm.
ATTERBOW: And then I'm especially pleased about 'The Destiny
    Waltz'. Do you know what pleases me the most about 'The
    Destiny Waltz'?

The inspector sits back in his chair, with a blank look.

INSPECTOR: No. What?

ATTERBOW: I'll never have to play it again.

Tiny pause. Atterbow simpers. The inspector looks at the policeman, who rolls his eyes.

INSPECTOR: Last night, between ten and ten-thirty p.m. –

ATTERBOW: 'By the Blue Hawaiian Waters'.

INSPECTOR: What?

ATTERBOW: You won't be hearing that from me, either. I'd rather piss in them instead, I'm very pleased to inform you.

INSPECTOR: And *I'd* be very pleased, sir, if you would inform me if there was any prior relationship between yourself and the deceased.

Atterbow's febrile manner changes. His silly little simper wipes off.

ATTERBOW: Sylvia? Do you mean – Are you referring to Sylvia? But I – no, no, no – I missed her! I missed her by a good inch! The bitch!

A gleam of pleasure from the inspector, and he leans forward, almost too eager.

INSPECTOR: I take it you are referring to Mrs Sylvia Berry of 32B Mar –

ATTERBOW: (*Shouts*) She's not dead! You're not telling me that! She's a bloody liar!

INSPECTOR: I didn't say she was.

Atterbow blows out air.

ATTERBOW: I thought for a minute there you were – (*Expression changes*) Deceased? What do you mean, deceased?

INSPECTOR: Her husband, sir.

ATTERBOW: What?

INSPECTOR: You knocked him down, sir. (*Deadly little pause*) You knocked him down and you killed him.

ATTERBOW: No, no, no no.

INSPECTOR: There's not a shred of doubt about *that*, sir. It is something else that is in question. And it's my duty to warn you, sir, that anything you say will be noted down. You follow me?

The inspector nods at the policeman.

ATTERBOW: No, no, no. I'm not having this. I'm in a lot of pain. You shouldn't be doing this. It's not right and proper, not to an injured man.

INSPECTOR: You referred to Mrs Berry just now, sir, as a bitch, sir. I take it that that means you had an intimate relationship with her, sir?

The question has no irony. Atterbow's manner has completely changed. He plucks with the hand of his good arm at the blanket on his bed.

ATTERBOW: There is a – surely I don't need to – there is a great gulf between – in age, in social position, in – what do you mean, intimate?

INSPECTOR: I mean intimate, sir.

ATTERBOW: I'll not have this, you know. I'll not be spoken to in this manner. (*Calls*) Nurse! nurse!

INSPECTOR: The nurse will be along in a minute, sir. We'll not be disturbed, so don't worry about it, mmm?

ATTERBOW: But I need my – ah – I need the bed pan.

INSPECTOR: A bowel movement, would that be? I'm not surprised.

ATTERBOW: The police force, I know, attracts men of low intelligence and dirty mouths –

INSPECTOR: We'll see about that, Mr Atterbow.

ATTERBOW: There's something I think you should learn and digest, my man. There's something I want to say to you.

INSPECTOR: I'd just like you to answer the question. How did Mr Berry feel about your relationship with his pretty young wife? Sir.

ATTERBOW: No. No. You listen to *me* for a change.

INSPECTOR: That's what I'm here for.

ATTERBOW: I have broadcast many, many times on both the Light Programme and the Home Service. And my photograph has appeared in the *Radio Times* on seventeen different occasions.

INSPECTOR: You hear all this, constable?

POLICEMAN: I do, sir.

INSPECTOR: (*To* ATTERBOW) You used to be well known to the general public, yes, indeed, sir. But – pardon me – what has that got to do with it?

ATTERBOW: It means I'm not just a nobody of the kind people like you try to bully and browbeat. It means that you'd do well to watch what you're saying. Intimate? Intimate? I'm old enough to be her father.

INSPECTOR: That's what several people have said already.

161

ATTERBOW: What? Which people?

INSPECTOR: In the course of our enquiries, sir.

ATTERBOW: Get out.

INSPECTOR: Now, now, Mr Atterbow –

ATTERBOW: No. I will say no more. I will say nothing more at all.
But in the meantime –

INSPECTOR: Till we meet again –

ATTERBOW: (*Rising tone*) In the meantime I would recommend to
you for the good of your own soul my gramophone recording
of the 'Sanctuary of the Heart'.

On cue, so to speak, Arthur Ketelbey's 'Sanctuary of the Heart'
rises up from the theatre organ, as night falls on the small Fulham
house.

But the perspective of the house is slightly wrong, in a
threatening sort of way, made worse by the music.

In the darkness the stairs stretch upwards at a steep angle,
'Sanctuary of the Heart' still swelling. In the hallway, a shaft of
light widens from Francis' door. Francis comes into the narrow
little hall, troubled. He puts his hand on the bottom of the banister
and looks up at the tilt of the stair. A moment – as 'Sanctuary of the
Heart' rolls on – then –

FRANCIS: (*Calls up*) No. Leave her alone. She can't help it! No.
Leave her.

In her bed, Sylvia is like a princess in a fairy-tale, fast asleep, her
hair tumbling on the pillow.

'Sanctuary of the Heart' continues.

VOICE: Sylvie – angel – Sylvia . . . ?

Sylvia moans and twists her head from side to side. Stooped over
her, Berry reaches out and puts the tips of his fingers on her face.

BERRY: They're cold – bloody cold – And it's all your fault, ennit?
Ennit?

Her eyes pop open, wide with fear, and she rears up in her bed.
'Sanctuary of the Heart' fades. She looks around the half-lit room,
panting a little. Slowly, her fear subsides.

SYLVIA: Oh, my Gawd.

She gets out of bed, in her baby-doll nightie, shaken, rather
pathetic, and pads across to where there is a bar of light under the
door of the living-room. Sylvia looks around all the unsightly
clutter. She has left the single overhead light on. Her face shows
what she thinks of it all. She goes through the already opened

curtain to the little kitchenette, to turn on the tap.

Downstairs, Francis is asleep, but an odd voice sounds in his head.

GENERAL: The Tenth Armoured Division from Libya, which, it has to be said, is not the strength it should be, with just the one artillery regiment, two tank regiments, one – only one – battalion of infantry and Diana Dors who, it has to be said, is a good shag – a good shag – a good sh.sh. shhh!

He wakes.

FRANCIS: What?

A moment. He gets out of bed, and switches on the harsh glare of the single overhead light. He goes back to the Put-U-Up, but lies now on top of the eiderdown, and broods. His expression becoming more and more sombre and introspective.

You mustn't think I don't mean what I say, Sylvia –

His thoughts take him back to the bar at the Palais.

(*Continuous*) – It's like this, you see. There is a redemptive power in love which transforms the

Crack! She smacks him straight round the mouth in a fury.

SYLVIA: Don't you talk to me like that!

In his bedroom, remembering, Francis shifts and sighs, no longer quite so sure of the truth of his earlier declarations.

A moment. Then he lets her chirpy little voice come back into his head again, from their encounter on the towpath near Hammersmith Bridge.

(*Over*) I just thought you wanted a shag, that's all.

Memory forms the towpath bench again, with Francis turning to look at her, tears in his eyes, voice barely able to get out of his throat.

FRANCIS: Oh. But I do-o-o-o –

She is half-amused, half-touched, and puts her hand to his face.

SYLVIA: Then you shall have one, you greedy little devil.

He swallows, moistens his lips.

FRANCIS: But – but –

SYLVIA: But what?

FRANCIS: Your husband –

SYLVIA: He's not there all the time, is he? And sometimes –

The towpath images fade, but her voice stays in Francis' head, as he lays on the Put-U-Up.

(*Over, continuous*) – I wish he wasn't there at all. Isn't that wicked.

163

Francis thinks about it.

FRANCIS: (*Sighs to himself*) Yes. It is.

Then his eyes go to the ceiling, as they must have done so many times before.

Upstairs, Sylvia sits in bed, sipping the cup of tea she has made herself. She puts the cup down. A moment. Then she starts to cry, looking at her wedding ring.

A 1956 hit comes at her: Don Cherry singing 'Band of Gold', complete with a ba-ba-baa fifties chorus and a mournfully insistent affirmation of love and marriage.

Moving with comic and yet earnest caution, Francis, in bare feet and pyjamas, is very slowly going up the dark stairs, as the music continues – He freezes, full of anxiety, head cocked to listen, as the chorus wa-wahs.

At the same time, in the other bedroom downstairs, Aunt Vickie sussurates soft little whiffles of sleep.

Beside her, Uncle Fred lies awake, hollow-eyed in the near dark, jaws clamped, wrestling with God and demons. 'Band of Gold' continuing.

Upstairs, tears trickle down Sylvia's cheeks as she thinks of the song and its messages.

Francis ultra-cautiously takes another upward step on the dark stairs. Downstairs Uncle Fred groans, long and loud, as the music stops.

AUNT VICKIE: Wassamatter – ?

Francis takes another step on the stairs in the music-less silence. A board creaks. He freezes, again.

Sylvia weeps in her bed, and unclenches her hand. In it, the wedding ring, which she has taken off in order to hold tightly.

SYLVIA: (*Chokes*) Oh, Pete . . .

Downstairs, Aunt Vickie, disturbed in her dreams, is rather fed-up, but she mustn't show it too much.

AUNT VICKIE: Can't you sleep?

UNCLE FRED: I can never sleep.

AUNT VICKIE: Ts!

UNCLE FRED: Don't you tut me!

AUNT VICKIE: Do you want me to make some cocoa?

UNCLE FRED: Cocoa!

AUNT VICKIE: Well – if you can't sleep –

UNCLE FRED: I never can sleep. (*Tiny pause, sepulchral voice*) It's that 'ymn.

AUNT VICKIE: That who?

UNCLE FRED: (*Angrily*) 'Ymn!

AUNT VICKIE: Yes, but who? Him upstairs – as was?

UNCLE FRED: Nah! Ymn number four four one.

AUNT VICKIE: (*Flatly*) Oh.

Pause. She visibly steels herself.

UNCLE FRED:

> 'In the silent midnight watches
> List – thy bosom's door!'

He recites as a child might, with plodding and awkward intonation. She is moved enough to touch him.

AUNT VICKIE: (*Wretched*) Don't, Fred.

UNCLE FRED: (*Rising tone*)

> 'How it knocketh, knocketh, knocketh,
> Knocketh evermore!
> Say not 'tis thy pulse is beating –'

AUNT VICKIE: I'll make some cocoa.

UNCLE FRED: (*With genuine dread*)

> 'Tis thy heart of sin
> Tis thy Saviour knocks, and crieth
> *Rise, and let Me in*!'

On the upstairs landing, Francis hovers at the door to the bedroom.

FRANCIS: (*Whispers*) Sylvia – ?

But it is too soft to be heard.

On the other side of the door, more in control of herself, Sylvia is putting the wedding ring back on her finger. But the doorknob is slowly, slowly turning, as in a B-Movie thriller. She hasn't noticed. And puts out the light, in order to settle down again for sleep. Francis edges very carefully into the now darkened room, ludicrously, more and more like a criminal.

(*Whispers*) Sylvia.

She shoots up in the bed with a little yelp, genuinely afraid.

A noise heard in the downstairs bedroom –

UNCLE FRED: *Wassat*!

Aunt Vickie had just been about to slip back into sleep, the cocoa not made, and forgotten.

AUNT VICKIE: What's what?

UNCLE FRED: That noise! Somebody is moving about.

AUNT VICKIE: I didn't hear nothing.

Uncle Fred is half-cowering down so that the sheet comes up to his nose.

Could it be – ask his eyes – that the Saviour, having knocketh-knocketh-knockethed, has at last entered?

Upstairs, Sylvia has put the light on. Her eyes are still wide with the jump of fear she had experienced.

SYLVIA: I thought it was – For a minute I thought Pete had – Christ! What do you think you are doing!

FRANCIS: Shhh! Shhh!

SYLVIA: Shhh your bloody self!

FRANCIS: Sylvia . . .

SYLVIA: What do you want – ? Frightening me half to death. I'm going to put a bloody lock on that door.

Francis is still standing by the door. He starts to move towards her, looking ashamed and full of contrition.

FRANCIS: I want to talk to you. There's something I've got to – to explain. It's only fair that I should clear it up. (*Looks at her*) I only hope you won't think too badly of me.

She stares at him.

SYLVIA: Why? What's happened? What have you done?

Helplessly, his eyes have fallen on her body, a lot of which can be seen in the baby-doll nightdress and the pulled back bedclothes. He swallows.

FRANCIS: I – (*Tries again*) This is hard. Oh, very hard. You're so lovely – By God, you are. But it's only fair, see, that I should tell you. (*With difficulty, and very Welsh*) I *thought* I was in love with you. No lies, mind. I said what I felt. But – Well, I been thinking.

Downstairs, a fed-up Aunt Vickie comes out of the bedroom into the narrow hall.

AUNT VICKIE: Well, it might help you get to sleep. *Both* of us.

She goes towards the living-room/kitchenette, to make cocoa – and then notices that Francis' door is open, with the light on. She goes into his room.

Frank. I'm making some . . .

She stops dead at the sight of an empty room.

Aunt Vickie comes out into the hall with a frown. She looks at the stairs, dismisses the thought, goes through to the living-room.

She puts on the light, and realises Francis is not there, either.

Frank?

The budgerigar gives a cheep.

Upstairs, Sylvia bursts out laughing as Francis, apologetic, hovers uncertainly over her. But the laughter – laced with pain, and with contempt, and even a little disappointment – becomes too shrill, and leads to tears.

FRANCIS: (*Shocked*) Oh, don't. Don't. Please.

Aunt Vickie stands at the foot of the stairs, looking up, utterly incredulous. She can hear Sylvia's laughter. Her face tightens, and she hisses 'My God!' under her breath.

In the upstairs bedroom, the laughter merges almost indistinguishably into hard sobs. Francis is moved, and forgets all that he had meant to say.

Oh, my poor love. My poor little love!

Her breast is exposed, quivering with her sobs. He looks at it. He cannot help it. His hands reach –

SYLVIA: Ow!

And then she starts to laugh, her mouth reaching for his, pulling him down beside her.

'The Man with the Golden Arm' thunders out, leaving them to their own devices.

Six

In the cinema, the 1956 newsreel shows the wedding in Monaco of Prince Rainier and Grace Kelly.

Troubled, scared Francis in the audience looks along the row at usherette Sylvia, avidly watching the screen. But when her eyes switch hopefully to Francis (during the marriage service), there is an empty seat. He has slunk away.

Then another summer morning over the tawdry little street of uniformly depressing terraced houses. Some early street activity, including a rag and bone man.

Music over, from the start: one of the many unbelievable hits of 1956 – 'Robin Hood' by Gary Miller with Tony Osborne and his Orchestra, and the Beryl Stott Chorus.

Francis is shaving at the sink in the tight little kitchenette of the downstairs flat, half lathered and wholly worried. Inappropriate images of the Wedding of the Year insist upon forming themselves in his mind. Prince Rainier of Monaco and Grace Kelly are being betrothed, in fairy-tale splendour. Newsreel realities turn into Francis' dread, as the new Princess Grace becomes Sylvia – and the Prince, Francis himself. Shaving, Francis makes a sudden wince – partly because of the images from his own head, but also because he has cut himself. The 'Robin Hood' music, coming from the wireless on the other side of the curtain, jollies on and on.

Another dread forms for Francis – He imagines Sylvia and himself are walking along the wretched street, pushing a pram. She is obviously nagging him about something.

The music continues. The baby in the pram throws out a rattle or dummy or soft toy on to the pavement, and yells its head off.

In the kitchenette, Francis is trying to staunch the small rivulet of blood as it trickles down his cheek, and the music continues, mindlessly cheerful, but now more obviously coming from the radio on the shelf in the small living-room on the other side of the half-pulled curtain.

Uncle Fred, standing, is putting his jacket on, ready to collect his sandwiches and go. Click! Off goes the radio.

UNCLE FRED: (*Mimics American accent, badly*) Robin Hood –

Robin Hood! Bloody rubbish, ennit? And it's not right, is it? Eh?

Aunt Vickie is wrapping up the doorstep sandwiches, preoccupied and so not quite aware of his tone.

AUNT VICKIE: Oh, I don't know – it's cheerful enough. Nice and breezy –

UNCLE FRED: But they're Yanks!

The inner rage — always a total puzzle to her – breaks through, and she becomes warily alert.

AUNT VICKIE: Yes. Well –

UNCLE FRED: Americans, them singers. So-called singers. What do they know about it?

AUNT VICKIE: (*Conciliatory*) Not much, I don't suppose.

UNCLE FRED: He's English, Robin Hood is. *English.* At least he was when I was at school! So it's not bloody right, is it? They take over everything –

Francis finishes shaving, the blood staunched with a bit of cigarette paper, listening with obvious disdain to Uncle Fred on the other side of the partly drawn curtain.

– and everybody and it's about time we stood up to them – as well as that sly A-rab whatsisname –

AUNT VICKIE: Nasser.

UNCLE FRED: He's not even a Christian.

She is putting the wrapped sandwiches into the reused brown paper bag.

AUNT VICKIE: Not many are.

UNCLE FRED: What?

AUNT VICKIE: (*Quickly*) It's a disgrace.

UNCLE FRED: What did we fight the war for? Who won it? So say. Now look what's going on. (*No break of tone*) Have you asked him yet? Have you asked him to go? Eh?

AUNT VICKIE: Who?

UNCLE FRED: That dirty little bleeder shaving the hairs off his dirty little chops.

Francis, emptying the bowl, stiffens, mortified.

Aunt Vickie is not happy about the crude directness – but she, too, is willing to judge severely Francis' presumed sin, sneaking upstairs to make love to Sylvia.

AUNT VICKIE: (*Sotto voce*) How could I – ? There hasn't been time . . .

Her eyes, and her wince, indicate Francis' proximity.

UNCLE FRED: No use you rolling your eyes up like that. What's right is right and what's wrong is wrong. There's no two ways about it, and there never has been. (*Takes sandwiches*) 'Am?

AUNT VICKIE: Ham.

UNCLE FRED: Mustard?

AUNT VICKIE: Lots.

UNCLE FRED: I'm a tolerant man – about little things, most things – and I like intelligent company – which I don't get much of –

AUNT VICKIE: Ta.

UNCLE FRED: But there are some things – some things – (*Spasm of fury*) In my own house. Right under my nose. I'll tell you – I'll tell you this –

AUNT VICKIE: Don't, Fred. You'll do yourself an injury getting in this sort of state.

UNCLE FRED: I'll do somebody an injury all right. Some sly little – dirty little –

Francis, trying to be brave, appears in the half curtained off entrance to the kitchenette.

FRANCIS: Who are you talking about?

UNCLE FRED: Who do you think?

FRANCIS: Well – what is it you think I've done? What are you trying to say – ?

UNCLE FRED: I'm not *trying* to say – What I want – What I'm telling you –

AUNT VICKIE: Fred.

But his finger is jab-jab-jabbing, virtually under Francis' nose.

UNCLE FRED: What *I'm – telling – you –*

FRANCIS: Tell me, then.

UNCLE FRED: You can't even wait for his body to go cold. Sneaking up the stairs to that Jezebel up there –

FRANCIS: Her name is Sylvia.

UNCLE FRED: I don't care what her bloody name is. What I do know is what she is. A slut. A mouthy little slut!

FRANCIS: You're talking about the girl I'm going to m.m.mum –

His jaw, his tongue, lock. The word won't come. There is a sudden, appalled silence, in which the struggling 'm.m.m.mum.m.' seems to go on for ever. 'Marry' is the blocked word.

And during the block, we see the moment from the previous

night when Sylvia's laughter merged into hard sobs and Francis plunged, enfolding her flimsily dressed body.

Oh, my poor love. My poor little love!

She weeps, twisting her head away, her body away: a movement which, in the little nightdress, reveals too much of a breast. Helpless now, Francis awkwardly gropes, enclosing her mostly exposed breast, but with characteristic lack of finesse.

SYLVIA: *Ow*!

The word is released as the moment dies –

FRANCIS: – Marry.

He suddenly plumps himself down at the table which holds breakfast things and the budgerigar cage, like one who will fall down if he doesn't sit down. There is a shocked little silence.

AUNT VICKIE: Frank. You don't know what you're saying.

UNCLE FRED: Marry! Her upstairs? You must be out of –

(*Cackles, nastily*) You going to do that before the funeral, or after?

The postman drops a couple of letters into the letter-box of number thirty two, the Fulham house. As the letters drop, Uncle Fred is already on his way out, half-way up the narrow passage, by the foot of the stair, calling back over his shoulder to the living-room.

– and the sooner the better! I'm having no more filth in *my* house!

FRANCIS: (*Off, shouts*) Don't worry! I'm going!

Uncle Fred snorts, picks up the two letters, puts one in his jacket pocket, and in a weird, aggressive whirl, like someone in a spasm from cyanide, throws the other letter half-way up the stairs.

UNCLE FRED: (*Yells*) Something for the tart!

And bang! – demented, surely – he bangs shut the front door on his sudden swift exit.

In the downstairs living-room, Aunt Vickie, standing, closes her eyes in pain, and sucks in her breath.

AUNT VICKIE: Sometimes –!

She opens her eyes, and looks steadily at Francis, who is still slumped in a curve of dejection at the table. He lifts his head, feeling her eyes on him, and stares at her. A small, strange, silent moment. Then –

FRANCIS: (*Quietly*) Aunt Vickie. He's mad, you know.

She doesn't answer, doesn't move.

He's – certifiable.

AUNT VICKIE: I wish he was d-

She stops herself.

FRANCIS: You wish what?

AUNT VICKIE: (*Recovering*) You're a fine one to talk. If you're
thinking of throwing your life away on that girl upstairs –
Frank! For goodness sake, stop and think! What will your
poor mother say?

FRANCIS: (*Glumly*) She – no. She won't be very happy.

AUNT VICKIE: And what about your career – you going to Oxford
and all that.

Francis looks at her, then sighs, or almost groans.

FRANCIS: (*Hollow*) I know.

Aunt Vickie sits at the table, next to him.

AUNT VICKIE: Listen, Frank. Listen to me.

FRANCIS: There's not much to say, is there? I've – (*Lifts shoulders,
straightens jaw.*) It's a question of honour now, Aunt Vickie.
I'm not one to trifle with a lady's heart.

AUNT VICKIE: Oh, you silly bugger.

FRANCIS: What – ?

AUNT VICKIE: If you could hear yourself. If only you could hear
some of the silly – silly – silly things you say. What have you
done? Made her pregnant or something?

FRANCIS: Aunt Vickie –

AUNT VICKIE: And how do you know it's yours? She's been
around a bit, that girl.

FRANCIS: (*Through his teeth*) Please. Please, don't.

AUNT VICKIE: You might be daft, Frank, but you don't have to
be blind as well. She'd have the rag and bone man if he gave
her his horse's feedbag.

FRANCIS: You don't know her. You don't know what you're
saying.

AUNT VICKIE: Christ, you've only known her five minutes.
(*Studies him.*) When did you start doing it, Frank?

He wants to hide, or cover his face.

FRANCIS: Start doing what?

AUNT VICKIE: (*Brutally*) Creeping up the stairs and having it off
with her.

FRANCIS: (*Cries*) Stop it.

AUNT VICKIE: Come on, Frank. The truth.

FRANCIS: You don't – You're – No! You've got it all wrong!
AUNT VICKIE: You're not trying to tell me you weren't up there last night.
FRANCIS: That was the first time. And I went up there because I – He stops.
AUNT VICKIE: Because what?
FRANCIS: (*Steadily*) I went up there because I wanted to tell her that I had realised that love is more el-us-ive than mere physical attraction, and that I didn't want to make the same mistake Pushkin had made.
AUNT VICKIE: What? Who – ?
FRANCIS: He met the most beautiful woman in Russia at a ball and – (*Swallows*) Never mind. The point is, I want –
AUNT VICKIE: The point is you went up there to talk *that* sort of – I don't know what – the day after her poor bloody husband is squashed flat outside the pub. I'll bet she was glad to see you!
FRANCIS: (*With difficulty*) She – well, she started to laugh, and –
AUNT VICKIE: I'll bet she did! Oh, Frank. Frank. You are such a –
FRANCIS: And then she cried. She cried enough to break your heart.

His soft, sing-song Welsh voice is too obviously sincere, too obviously vulnerable.

If there's one thing I can't abide, Aunt Vickie, it's a woman in tears like that. It pulls at you – tugs at you – and I forgot everything I had gone up there to say – everything – and I – (*Falters*) Well she looked so lovely and I – well, I – shhh shhh! I said or sort of wanted to say and – and I – put my arms around her, the poor little, lost, grieving – (*Stops, changes tone*) I didn't realise how much of the animal is in me, Aunt Vickie. A beast, I am. (*Gets up, and in a doomed, awed, near-whisper*) She was in her nightie, see. And I was in my pyjamas.

Colonel Bernwood, as harassed as ever, is stooped over his desk, alone in the big room at the war office. He is in very early. The clock on the wall shows it is 8.10 am, and he looks as though he has been there for a long time.

Outside the office, there is a long and wide corridor, along which comes Private Hopper, reading *Melody Maker*, and not looking where he is going.

He stops, absorbed, makes a 'mm-huh' sound of assent or

approval at what he is reading, then goes on his way, folding the paper up and beginning to half-sing the Elvis Presley 1956 hit 'Heartbreak Hotel', in his own voice. He virtually kicks open the door into the big room.

Crashing in, Elvis on his lips, Hopper stops dead, astonished that Bernwood should be there. He swallows down the 'I-ah-could die – !'

HOPPER: Sorry, sir.

Bernwood lifts his head from his pile of papers and looks at him in his vague, rather puzzled way.

BERNWOOD: What is the matter? Are you ill?

HOPPER: I – no, sir.

BERNWOOD: Not the stomach ache?

HOPPER: No, sir.

BERNWOOD: (*Abstracted*) Good. Goo-oo-ood – –

He lowers his head again, with a diligent sigh. Hopper looks at him warily, then quietly gets his papers etc. out of his desk, keeping an eye on Bernwood and moving as one might in a sick room.

Scratch-scratch-scratch. Then – a pen lifted, and:

Ah – Hopper – ah –

Hopper tenses, waits, but Bernwood seems to forget all about it, and resumes writing. Hopper covertly eyes him, comically.

Hopper's wariness slackens. He sighs a National Serviceman's sigh, fed up with this bondage.

HOPPER: (*Under his breath*) Roll on.

Start rocky-rhythm introduction to Jerry Lee Lewis' 'It'll Be Me' as the fierce arrow of Hopper's glance falls on Bernwood, making the colonel lift his bemused head exactly as the vocal begins, apparently in Bernwood's mouth.

Lips not moving, Hopper's lips are not moving, but he is putting his fear of being kept on in the army into the music.

The room darkens, and a searchlight seeks him out, controlled by Bernwood. As 'It'll Be Me' throbs on, with its implicit threat, Hopper runs from the room into the long corridors and flights of stairs beyond. But (in his dread) the lights seek him out, and all the officers from the big room – using their umbrellas as rifles – are out to get him. They fire!

In the big room, Hopper is firmly in the grip of his rhythmic fantasies, at his desk. He too opens his mouth to be Jerry Lee

Lewis, more confident now, and placing himself back on stage at the Palais, in another mythic triumph. Hopper beats hell out of the piano, and makes the Palais girls swoon with his frenzied vocal.

With bowler hats and tightly furled brollies, Hedges and Church arrive for the start of their working day, obviously 'singing' the same number. At which point, in the original recording, the vocal yields to a feisty, hard-driving half a minute or so of piano and instrumental –

Hopper is eagerly picking up on the beat, and – flying with it – extending it once more into 'real' band playing in the Palais.

Back in the big room at the war office, the thumping, non-vocal section of 'It'll Be Me', apparently performed, with mock instruments and evil expressions, by Bernwood, Hedges, Carter and Church.

Hopper cannot quite sustain the glee and the physical contortions. His face shows signs of wistful melancholy again, and as the Jerry Lee Lewis vocal resumes, Hopper does not move his lips in synchronisation. Instead, he remembers, and improves, the way he stood at the window of his bed-sitter, high up in the house, looking down at the street, and a tree whose branches make shifting patterns of shadow in the street lamp's light.

Lisa emerges from the net of shadows by the tree, and looks up at Hopper's window, as 'It'll Be Me' continues.

Looking out of the window, hope flies and then dies for Hopper, seeing the lamp, the tree, the mesh of shadows, but no Lisa. And he 'sings' Jerry Lee Lewis, pulling a wry face.

But in the big room back at base, Hopper stops 'singing' and looks around at the diligent faces in the office, fed-up, as the music continues, over, but starting to fade as his mind lets it go. He eventually realises that Church is looking at him, sardonically.

CHURCH: Concentrating, are we?

HOPPER: Yessir!

He quickly bends to his work.

CHURCH: I very much hope so, Hopper. You'll not leave this room until those pages are translated.

HOPPER: Yes, sir.

HEDGES: We'll all be here until midnight, if you ask me. When is Berry's replacement coming? I need some beavering. *And* somebody to empty my out-tray. Though I suppose whatever scruffy little bugger they do deign to send us will be just as keen to fill my in-tray as well.

CHURCH: Harry. We need some more hands. Really – we do!

BERNWOOD: (*Looking around*) Only one clerk? Why is that? We can't cope with all this with only one clerk.

CHURCH: (*Sigh*) Private Francis is waiting tables in the conference room – Operation Musketeer – yes?

BERNWOOD: (*Testy*) Yes, yes.

CHURCH: And Corporal Berry is dead.

Tiny pause. Church, Hedges and, more covertly, Hopper stare at Bernwood, fascinated.

For a brief moment Bernwood's eyes glaze, and even moisten, and faintly the opening notes of 'In a Persian Market Place' sound on the theatre organ with ghostly insistence.

Bernwood, carefully watched, gains control of his wayward mind.

BERNWOOD: Ah. Yes. Poor chap. Poor chap. I've – ah – that reminds me. I've drafted a letter to his – I believe he was married – Right thing to do, yes? After all, he – Do we have his address on file?

CHURCH: Bit awkward.

BERNWOOD: How do you mean?

CHURCH: Chap you'd ask that sort of thing is Berry himself.

BERNWOOD: (*Puzzled*) Ah. Yes. Quite a – Bit of a conundrum, what?

HEDGES: Which is a good example of why we need a new general office clerk and tea-wallah, Harry. Now. Today.

HOPPER: (*To* BERNWOOD) Permission to speak, sir?

BERNWOOD: Yes, yes.

HOPPER: Private Francis lodges in the same house as the corporal did, sir.

BERNWOOD: (*Testy*) What of it?

HOPPER: Well – he – sir, he would know the address since he lives there himself, sir.

Tiny pause.

BERNWOOD: Good thinking, Hopper!

HOPPER: Thank you sir.

CHURCH: (*With irony*) Absolute bloody genius, Hopper. Why don't you find the lowest common denominator next?

They've been looking for it for years.

Hedges snorts a laugh.

BERNWOOD: (*Oblivious*) Private Francis. Yes. But – Oh, yes, yes, – he's in the conference room, isn't he? Where is this *house* or – whatever it is?

HOPPER: Fulham, sir.

BERNWOOD: Fulham.

Bernwood says the word as though it were Bali or Xanadu.

HEDGES: (*Chuckles*) Oh, there are some amazing places in the world, Harry.

Bernwood is stung, and speaks almost angrily, and with uncharacteristic decisiveness.

BERNWOOD: A quip a minute, aren't we? I was just working out that it was possible for Hopper here to get there and back during his luncheon hour. Tube or bus. Office tea kitty. Deliver CO's letter of condolence. Right?

HOPPER: (*Not pleased*) Yes, sir. (*Then*) Excuse me, sir.

BERNWOOD: Yes, yes.

HOPPER: Since Private Francis lives in the same place, sir, and will be going home this evening, sir, why not let him –

BERNWOOD: (*Cuts in*) Francis may be very late. Very late. The way those sessions are going. And I would prefer Mrs – ah – Berry received her late husband's Commanding Officer's letter of sympathy sooner rather than – (*Turns to others*) Spoke to Archie last night. They seem bogged down upstairs. No spring in the heel. We can't seem to – it's all very shocking – Wallace. Did you know we only had five squadrons of troop-carrying planes? The Hastings and – ah –

CHURCH: Vickers Valetta.

BERNWOOD: That's the one.

HEDGES: Harry. What do you mean?

BERNWOOD: Well, that's only enough to lift *one* parachute battalion with all its support arms.

HEDGES: (*Frowns*) Come on. You're not serious.

Bernwood is clenching and unclenching his hands, in increasing distress.

BERNWOOD: Time is of the essence. Time is of the essence. But they're running into one damned deficiency after another. I can't believe it! There's Nasser putting his fingers to his nose and we can't seem to get our hands out of our pockets!

In the conference room, floors above, a senior parachute officer is under some pressure, standing well down the very long table, as Francis and other clerks distribute fresh papers at each position.

PARACHUTIST: The Soviet and Czech tanks which would be deployed against us by the Egyptian Army are not vulnerable to the kind of weapons which Sixteenth Parachute Brigade could transport by air for any drop. That is, except the BAT – the recoilless anti-tank weapon – but –

(*Coughs, apologetically*) The ammo it uses has not been tested under heatwave conditions. I'm afraid that we would need the American 106 millimetre RCLs – which is jeep mounted.

A COLONEL: But the Americans are – well. They're not cooperating, are they?

A BRIGADIER: No – but we could raid NATO stocks in Germany. Sort of – *borrow*, mm?

Some subdued but dispirited laughter. The clerks – including Francis – retreat to stand against the walls, awaiting their next tasks.

A LT COLONEL: Jeep-mounted, did you say? What about our new vehicle – the Champ? Haven't we dispensed with the jeep?

PARACHUTIST: We have. But – (*Spreads his hands*) Look. I'm not denying that everything I've said this morning from the Parachute Brigade angle is not disappointing for you and irritating, too – and that's a measure of how *we* have been feeling for quite some time, to be honest. You ask about the Champ – the new British equivalent of or update on the American jeep – well – the damned thing is too bulky when lashed for a parachute drop – you follow that it has to be lashed on a platform under the plane – yes, well – it's too big. The landing wheels of the bloody plane won't touch the ground. (*Tiny pause*) Excuse my French.

Of course it's only our people who have to lash the cargo under the plane. We ought to be able to load and discharge through the tail of the plane. The Americans do. And so – if you'll excuse my French – so can the French themselves with their Noratlas plane. And *now* we're told – on top of all that – that the new self-loading FLN rifle is being withdrawn from our para battalions because *sand* will jam the re-loading mechanism.

GENERAL: (*Mildly*) I think we need a rather more positive tone, don't you?

PARACHUTIST: I'm sorry, sir. I've been asked to put the position as the Parachute Brigade sees it. We *want* to go in. By God, we do. But of the Sixteenth Brigade, two of our battalions have been in Cyprus for a year and have done no drops. We don't parachute against EOKA. We're rusty and under-equipped, that's the fact of the matter. If you are asking us to drop on the Canal base to cut down the delay in mobilisation and movement of the main body of our forces, then you are also in logic saying that the paratroopers would have to hold out for – how long? As long as Arnhem?

There is a murmur of something like anger.

Private Francis, standing against the wall, is preoccupied with his own life:

UNCLE FRED: (*Over*) What did we fight the war for? Who won it? So say. Now look what's going on. Have you asked him yet?

AUNT VICKIE: (*Over*) Who?

UNCLE FRED: (*Over*) That dirty little bleeder shaving the hairs off his dirty little chops. Have you asked him to go? Eh?

Recollections and shames fade to let in the troubled and despondent general in the conference room.

GENERAL: It seems to me we are beset by difficulties which are not wholly of our own making.

FRANCIS: (*Under his breath*) Amen.

In the hospital, a bored, uniformed policeman sits on a canvas and tubular steel chair, his helmet on the linoleum, outside the side-room where Atterbow languishes.

POLICEMAN: No. I don't want to do this. I'm not going to think about it.

ATTERBOW: (*Off*) Come on! In charge flanked by a European officer. Six letters.

POLICEMAN: (*To himself*) Oh, shut up.

Atterbow, sitting up in bed, stitched and plastered, is doing the *Daily Telegraph* crossword.

ATTERBOW: Well, what's short for 'in charge'? Come on. That's the way you work these things out. 'IC', that's short for 'in charge', now isn't it?

The policeman shifts in his chair, bored.

POLICEMAN: I don't know. I don't care.

ATTERBOW: (*Off*) Ah, but the answer will amuse you. You've got
    IC in the middle of the six letter word, right?

The policeman's bored and irritated expression swiftly changing,
taking on a gleam.

Coming towards him, along the corridor, her high heels once
again clicking, is Sylvia.

In his side-room, Atterbow taps the pencil against his teeth.

So what we've got left is a European who is a four-letter
    word. And I can think of quite a few of those, eh?

His chuckle dies at the sound of a voice outside his small, doorless
room. He drops the pencil and makes a pointless attempt to
smooth down his few wisps of hair.

SYLVIA: (*Off*) This where Harold Atterbow is – ? They told me.

The policeman has jerked to his feet, very taken by her obvious
physical attractions.

POLICEMAN: Might I ask who you are, Miss?

SYLVIA: Waffor?

POLICEMAN: Because it's my job, miss. (*A sort of wink*) I'd like to
    know anyway. Wouldn't I?

She nods at the little doorless room.

SYLVIA: In there, is he? What the police out here for? he nicked,
    or what?

POLICEMAN: Yeh. For doing crosswords and disturbing my
    peace.

SYLVIA: Wha – ?

ATTERBOW: (*Off*) Let her in! Let her in!

POLICEMAN: You related to him?

SYLVIA: Not bloody likely.

POLICEMAN: He's charged, all right. Manslaughter. But it might
    be even more serious than that.

SYLVIA: Good!

ATTERBOW: (*Calls*) Don't say that! Oh, don't say that, Sylvia!

SYLVIA: (*Louder*) I'll say what I like, you dirty old drunk.

POLICEMAN: Blimey. You *sound* like a relative. What you want to
    see him for, sweetie-pie?

SYLVIA: He's writ to me, ennhe?

She is getting that morning's letter out of her bag.

POLICEMAN: Yeh? What about?

Atterbow, straining to listen, mutters a barely audible 'No, no', very tense, and starts to scribble on a bedside pad.

    The policeman, looking at the envelope, changes his manner.

        Oh. I'm sorry, Mrs Berry. I didn't realise you were – You have my condolences.

SYLVIA: (*Matter of fact*) Ta. Can I go in then?

POLICEMAN: (*Unsure*) Well – I –

But she goes in. He hesitates, shrugs, sits, and pulls his chair even nearer to the doorless entrance, to listen and make notes.

ATTERBOW: (*Loudly, very formally*) Good morning, Mrs Berry. I'm glad you could come. (*Lip-mimes, urgently*) Be careful. He's listening.

SYLVIA: What?

Atterbow puts his finger to his lips, eyes darting with urgency and anxiety.

ATTERBOW: (*Silent lip-moves*) One hundred pounds.

SYLVIA: What?

He rolls his eyes in despair, but speaks properly again, very formally.

ATTERBOW: I don't know you very well, Sylvia. Not very well at all. But I just wanted to give you my commiserations, and, ah –

At the same time as he speaks, he holds up his scrawl for her to see on his page of Basildon Bond. It says . . .

               '£100 if keep mouth shut about us.'

Her face changes.

SYLVIA: Yeh. Well. Of course. I'm upset. It's hit home hard, ennit?

Outside, the policeman listens very intently, his notebook at the ready.

ATTERBOW: A terrible thing. A terrible, terrible accident. And of course I feel very badly about it myself. I'd never had the pleasure of meeting your husband, of course – And it's a bit late, now.

He is frowning as he talks , because she has taken his pencil and is writing something herself. Worse, she has torn off the top sheet with his offer, and tucked it up her front.

SYLVIA: (*As she writes*) He was a nice bloke, my Pete.

She holds up the sheet she has written on:

              '£200 or your for
                 it you buger
           and no more skrewing'

182

Back in Fulham, Hopper comes down the side street of the little terraced houses, looking at the house numbers. In one of which, Aunt Vickie is relaxing with tea and a Sweet Tea finger, to dunk. The budgerigar chirps, caged on the table.

AUNT VICKIE: What you got to chirp about, eh? (*Sighs, sips, bites*) If I was on that table in this bloody house, you wouldn't catch me chirping. Oh – wouldn't it be nice to fly away. Wouldn't it, just!

There is a knock on the front door.

Hopper waits at the front door, being Elvis under his breath. The door opens.

Yes?

HOPPER: Hello. I'm looking for –

AUNT VICKIE: She's not here.

HOPPER: (*Blinks*) What?

AUNT VICKIE: The girl upstairs.

HOPPER: Mrs Berry.

He is taken aback by her fierceness.

AUNT VICKIE: Every time I sit down with a cup of tea.

And she shuts the door without any more ado.

He stands on the narrow step, astonished and angered.

HOPPER: Christ Almighty.

He looks at the sealed letter he is holding, turns it over in his hands, looks at his watch, shrugs, and puts it through the letter-box, turning away. He strides back the way he has come, somewhat disgruntled.

Coming towards him, tip-tap-click-clack, by no means so ill-pleased, is Sylvia, returning from her morning visit to the hospital.

Hopper looks at her as they come almost alongside each other. And with a similar Don't-I-Know-You-Don't-You-Look-Good, Sylvia looks hesitantly sidelong at him.

But they pass.

Hopper's stride slows, his expression changes. Behind him, the click-clack of her high heels becomes less frequent. Hopper then allows himself the kind of smirk which shows that he thinks he is in a musical: a home-made one, spun from his ever-present fantasies. Start guitar introduction to 'Love Is Strange' by Mickey and Sylvia, fifties duo.

Sylvia stops. She smiles – shifting into his head. She turns, with a lilt of her limbs, and looks, and then – bang! Hopper makes her 'sing' the love lyric, and then himself joins in as they dance towards each other, full of mutual adoration. The street itself is transformed. Drab houses are gone. Love gilds all, musical style. Hearts and flowers and new clothes.

Eventually, the music ends – after much parodied kissing and amiable sexuality – and the two are as they were before the song. And each stops walking, each half-turns –

HOPPER: Excuse me – but – ah –

SYLVIA: Yeh. You – um – You were –

HOPPER/SYLVIA: At the Palais!

HOPPER: (*Laughs*) Sylvia Berry – yeh? –

SYLVIA: (*Laughs*) Frank's friend – what was it – *Mickey* – yeh?

HOPPER: Mike.

SYLVIA: *Mike*. Yeh. Mike Rophone!

But her silly little laugh dies, remembering bereavement. Hopper responds as though her laugh had been his fault.

HOPPER: Sorry. Yes. Sorry, I – (*Gulps*) Listen. I – well – it's a
    terrible thing what happened to – I mean *terrible*.

SYLVIA: Yes. It was. Over there, that's where it was – (*Points to the
    pub corner*) There's still blood and that on the pavement. It's
    disgusting.

HOPPER: Only I – just been to your place. Delivered a letter.

SYLVIA: Yes?

HOPPER: From – his – from your – from his CO – Colonel
    Bernwood. You know, his sympathies.

SYLVIA: Is that all?

HOPPER: Pardon?

SYLVIA: Well, you can't spend *them*, can you? Sympathies.

HOPPER: No. True enough. (*Looks at her*.) Things going to be a bit
    rough, are they?

SYLVIA: (*Sounding brave*) Oh. I'll manage. Somehow.

They look at each other. A moment.

HOPPER: You're – ah –

SYLVIA: Yes?

They seem to examine each other, yet more. A moment.

HOPPER: Frank. He's – you and Frank –

SYLVIA: Frank? Oh, he's nice enough. Your mate, ennhe?

HOPPER: Well – in a way – no, not really – I mean, I wouldn't go so
    far as that. (*Pause*) I can see why he fancies you. If I may say so.

184

SYLVIA: (*Comically*) You may.

Pause. They continue to look at each other.

HOPPER: You go there a lot, do you? The Palais, I mean.

SYLVIA: Well, I got the funeral and all that to think about –

HOPPER: (*Quickly*) Oh, I – I didn't mean –

SYLVIA: Oh. No. See what you mean. No, I don't go a lot. Nobody to go with, have I?

HOPPER: What about Frank?

SYLVIA: (*Laughs*) He's a bit doo-lally.

HOPPER: (*Laughs*) He is a bit.

They both stop laughing, still looking closely at each other.

Oh, my God.

Meanwhile, in a mustily gentleman's club sort of place, in the lunch hour. Bernwood in a deep armchair, a small table in front of him, sipping Scotch, and looking even more twitchy than usual.

An elderly gent shambles past, walrus-moustached, rheumy-eyed.

ELDERLY GENT: How are you, old bean?

BERNWOOD: Fine. Fine.

ELDERLY GENT: Don't let them worry you.

BERNWOOD: Who?

But the elderly gent has shuffled past, with the hint of a chuckle. Bernwood stares at his hands, then looks up glowering.

Don't let who worry me? Who? *Who?*

Far too angry, far too loud. Sedate heads lift all around, not pleased. The elderly gent continues on his way, without turning around.

Bernwood, half-risen, quivering, realises that he is far too tightly wound, and sinks back into old, soft leather with half-furtive, half-apologetic looks at the others in the large, musty, out-of-time room.

Sanders, the elegant, limping MI6 Brigadier, stands between a pair of fluted pillars, surveying the scene with a sardonic eye. He sees Bernwood, crunched into the armchair, twists a possibly scornful little smile, and makes his way across half-an-acre of stale air towards him.

Bernwood, staring into space, too slowly becomes aware of Sanders, standing, looking down at him with the same small twist of a smile.

Cecil! Made me jump.

Sanders sits in the opposite armchair, adjusting the crease of his trousers, and flicking away imagined fluff from his knee.

SANDERS: Come, come, Harry. You didn't jump. Altogether a slower movement. Not unlike the head of a tortoise.

BERNWOOD: What?

SANDERS: Emerging from its carapace.

BERNWOOD: What?

SANDERS: Shell, Harry.

Bernwood stares at him for a moment, then dismisses something puzzling.

BERNWOOD: Good of you to find time to see me. What'll you have?

Sanders looks around, as though doubtful whether this place will quite serve his needs.

SANDERS: Oh, I'll make do with a Glenmorangie, if they have it.

BERNWOOD: (*Indignantly*) This place has one of the finest selections of single malts in the kingdom, Cecil.

SANDERS: Oh. Good. I was not casting aspersions on your club, by the way. Heavens above. (*Looks around, comically*) Very fine old place.

Bernwood raises his hand to seek the attention of a steward, who looks as though he should be a Chelsea Pensioner.

BERNWOOD: Cecil. I want to know what's going on. Up above.

SANDERS: Amongst the cherubs and archangels, Harry? Oh – same old bugger, I should think.

SANDERS: Cecil.

SANDERS: With lutes and flutes and harps thrown in. My God – that steward is absolutely intent on taking no notice of you. Why is that?

Bernwood has kept his hand up, almost as though it doesn't belong to him.

BERNWOOD: I wish you'd – Cecil. Please. You have the ear of so many in – (*Lowers his voice, leans in*) The planning conference is not going well, apparently. Mobilizing, moving, equipping the chaps. Constant changes of timetable and destination. The whole army wants to go in through Alexandria, but it has to be Port Said, Cecil. Is all this *bluff*, or what?

SANDERS: Harry. Could you arrange to have that Steward

transferred to Madame Tussaud's?

Bernwood still has his hand up. Sanders has a new, hard look in his eyes, and they are fixed on Bernwood.

BERNWOOD: I hope I'm not out of order, Brigadier.

SANDERS: Why don't you concentrate on your own job? Mm?

BERNWOOD: I can't. (*Twitches*) I just – I can't, Cecil. (*Looks at him, hesitates.*) For a moment yesterday, I almost did something which I never contemplated I could ever – When you collate all the bumf that crosses my desk, Cecil, you get a sort of, sort of extra sense, sixth sense, about what this little unexplained bit *might* mean.

Sanders is looking at him closely, and with a hint of accusation.

Well – I've formed the opinion that the Red Army is not simply *adjusting* its old position in the usual – (*He often doesn't finish his sentences*) It's not for me to make sense of any of this, of course. But it *is* my job to oversee the collation, and pass on the – ah – Anyway. God help me, Cecil, I was severely tempted.

Tiny pause. Sanders, understandably, is puzzled. All this time, too, Bernwood's hand hangs in the air, as though he doesn't know it's there.

SANDERS: By what?

BERNWOOD: To withhold the conclusion.

SANDERS: (*Still puzzled*) Why? What do you mean?

BERNWOOD: I mean –

SANDERS: For heaven's sake, put your hand down!

BERNWOOD: What? (*Looks at his hand, in surprise*) Oh. Yes. But – ah – but what about your drink?

SANDERS: (*Exasperated*) I think the steward needs it more than I do. (*Sniff of disdain*) Poor old bugger.

Intense, fretful Bernwood cannot keep his mind on anything else.

BERNWOOD: Cecil. The accumulating evidence on my desk, from my team, shows that the Soviets may well be disposing themselves to make threatening gestures in the Middle East – the increase in 'volunteers', so called, in Egypt and the movement of troops south to –

SANDERS: (*Dismissively*) Yes. Oh, yes. Yes.

BERNWOOD: I wanted to hold this stuff back. My bit of it, anyway.

SANDERS: Harry. Are you all right?

Sanders reaches across and downs Bernwood's scotch in one gulp. Bernwood doesn't even notice. He is crunching up inside again.

BERNWOOD: They're such a lily-livered lot, you see. The politicians. They'll back down, Cecil. And I know this, I know it for sure – if we don't stand up for ourselves, for our history, our rights, our – If we don't go in, and – (*In anguish*) Cecil. Cecil. They're looking for an excuse *not* to invade Egypt! And I think that's the –

SANDERS: (*Crisply*) Rot! Ab-so-lute rot!

BERNWOOD: (*Blinks*) What – ?

SANDERS: (*Angrily*) Precisely the opposite is the case! What we desperately – badly – want is an excuse to go in, not to stay out.

Bernwood stares at him as he might at his fairy godmother.

BERNWOOD: Are you –

SANDERS: Nasser's no fool, you know, in a way. He's been the soul of moderation vis-à-vis the UN, all that – the oily bastard.

BERNWOOD: Terrible. Terrible.

SANDERS: If only the ships weren't still passing through the Canal. Harry – we said they couldn't run the installations – couldn't provide the pilots – there were more than 200 of them, and only forty of those were Egyptian. When all the others left – well. It had always been supposed that it took two years to bring a navigator up to scratch. What happens? The very next bloody day after our bloody people left? Harry. They piloted more ships through than the daily average.

BERNWOOD: It's – well, it's uncanny.

SANDERS: So, bang goes that excuse. And our civilians employed by Suez Contractors Ltd – you know, at Tel-el-kebir, Fayid, those places – we could move in if they – Harry. They've not been harassed. Not a dicky bird.

BERNWOOD: What's he playing at, Cecil?

SANDERS: The simple fact of the matter is that we're hard pressed to justify what it is we know we want to do. And the Americans – well – (*Spreads his hands*) They're very pi about it all. They're twisting our arms. Harry. They really do not want us to do this. The ungrateful sods.

BERNWOOD: I don't even pretend to understand it, but – when

all's said and done, we have to look after ourselves. Either we are or we are not our own master. This is the time to find out. It's been – yes, keeping me awake at – I love this old land of ours, Cecil, and any humiliation of it is a – But I'm glad about this chat. I find it very – Your feeling is that we really are not just going to blub? We're going in?

SANDERS: We're going in.

BERNWOOD: (*Beams*) Dear God above! That's a load off my – You're sure? Absolutely sure?

Sanders lifts himself out of the chair. Bernwood, in his pleasure, is too loud.

SANDERS: Hush, hush, old stick. (*Looks down at him*) The bombers are due over Cairo next Thursday.

Bernwood jerks with pleasure, as though an electric current was passing through his limbs.

BERNWOOD: Oh, that's – that's – My goodness!

SANDERS: (*Cruelly*) They're going to drop leaflets, Harry. With cartoons of Nasser running away.

The tardy, elderly steward at last arrives, as Bernwood deflates.

STEWARD: You required something, sir?

SANDERS: No. But *he* does.

Some days later, and the American girl Lisa sits in the front passenger seat of an otherwise unoccupied and smart, well-finned 1955/6 car. She has the red Penguin, *The Seagull and Other Plays*, and is reading. She holds a finger in the book, then closes it, marking her place, and tries to see whether she has learnt something.

LISA: 'For the sake of being happy like that – of being a writer or an actress – I would put up with – ' (*Has to think*) 'I would put up with unfriendliness from my family, with – um – With poverty and disappointment, with living in a garret and – – um – '

She looks out of the car window, a bit bored. The car is parked on gravel, at the wrought iron gates to a huge cemetery.

Lisa starts again, but in a flatter tone.

'Poverty and disappointment, with living in a garret and – having nothing to eat but rye bread . . .'

She sighs, puts the book down, and gets out of the car, a little fretful. Like one waiting, and not too patiently, she stands by the car, then walks up and down a little, her feet crunching on the gravel path of the cemetery.

(*Over*) 'I would gladly suffer dissatisfaction with myself in the knowledge of my own imperfections, but in return I would demand –'

She stops.

(*Out loud*) What? But – *what*?

An elderly couple, bearing a huge bunch of flowers, look at her as they pass, going into the cemetery. She thinks she might have seemed rude, and smiles at them, awkwardly.

Deeper into the cemetery, beyond stone angels, Celtic crosses, memorial slabs, urns etc., Corporal Berry is being laid to rest in a C of E Service.

The concluding words of the interment drift across the expanses of the big cemetery, which, at one end, runs alongside the Fulham Palace Road.

Sylvia is looking fetching in black – and conscious of it. A slow tear is allowed to trickle, but not so as to disturb her make-up.

The small cluster of mourners, now that all preacherly words have been delivered, and the vicar is shaking various hands, is about to go through the sad little ritual of going to the lip of the open grave and staring down into it, in farewell.

Hopper's eyes are on Sylvia in an overtly concerned sort of way.

Francis shifts from foot to foot, ill at ease – and glancing with an almost furtive anxiety at the lovely Sylvia.

A stunned but rather seedy couple who must be Berry's parents try to evade the vicar's dog-like persistence.

VICAR: – And you must have been very proud of – as we are of all our servicemen –

And, next to Hopper, the only one of the big room officers to turn up on this Saturday afternoon: Colonel Trekker, in his US Army uniform.

From the distance, there is a great roar from about thirty thousand mostly male throats.

TREKKER: (*To* HOPPER, *low-toned*) What the heck is that –

HOPPER: Football, sir.

TREKKER: You mean, soccer?

HOPPER: Yes, sir.

TREKKER: But it's summer.

HOPPER: It's the first Saturday of the season, sir. Fulham must have just got a goal.

TREKKER: Yes?

HOPPER: Oh, they're good, sir. They've got the highest scoring attack in the football league. Jezzard, Haynes, Robson, Leggett – They're really something, I –

He stops himself, feeling inappropriate.

They both watch the delectable young widow approach the grave. She stares down, covertly looks at the others, then lets a sob rise.

SYLVIA: Oh, Pete. Pete! Come back, Pete!

As Hopper watches a theatrical Sylvia, his own eyes all but moisten, and he mistakes desire for sympathy.

His mind spirals away into song, his eyes clamped on Sylvia. Begin 'Sh'Boom' by the Crewcuts with Hopper, the vicar, Sylvia and the mourners 'singing'.

The vicar, hovering near the grave as though for a tip, has also been sneaking less than spiritual glances at Sylvia.

Francis switches his gaze from the vicar to Sylvia – but with desperation and deepening gloom. But his lips stay sealed as the song thumps on.

All around the open grave now take on the ling-a-lang-boom-ba-doo chorus.

As the Crewcuts' song rocks on, it seems to envelop the stone angels, weeping cherubs, marble urns and tilting gravestones – a sort of rock of ages. During this, they are each taking turns to go with due solemnity to the very tip of the grave, even as they 'sing' 'Sh'Boom'.

At the edge of the grave, standing close now to the tear-streaked Sylvia, Hopper gives a quick, almost furtive look down into the earthy, coffin-laden depths, then lifts his eyes, straight to Sylvia, and bangs out the most yearning lines of the song.

Sylvia, aware of his intense scrutiny, looks sidelong at him, on the very lip of the grave. Even now, even here, she cannot help a little gleam of sexual interest, and a hint of promise.

Francis now steps forward in an uneasy gait to stare down reluctantly into Berry's grave as the song continues without a break –

Sylvia hasn't a glance to spare for Francis. Her eyes are on

Hopper, and her eyes gleam, as the song continues, over.

Hopper opens his mouth to complete the song. But then he stops, the music stops dead, his eyes suddenly startled, as –

With a shout of consternation, Francis, ever awkward, has lost his footing in the soft earth at the edge of the grave, and is falling headlong into the uninviting trench.

Thunk! he hits the coffin.

At virtually the same moment, as though in applause, Fulham score another goal, and there is a great roar from thirty thousand throats.

HOPPER: Two-nil!

FRANCIS: (*Off*) Ouch! Oh, my – Ow-www – !

SYLVIA: (*Hisses*) The awkward bugger.

Everyone rushes to the grave, to peer down in the earthy depths, where hapless Francis sprawls on top of the coffin. He is in obvious pain, and one of his legs looks peculiarly buckled.

The looming faces peering down are a mixture of indignation and suppressed hilarity.

Francis tries to hold in his pain, tries to compose his face , tries to alleviate his total embarrassment – and as always when under stress, he has both a stutter and a markedly singsong West Walian lilt.

FRANCIS: I'm very sorry in-deed – I was thinking about
  m.mum.m- mortality, see, and my f.fuf.foot slith-ered (*But
  the pain is too great*) Ooh Christ, mun – I think – Ow, oooh – I
  think I've bro-ken my bloodeee leg.

ALL: Sh'Boom!

Hundreds of yards away, Lisa has wandered into the cemetery, in a vaguely fretful manner. She is examining a large, discoloured stone angel, dropping over an ill-tended grave.

She sighs, momentarily affected, too, by mortality. Then – a theatrical young woman –

LISA: (*Quietly*) 'I would put up with unfriendliness from my
  family, with poverty and disappointment, with living in a
  garret and having nothing to eat but –'

Imitating the actress who played Nina in the play, in movement as well as words, she breaks off at what she sees –

Far along the path into the depths of the cemetery, in an avenue of gravestones and stone carvings, uniformed Trekker and Hopper, struggling a little, have made a cradle of their linked hands to carry Francis. Sylvia walks behind the three men, looking disgruntled, as though her big moment has been stolen.

Francis, in pain, and embarrassed, diverts his ludicrously literary mind on to the slow perspective of the passing graves, as the two carrying him pant a bit with the effort.

FRANCIS: So many graves. So many, many graves!

HOPPER: (*Irritated*) Yeh. Well, it's a cemetery, ennit?

FRANCIS: (*Intones*) 'Death closes all – '

TREKKER: What?

FRANCIS: Tennyson, sir.

TREKKER: (*With edge*) You remind me of my niece.

Hopper's face shows a 'you can say that again'. But Francis, wincing a little, and looking at all the graves, seems unaware of the irritation he is causing.

FRANCIS: 'Death closes all: but something ere the end,
  Some work of noble note, may yet be done,
  Not unbecoming men that strove – '

TREKKER: (*Snarls*) Shut up!

FRANCIS: Sah!

Minutes later, and Francis has just been put in the back seat of Trekker's car. Lisa, not pleased, is in the front passenger seat. Trekker, opening the driver's door, looks at Hopper and the hovering Sylvia.

TREKKER: I'll soon find where it is. Sooner he's checked over the better. I must say this is not the sort of day I – (*But his eyes fall on* SYLVIA) Well, Mrs Berry – I'm sorry we didn't meet under happier circumstances. I know what you must be feeling.

SYLVIA: Thank you, Colonel.

So demure, and impressed by his rank and uniform she all but curtsies. Trekker shakes her hand.

TREKKER: My best wishes to you, and most sincere condolences.

SYLVIA: And to you, sir.

Trekker, clearly longing to get away, gets into his car. As the car pulls away –

TREKKER: (*To* FRANCIS) You OK in back, there?

FRANCIS: Yes, thank you, sir.

But he is obviously in pain. Trekker looks sidelong at Lisa, apologetically.

TREKKER: We just have to find this hospital, Lisa –

LISA: (*Tight-lipped*) That's OK.

TREKKER: We won't be too late, honey –

LISA: But *late*, though.

Sylvia and Hopper watch the departing car, then turn to look at each other.

HOPPER: Decent bloke, that Yank. The only one of the officers to bother to turn up. God knows what he thought of Frank – isn't he a berk? Oops. Sorry.

SYLVIA: What for?

HOPPER: Well, you and him – I mean, he's sweet on you. Isn't he?

SYLVIA: Is he?

HOPPER: (*Probing*) And you on him. Aren't you?

SYLVIA: Am I?

A little pause. They keep their eyes on each other.

HOPPER: But I mean to fall into the –

She starts to laugh, then adjusts to the grieving young widow mode.

SYLVIA: Poor old Pete. He would have killed him. If he could have got out of that coffin.

HOPPER: Not half!

Silence.

SYLVIA: Well. I'd better be on my way – so – thanks for coming –

HOPPER: (*Quickly*) You've been very brave.

SYLVIA: Me?

HOPPER: I think so!

SYLVIA: Which way you going? Only – I could do with some company.

In Trekker's car, Francis is very quiet in the back, gritting his teeth. Trekker checks in his interior mirror – a kindly man – and frowns to himself at Francis' obvious but bravely controlled distress. Lisa, being of an artistic or literary disposition, is far less concerned by real life human feelings.

LISA: (*To* TREKKER) You know you said you'd never seen a cloud shaped like a piano?

He looks at her, almost with distaste.

TREKKER: Please, Lisa. Enough.

LISA: (*Triumphantly*) Well – I just saw one!

Francis frowns to himself for a beat – and then, forgetting pain, beams recognition.

FRANCIS: Ah – but did you smell heliotrope in the air?
Startled, incredulous, Lisa whips her head around.
LISA: What?
Francis misunderstands. Being British, he must not forget rank.
FRANCIS: I beg your pardon. I – I – forgot who I – s.sorry –
LISA: (*Still incredulous*) You know *The Seagull*?
FRANCIS: Permission to speak, sir.
TREKKER: Holy Mose. Go ahead!
FRANCIS: (*Smirks to* LISA) Trigorin says it. He makes a mental
     note so that he can use it – um – what's he say – 'I snatch at
     every word and sentence I utter.' It's when he's speaking
     to –
But in his characteristic excess of enthusiasm he has moved his
limbs too much, and has to stop with a gasp of pain.
LISA: (*For the first time*) Hey. Are you all right?
FRANCIS: (*Gasp*) Yes, miss.
Equally characteristically, her brief concern is swiftly overtaken
by her literary enthusiasms.
LISA: Is he your favourite writer? Chekhov.
FRANCIS: (*With difficulty*) Amongst the Russians? Oh – almost. In
     drama. But for me the one I – in Russian, I mean – is
     Alexander Pushkin. He's the –
LISA: (*Little American yelp*) Pushkin! You go for Pushkin?
Driving, Trekker rolls his eyes, for his own benefit. 'In a Persian
Market Place' surges on a theatre organ, over.
   Summoned up on its tides, so to speak, a bored policeman sits
outside Atterbow's doorless little room, helmet on the floor. The
organ music fades.
ATTERBOW: (*Off*) Seven letters. Come on. Third one is an S and
     the last one is a D.
The policeman takes no notice. He watches a nurse pass, with
interest.
   Sitting up in bed, with pencil stub and *Telegraph* and packet of
'Passing Clouds' cigarettes, Atterbow indulges his nasty streak.
But he is not alone: a timid, depressed little woman, Mrs
Atterbow, sits on the only chair with her handbag on her knees.
     (*Calls*) What's the matter? Too difficult for you, eh? You'll
     never make inspector, will you?
MRS ATTERBOW: (*Sotto voce*) Sshh, Harold. You'll only offend
     them. You can't afford to do that.

ATTERBOW: Pooh. Their case is collapsing. It's a colander – won't even hold a widdle.

MRS ATTERBOW: Harold.

ATTERBOW: It'll probably be reduced to dangerous driving. You'll see, there won't be a damned rozzer out there on Monday morning. What you mean, *Harold*?

MRS ATTERBOW: The way you speak.

ATTERBOW: (*Unpleasantly*) What about it? (*Before she can answer*) Oh, go home. Leave me be. Go! I'm fed up with women, I can tell you. Utterly fed up! I'm giving up the organ. I'm giving up the ladies. I'm going to volunteer for the bloody army, and be a *man*.

MRS ATTERBOW: (*Miserably*) Ts. Ts.

ATTERBOW: What you tutting about? Bitch.

MRS ATTERBOW: You're too old, Harold.

ATTERBOW: Not to fight the bloody wogs and gyppoes I'm not!

Outside, the bored policeman watches an operating trolley's distant approach. A porter pushing a young man, and walking with him a pretty young woman and an American colonel, in uniform. Two of them are obviously talking very, very earnestly.

The small group swings away at a junction in the corridor, taking them out of sight, in a distant squeak of rubber wheels.

Come on! Something – something – S – something – something – something – D.

POLICEMAN: (*To himself*) Try 'bastard'.

Another bright day, sun on the war office windows, and in the big room everyone except Francis (hospital) and Berry (dead) in place: Bernwood, Hedges, Carter, Church, Hopper, Trekker.

But there is a newcomer. A Private Mason, Intelligence Corps, standing to nervous but clearly bemused attention in his cumbersome Full Service Marching Order in front of Bernwood's desk.

BERNWOOD: A time of exceptional pressure, ah, um, Mason – we're here in this little room to keep a pretty damn sharp eye on the Red Army while we biff the Egyptians – yes? – Think of it as a – as a – Well, I think that about – you should be pretty clear about everything, um, Mason.

Mason, clearly, is totally confused. A tiny pause. Then he realises he must respond.

MASON: (*Bellows*) Sah!

BERNWOOD: (*Twinkles*) Wondering why you're here, eh?

Mason finds the sudden twinkle even more disconcerting.

MASON: (*Bellows*) Sah!

Colonel Trekker rolls his eyes. Oh, boy, this man's army, says his face.

BERNWOOD: We've had a series of unfortunate – This office has a
    high casualty rate, Mason. We're going down like flies.
    That's why you are here at such short – yes?

MASON: (*Alarmed*) Sir.

BERNWOOD: One death, and one set of broken bones. That's two
    out of three of our clerks. And the other has only a day or
    two left. An unacceptably high ratio, Mason, when we're up
    to our eyes in work. All I can hope is that, *you*, at least – ah –
    (*Picks up the word*) *survive*.

Mason's face is showing comic alarm ('What is this, the front line?' thoughts). It is made worse for him as it was for Francis a few weeks ago, by the manner in which Bernwood now bends his troubled head to the charts on his desk without further ado, leaving him stranded. Mason shifts uneasily, in his heavy equipment.

CHURCH: Over here, soldier. Come along. Sharp about it!

MASON: (*Relieved*) Sah.

Hopper has been watching the newcomer with a here-we-go-again, amused disdain. But his thoughts are mostly elsewhere. They take him back to the upstairs flat in the Fulham house:

    After the funeral – Sylvia still in black. In the tiny living-room, with its curtained-off kitchenette, Hopper takes a glass from her.

SYLVIA: Pete always kept a half bottle of Bell's for special
    occasions. Not that we ever had many.

HOPPER: Cheers.

SYLVIA: Cheers.

Hopper, still feeling self-conscious, looks around the dingy little room.

HOPPER: What will you do? Will you stay here, or what?

SYLVIA: I dunno.

Suddenly, she sounds utterly forlorn – and genuinely so.

HOPPER: Well. There's no need to hurry about that sort of –

He looks down into his glass, not knowing what to say or do. Still standing, and feeling empty, she looks at him, assessing him.

SYLVIA: Frank says he'll look after me.

HOPPER: He can't even look after himself!

Said so swiftly, and spontaneously, that they are both momentarily surprised. And then they both laugh.

SYLVIA: He's – nice, though. Kind.

HOPPER: (*Grudgingly*.) Oh, yeh – he's nice enough.

SYLVIA: You sound jealous.

This is said in her flirtatious style, and he knows it – yet still likes it.

HOPPER: Do I? Perhaps I am. Who knows.

Silence. He drinks. She watches.

SYLVIA: It don't seem right on the day they put poor old Pete into the ground – but – God, you got to live, encha?

HOPPER: That's right. No – but it is.

SYLVIA: I was going to suggest – well. I wouldn't mind putting a record on. Do you like music?

HOPPER: Do I like music!

SYLVIA: Yeh – but what sort?

HOPPER: (*Passionately*) The sort where moon don't rhyme with June and you're not up to your backside in bloody buttercups. Songs that –

Remembering his own words, Hopper feels entombed in the war office.

(*Remembering*) – aren't about your mum and dad. A bit rough. A beat that busts up the old way – the old stodge –

He looks around each desk and face –

Starting with Church talking to the new man. Then Bernwood anxiously stooped, Trekker, Carter with cold eyes, and Hedges, in red braces.

(*Remembering*) – the Empire and knowing your place and excuse me and the dressing-up and doing what you're told and not once being asked and not once –

HEDGES: Hopper.

HOPPER: Sah!

HEDGES: How about the barely bloody drinkable?

HOPPER: Sir.

He gets up, briskly.

At more or less the same time, the injured Francis in his hospital bed is suddenly very pleased with life.

FRANCIS: (*Beams*) Oh, thank you!

As he takes a cup of tea from a nurse, his legs under a bed cradle, and the red Penguin *The Seagull* in his hands. He sips, burns his mouth, winces, but his eyes soon fall back on the page.

> (*Reads*) 'Oh, how happy I am to think that we shall be seeing each other soon! I shall see those wonderful eyes again, this indescribably beautiful, tender smile . . . these sweet features, the expression of angelic – '

In the big room that Francis has escaped, Hopper flips off the whistler on the kettle, and pours boiling water.

HOPPER: Shoot me a slug from the wonderful – (*Sexual smirk*) wonderful! wonderful! – 'Is There Anything You Need for the Weekend, Sir?'

The introduction to 'Lotta Lovin'' by Gene Vincent and the BlueCaps crashes in, vibrant fifties proto-rock.

Hopper puts a condom into each cup and whirls around from the table to belt out the urgent lyric, Gene Vincent to the bone. He remembers how in her funeral black, Sylvia played this particular record on the portable Dansette, and turned to smile at Hopper, playing so provocatively with her gloves.

They look at each other as the music throbs on. He puts his glass down, questioningly. Her smile dies, and she seems to stiffen.

Suddenly, they are in each other's arms, in a demandingly sexual urgency, making love against the wall as the record plays.

Carrying the cups around to his masters, Hopper continues to 'sing' the sexually urgent Gene Vincent vocal, making the officers 'doo-wah!' the necessary choruses. Inspired, now, Hopper can somehow integrate other fragments, other places into the hard-driving rhythms of the song: thus, in the conference room, in full red-tabbed uniform the general wields his pointer and takes up the lyric – but the huge map is now an equally large picture of Sylvia in a Diana Dors pose.

In the big room downstairs, the officers dance in a circle around Hopper, threateningly, using the teacup condoms like slings. And then, as the beat drives on, and a flicker of conscience is overridden by renewed desire in Hopper's head, Sylvia stands provocatively at her husband's open grave, inviting yet more pleasures.

The music delivers us to the hospital, where a very pleased Francis, in bed, puts his book down and eagerly watches Lisa come through double-doors and down through the ward towards him, bearing her books and her smile. As she reaches the bed, the music stops. Ward sounds come clear.

LISA: Hi!

FRANCIS: It's w.wuh.wonderful of you to visit me –

LISA: Why not? You're the first guy I've ever been able to talk with about all the things I – Got you some books. Lermontov. Proust. Nietzsche. And some T. S. Eliot if you want something lighter –

FRANCIS: (*Overwhelmed*) Oh, but that's – that's – oh, thank you! Thank you!

He grabs at one of the books, opening it straight away. She watches with a proprietorial little smile of fellow-feeling.

LISA: You know, you're really *nice*.

FRANCIS: And – and so are *you*!

LISA: Gee – we got so much to talk about.

FRANCIS: Yes. Yes! Nietzsche for one!

LISA: Oh, the maxims. Sure.

FRANCIS: Um. 'Ultimately one loves one's desires and not that which is desired.' That's one.

LISA: Is it true, though?

FRANCIS: (*Solemn*) The two are very difficult to separate. I mean – I mean, I have myself been in love with the idea of love – oh, but that is the path to shame and perdition, Miss Trekker.

LISA: Lisa.

FRANCIS: Oh, but – Yes. Thank you. Thank you very much.

LISA: I know what you mean. 'In love with the idea of love.' Gee. Yes.

FRANCIS: You do?

LISA: But when you meet the real thing –

FRANCIS: Yes!

LISA: It sort of – the horizon tilts.

FRANCIS: (*Awed*) The horizon tilts.

LISA: Or – the earth moves.

FRANCIS: Hemingway!

LISA: Hemingway!

They look at each other. They laugh.

FRANCIS: Oh, it's so good to have a real conversation, *Li-sa*.

LISA: (*Pleased*) Why do you say my name like that, *Frank*?

FRANCIS: Because I've been practising how to say it. It fills my
   mouth in the shape of a – of a – Well, Keats put it better.
   The grape, you know.
LISA: Keats! Oh, yes! He makes the back of my eyelids sort of –
   sting. (*Laughs*) You know, my father said I'd never – Hey,
   sorry, this sounds really intimate – 'Lisa,' he said, 'you'll
   scare off every danged boy you meet with your danged
   books.' (*Laughs*) He's a Philistine, daddy.
FRANCIS: What does he do? For a living, I mean.
LISA: Oil.
FRANCIS: Beg pardon?
LISA: (*Wrinkles her nose*) Oil wells in Texas. (*Little shrug*) He owns
   a lot of wells.

One brief swoop at Francis' incredulous face, and explode into an
oil gusher. Dramatic, almost violent – black gold going whoosh! –
and moments later, crash in the big 1956 hit by Anne Shelton –
'Lay Down Your Arms', merging into a Suez montage:

   Ship crawling through Canal. Nasser and cheering Arabs.
Pyramids. Tanks. Troop embarkations. Parliament. Eden. The
landings. The bombings. And all through 'Lay Down Your
Arms' beating on –

   Ending on the Sphinx: the huge statue near the pyramids at El
Giza in Egypt, music continuing. Going closer, closer, until –

   The head of the Sphinx opens – as in a pier photo booth – and
Hopper's head pokes through the picture, and he 'sings' part of
the 'Lay Down Your Arms' lyric.

   A second trap opens in the Sphinx, and Francis' head pokes
through, so that both of them can continue the Ann Shelton lyric.
A scene which now seems to be on a cinema screen – but in 3-D –
so that when the watching audience is discovered, row upon row,
they are wearing the free cardboard-framed 3-D spectacles, a
transient phenomenon of the time.

   Returning to the screen, Privates Francis and Hopper 'sing' out
the conclusion of 'Lay Down Your Arms', but now Sylvia and
Lisa are the recipients of the song, entwined in the aisle. The
officers from the big room, led by Colonel Bernwood, come
marching in, brisk and aggressive.

   Eventually everyone is on the stage, including Uncle Fred and
Aunt Vickie. The organ rises, with Atterbow playing.

   The chorus fades. The lights begin to dip in the cinema. A

Union Jack glows on the face of the Sphinx. The dying music has a ghostly resonance. Now, only the Sphinx and the Pyramids remain, enigmatic shapes in the semi-darkness. The tale is over.

FABER AND FABER FILM BOOKS

'The essential reading list for any modern movie lover.' *Empire*

Recent titles in the Faber collection of screenplays and film studies include:

Potter on Potter edited by Graham Fuller
Malle on Malle edited by Philip French
Frank Capra by Joseph McBride
The Patty Diphusa Stories by Pedro Almodovar
Simple Men and *Trust* by Hal Hartley
The French Brothers Wild and Crazy Film Quiz Book
Taxi Driver by Paul Schrader
The Trial by Harold Pinter
Levinson on Levinson edited by David Thompson
Antonin Artaud by Stephen Barber

For a complete stock list, please write to:

Promotions Department
Faber and Faber Limited
3 Queen Square
London WCIN 3AU